# Attack Vectors

## The History of Cybersecurity

Morey Haber

Apress®

## *Attack Vectors: The History of Cybersecurity*

Morey Haber
Heathrow, Lake Mary, FL, USA

ISBN-13 (pbk): 979-8-8688-1708-3  ISBN-13 (electronic): 979-8-8688-1709-0
https://doi.org/10.1007/979-8-8688-1709-0

## Copyright © 2025 by Morey Haber

This work is subject to copyright. All rights are reserved by the Publisher, whether the whole or part of the material is concerned, specifically the rights of translation, reprinting, reuse of illustrations, recitation, broadcasting, reproduction on microfilms or in any other physical way, and transmission or information storage and retrieval, electronic adaptation, computer software, or by similar or dissimilar methodology now known or hereafter developed.

Trademarked names, logos, and images may appear in this book. Rather than use a trademark symbol with every occurrence of a trademarked name, logo, or image we use the names, logos, and images only in an editorial fashion and to the benefit of the trademark owner, with no intention of infringement of the trademark.

The use in this publication of trade names, trademarks, service marks, and similar terms, even if they are not identified as such, is not to be taken as an expression of opinion as to whether or not they are subject to proprietary rights.

While the advice and information in this book are believed to be true and accurate at the date of publication, neither the authors nor the editors nor the publisher can accept any legal responsibility for any errors or omissions that may be made. The publisher makes no warranty, express or implied, with respect to the material contained herein.

Managing Director, Apress Media LLC: Welmoed Spahr
Acquisitions Editor: Susan McDermott
Development Editor: Laura Berendson
Project Manager: Jessica Vakili

Distributed to the book trade worldwide by Springer Science+Business Media New York, 1 New York Plaza, New York, NY 10004. Phone 1-800-SPRINGER, fax (201) 348-4505, e-mail orders-ny@springer-sbm.com, or visit www.springeronline.com. Apress Media, LLC is a Delaware LLC and the sole member (owner) is Springer Science + Business Media Finance Inc (SSBM Finance Inc). SSBM Finance Inc is a **Delaware** corporation.

For information on translations, please e-mail booktranslations@springernature.com; for reprint, paperback, or audio rights, please e-mail bookpermissions@springernature.com.

Apress titles may be purchased in bulk for academic, corporate, or promotional use. eBook versions and licenses are also available for most titles. For more information, reference our Print and eBook Bulk Sales web page at http://www.apress.com/bulk-sales.

If disposing of this product, please recycle the paper

*Editors:*

*Matt Miller, Director of Content Marketing and SEO*

*Laura Bohnert, Senior Marketing Content and Public Relations Manager*

*Emmilyn Yeoh, Technical Writer*

*Special Thanks To:*

*Brent Thurrell, Chief Revenue Officer, BeyondTrust*

*Dedication:*

*"This book is dedicated to my Mom, brothers: Larry, Arthur, and Richard, and my unwarranted alias John Titor. Their love of history, and the arguments that ensue, will always be a source of delight and unwelcome ephemeral stress."*

*—Morey Haber*

# Table of Contents

About the Author .................................................................................. ix

About the Technical Reviewer ............................................................. xi

Foreword ........................................................................................... xiii

Introduction: Part I ........................................................................... xvii

Introduction: Part II ......................................................................... xxvii

**Chapter 1: The History of Attack Vectors ......................................... 1**

Foundations .............................................................................................. 1

Vacuum Tubes to Transistors (1950s–1960s) ........................................... 3

Mainframes and Early Cybersecurity (1970s–Early 1980s) ...................... 7

Personal Computing (1980s) ................................................................... 12

The Internet and Emerging Threats (1990s) ........................................... 17

Cybersecurity and Dot-Com (Early 2000s) .............................................. 23

Risk Management (Mid-2000s–2010s) ................................................... 28

Modern Threat Landscape (Late 2010s–Today) ..................................... 36

**Chapter 2: Business Justification .................................................... 43**

**Chapter 3: Definitions ..................................................................... 49**

Bugs ....................................................................................................... 49

Vulnerability ............................................................................................ 54

Exploitation ............................................................................................. 58

v

TABLE OF CONTENTS

    Obfuscation .................................................................................. 60

    Virus ............................................................................................. 63

    Worms ......................................................................................... 67

    Bots .............................................................................................. 69

    Rootkits ....................................................................................... 72

    Configuration .............................................................................. 75

    Attack Vectors ............................................................................ 77

**Chapter 4: Malware** ................................................................... **83**

**Chapter 5: Exploits** ..................................................................... **93**

**Chapter 6: Breaches** ................................................................ **103**

**Chapter 7: Regulations** ............................................................ **113**

**Chapter 8: People** .................................................................... **119**

**Chapter 9: Syndicates** ............................................................. **123**

**Chapter 10: Social Engineering** .............................................. **133**

**Chapter 11: Solutions** .............................................................. **143**

    Endpoint Security ..................................................................... 143

        Antivirus ............................................................................. 144

        Anti-spyware ..................................................................... 146

        Endpoint Protection Platforms ......................................... 149

        Endpoint Detection and Response .................................. 151

    Networks .................................................................................. 154

        Firewalls ............................................................................ 154

        Intrusion Detection Systems ............................................ 159

        Virtual Private Networks .................................................. 160

        Content Filters .................................................................. 164

## TABLE OF CONTENTS

Secure Remote Access .................................................................................. 166
Security Information Event Management........................................................ 168
Vulnerability Management ............................................................................. 171
Penetration Testing ....................................................................................... 174
Data Loss Prevention .................................................................................... 176
Identity and Access Management ................................................................. 181
    Identity Security ....................................................................................... 185
    Identity Governance................................................................................. 187
    Identity Provider ...................................................................................... 189
    Single Sign-On......................................................................................... 191
    Multifactor Authentication ........................................................................ 193
    Privileged Access Management .............................................................. 196
Quantum Computing ..................................................................................... 199
Artificial Intelligence ...................................................................................... 201
End-of-Life Solutions ..................................................................................... 204

**Chapter 12: The Human Threat** ............................................................. 209

**Chapter 13: Lateral Movement** ............................................................. 217

**Chapter 14: Return on Investment** ....................................................... 231
    Example 1: Ransomware Incident Containment with an EPM Solution ............ 233
    Example 2: Preventing Paths to Privileged Escalation with an ITDR Solution....... 234
    Example 3: Malicious Command Execution Due to Remote System Access..... 235

**Chapter 15: It's Not If, But When** .......................................................... 239

**Chapter 16: Supply Chain Attacks** ........................................................ 245
    Step 1: Confirm the Breach and Understand the Scope................................... 246
    Step 2: Activate Your Incident Response Plan ................................................ 247

TABLE OF CONTENTS

Step 3: Informing Stakeholders ..................................................................247
Step 4: Defense-in-Depth Review ..............................................................248
Step 5: Third-Party Risk Management Program ........................................249

**Chapter 17: Been Hacked? ...............................................................251**

**Chapter 18: History Lesson ..............................................................257**

**Chapter 19: Conclusion ....................................................................265**

**Appendix A: Malware .......................................................................271**

**Appendix B: Exploits .......................................................................299**

**Appendix C: Breaches .....................................................................315**

**Appendix D: People .........................................................................329**

**Appendix E: Crime Syndicates ........................................................361**

**Appendix F: Social Engineering .....................................................369**

**Index ..................................................................................................379**

# About the Author

**Morey Haber** is the Chief Security Advisor at BeyondTrust. As the Chief Security Advisor, Morey is the lead identity and technical evangelist at BeyondTrust. He has more than 25 years of IT industry experience and has authored four books: *Privileged Attack Vectors, Asset Attack Vectors, Identity Attack Vectors,* and *Cloud Attack Vectors.* Morey has previously served as BeyondTrust's Chief Security Officer, Chief Technology Officer, and Vice President of Product Management during his nearly 13-year tenure. In 2020, Morey was elected to the Identity Defined Security Alliance (IDSA) Executive Advisory Board to assist the corporate community with identity security best practices. He originally joined BeyondTrust in 2012 as a part of the eEye Digital Security acquisition where he served as a Product Owner and Solutions Engineer since 2004. Prior to eEye, he was Beta Development Manager for Computer Associates, Inc. He began his career as Reliability and Maintainability Engineer for a government contractor building flight and training simulators. Morey earned a Bachelor of Science degree in Electrical Engineering from the State University of New York at Stony Brook.

# About the Technical Reviewer

**Derek A. Smith** is a cybersecurity and AI strategist with over 20 years of experience in federal cybersecurity leadership, identity security, and cyber threat operations. He currently serves as Deputy Director for the DHS HART biometric program and has held key roles at the IRS, Booz Allen Hamilton, and CSC. He is also President of the Certify IT Academy, LLC, specializing in cybersecurity training. A former special agent with the US Treasury, Postal Service, Department of Education, Air Force OSI, and Army CID, Dr. Smith has deep expertise in identity access management (IAM), cloud security, and privileged access. He is the **Lead Cybersecurity Professor at Virginia University of Science and Technology** and serves as the **National Branch Chief for Security Awareness and Training** for the US Coast Guard Auxiliary. Dr. Smith is also the author of over a dozen cybersecurity books and a nationally recognized speaker on AI-integrated cyber defense.

# Foreword

I am both honored and horrified to have been invited to write the foreword of this important book, *Attack Vectors: The History of Cybersecurity*, by my dear friend and colleague, Morey Haber. I'm honored because I know how rare it is for someone as learned and accomplished as Morey to entrust a task like this to a nonpractitioner, and dare I admit, a salesperson. I am also horrified because it is not lost on me that I am participating in what is essentially a history book of cybersecurity, and during my own career, I have experienced, firsthand, most of what lies within these pages! A bittersweet reminder of the march of time, I guess, and memento mori.

Having never written a foreword before, I was advised by those more seasoned in such matters to first focus upon illuminating the character and essence of Morey for those who have not had the pleasure and privilege of spending time with him in person. So, with "bring him to life for the reader" ringing in my ears, I immediately embarked upon making this foreword a literary representation of the man himself–organized, insightful, semihumorous, and … short.

For the last 15 years, a significant part of my life outside of driving growth at BeyondTrust has been devoted to mercilessly teasing Morey about his diminutive stature, questionable dress sense, and that he might in fact be John Titor of renowned time travel fame (if you know, you know). We are BeyondTrust's balder versions of Arnold Schwarzenegger (unfortunately, without the muscles) and Danny DeVito from the 1988 movie, *Twins*. But appearances, as they say, are often deceptive, and in Morey's case, it's a perfect disguise for the intellectual giant that resides within.

# FOREWORD

Morey is a mentor, teacher, and cyber guru not only to me, but to all my colleagues, our partners, and thousands of security professionals around the world. Throughout his career, Morey has authored six—now seven—books, including *Privileged Attack Vectors*, *Asset Attack Vectors*, *Identity Attack Vectors*, and *Cloud Attack Vectors*. These works have established him as a leading voice in the field of cybersecurity, dissecting various attack vectors and analyzing the methods used by threat actors to exploit vulnerabilities. This book continues that tradition, offering a deep dive into the history of cyberattacks and the lessons they hold for today's cybersecurity professionals, of all types and backgrounds. Whether you are a seasoned CIO or just starting your career in cybersecurity sales, this book is what I would consider required reading.

The book begins with a historical overview, tracing the evolution of cyberattacks from the earliest worms and viruses to the sophisticated, state-sponsored threats of today. Morey emphasizes the importance of understanding the consistent patterns of exploitation that have persisted over time, even as technology has evolved. By examining the tactics and strategies of past threat actors, readers can gain valuable insights into anticipating and mitigating future attacks.

Morey also highlights the role of human nature in cybersecurity, noting that psychological factors, such as curiosity, arrogance, ignorance, greed, and complacency, have remained consistent drivers of cyberattacks. This perspective underscores the continued need for a holistic approach to cybersecurity that considers both technical and human factors.

In addition to historical analysis, the book provides the reader with practical recommendations for improving cybersecurity posture. Morey advocates for a strategy of incremental improvements, emphasizing that small, consistent steps can yield significant results over time. This approach is grounded in the concept of "1% improvements", also referred to as marginal gains theory, where organizations focus on making small, manageable changes that collectively enhance their overall security.

As you embark on this journey through the history of cyberattacks, guided by Morey's expertise, you will gain a deeper understanding of the Machiavellian threats we now face as individuals, corporations, and societies, and the strategies that we must employ to defend against them. This book is not just a historical account; it is a blueprint for building a resilient cybersecurity posture in an increasingly complex and interconnected world.

Having mentioned him, I am reminded of this quote from Machiavelli (who at five foot nine inches, tall for his day, would have towered over Morey) that perfectly summarizes the need for us all to keep an eye on the lessons of the past when looking to an uncertain and often intimidating future:

*"Whoever wishes to foresee the future must consult the past; for human events ever resemble those of preceding times. This arises from the fact that they are produced by men who ever have been, and ever shall be, animated by the same passions, and thus they necessarily have the same results."*

–Machiavelli
**Sincerely, (the taller twin)**
**Brent Thurrell, Chief Revenue Officer, BeyondTrust**

*And, Morey's rebuttal: "I identify as being tall."*

# Introduction: Part I

Welcome to the latest installment in the "Attack Vectors"[1] series. If you have followed my work in the past, you might already suspect the underlying premise of each book: that our battlefield has evolved beyond the physical realm of munitions and science fiction into a sophisticated, nearly invisible domain of digital cyberwarfare. A growing, modern theater of war is a domain governed by lines of code, social engineering, and a continuous tug-of-war over the world's most sensitive data by script kiddies, organized cybercrime syndicates, and nation-state-sponsored espionage.

Over the years, I've approached cyber threats from multiple angles, dissecting various attack vectors—from assets to identities—analyzing the methods used by threat actors, and mapping technology to prevent exploitable vulnerabilities. Today, as we venture deeper into our dependencies on electronics and the Internet, it becomes even more critical to look back at what has happened in the past and the people that have made a difference securing our future. The history of cyberattacks is more than a tale of cunning threat actors and unsuspecting victims; it's the blueprint by which we forge our strategies for tomorrow.

As technology continues to evolve, the global threat from cyberattacks has become an arena where anyone and anything could be a target. What is not part of the attack surface is becoming vanishingly small. Today, almost nothing is immune, not even disconnected (air-gapped) systems.

---

[1] https://link.springer.com/search?new-search=true&query=Haber+attack+vectors&content-type=book&dateFrom=&dateTo=&sortBy=relevance

## INTRODUCTION: PART I

Threat actors utilize everything from zero-day exploits and social engineering tactics to state-sponsored advanced persistent threats (APTs). What unites these threat actors over time is the consistent intent to infiltrate, disrupt, exploit, monetize, and coerce victims.

Most discussions about cybersecurity in the modern context revolve around new vulnerabilities (whether software, hardware, or identity-based) and the advanced methods used to infiltrate systems, but we often lose sight of the historical dimension, a dimension that can prepare us with valuable lessons and insights from the past. The truth is, patterns of exploitation have remained remarkably consistent, even as technologies have evolved to defend organizations. By dissecting the history of cyberattacks and their defenses, we can interpret these patterns, anticipate adversarial moves, and sharpen our defense mitigation strategies in an attempt to stay one step ahead. And, in this book, the intention is also to do so while attempting to interject a little humor to keep the discussion lively.

To be fair, one might ask: "Why revisit previous attack vectors when the pace of technology seems to be racing forward exponentially?" My response is that no new threat emerges from a vacuum or is truly unique. New attack vectors almost always leverage concepts that build upon the past. Every sophisticated attack we see today has at its core the same fundamental elements that formed the basis of earlier exploits: reconnaissance, intrusion, exploitation, exfiltration, and obfuscation. These steps might be dressed as novel zero-day exploits, AI-driven reconnaissance, or multistage malware, but the underlying architecture of an attack remains the same as it was decades ago. If we can study how earlier generations of cybercriminals orchestrated their efforts, we can better identify the traits that future threat actors may leave behind.

# INTRODUCTION: PART I

Figure 1 illustrates the basic cybersecurity attack chain that can explain almost every attack that has occurred to date. In addition, Asset, Privilege, Identity, and Cloud Attack Vectors are all topics covered in the "Attack Vectors" series of books[2] over the last decade.

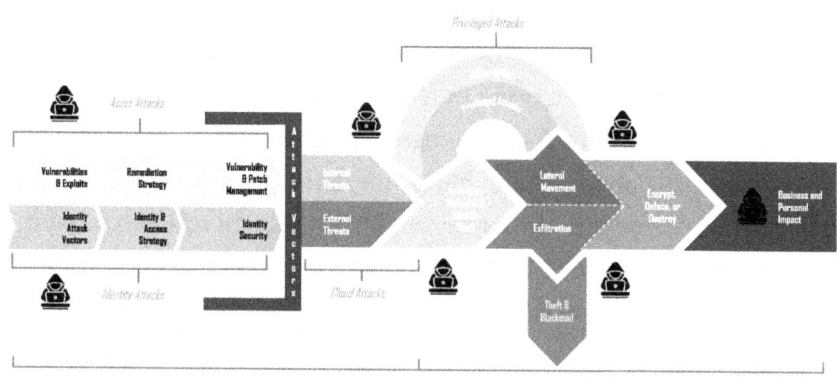

*Figure 1.* *Cyberattack chain*

To begin, let us start our discussion by looking at the earliest worms and viruses that propagated through rudimentary dial-up bulletin board systems[3] (BBSs) even before the Internet. Though communication technology was different, the human psychological traits used in social engineering were the same: curiosity, arrogance, ignorance, greed, and complacency. The progression from those early days to today's advanced persistent threats demonstrates an evolution in resources, sophistication, and targets, but the ideological underpinnings and strategic objectives

---

[2] https://link.springer.com/search?query=Haber+attack+vectors&lang=en_US&content-type=book

[3] https://www.theatlantic.com/technology/archive/2016/11/the-lost-civilization-of-dial-up-bulletin-board-systems/506465/

remain strikingly similar: seizing data, manipulating systems, denying services (or holding them for ransom), or forcing some form of political gain. By unearthing the lineage of these tactics, we gain the ability to foresee how they might evolve into future campaigns and what tactics emerging threat actors may embrace. And, while technology has evolved, human failings have not, and these failings play a key role in our discussion.

Make no doubt, cybersecurity is largely about prevention. Understanding where attacks come from, how they unfold, and the historical successes and failures of past defenders not only sharpens our technical defenses but informs our thinking about risk management, crisis response, and long-term cybersecurity planning and budgeting. Every time we reopen a case study from a past incident, we can assemble tactics and strategies that might still be utilized today. Indeed, while technology progresses, human nature drudges along at a more methodical pace, meaning our vulnerabilities—both technical and psychological—often remain the same or even go backwards as we search for facts and tackle FUD (Fear, Uncertainty, and Doubt). Understanding this is key to building a cybersecurity mindset that separates the truth about an attack from the noise of noticeable outcomes.

History can also be a warning sign to complacent defenders. Many organizations assume their sophisticated investments from next-generation firewalls (NGFWs), endpoint protection, or zero trust architectures are sufficient to mitigate the risks from even the most persistent threat actors. Yet, time and time again, we see breaches where threat actors find the smallest possible chink in the armor. It is always a matter of when, not if, an attack will occur. Whether through unpatched software, unprotected creases in the identity fabric between siloed systems, social engineering, stolen credentials, or targeted phishing campaigns, threat actors will reliably find vulnerable spots and exploit them. The pages of cybersecurity history are littered with cautionary tales of organizations that relied too heavily on a single defensive strategy, vendor, or solution. Many spent millions on cutting-edge solutions, yet overlooked fundamental best practices, consequently incurring catastrophic breaches.

## INTRODUCTION: PART I

When we trace the evolution of notable cyberattacks through the years, a clear pattern emerges.

In the early days of the Internet (late 1990s), many intrusions stemmed from curiosity, mischief, and simple bragging rights. A hacker (not a threat actor) might infiltrate a system simply because they could. The difference between the two is an important distinction. A hacker is a person skilled in information technology who achieves goals and solves problems by nonstandard means. These are typically nefarious in nature by today's standards. A threat actor by comparison is an entity (group or person) that poses a risk to computer systems, networks, and data and is a super set of hackers. As the dot-com era gained momentum (early 2000s), motivations grew more complex and widespread: financial theft, corporate espionage, and even sabotage of critical infrastructure for revenge, potentially even from a disgruntled employee. The evolution of simple hacking to organized cybercrime (threat actors) syndicates has warranted a change in the way we identify threats and the adversaries behind them.

Therefore, it didn't take long before state-sponsored attacks entered the scene. Governments recognized that crippling an adversary's power grid or stealing sensitive military technology could be accomplished far more efficiently through cyberspace than via bombs, spies, or other types of physical espionage. In my opinion, this is when the landscape began to change for the worse. Governments got involved, which kicked off a long-drawn-out period of cyberwarfare that we still experience today.

Throughout the "Attack Vectors" series of books, I have called attention to these shifts, not merely to alarm readers or proclaim a new digital arms race, but to illustrate how each step in the historical progression informs the next generation of threats. Understanding how amateur hackers (as in the 1995 movie *Hackers*[4] starring a young Angelina Jolie) once defaced websites for notoriety offers insight into how larger groups might now attempt to cause mass disruption by targeting a company's

---

[4] https://www.imdb.com/title/tt0113243/

public presence and creating a "watering hole" for future attacks. Similarly, once-novel worms that spread from machine to machine without user intervention paved the way for today's ransomware epidemics, shutting down city councils, hospitals, and entire corporate networks.

Cyberattacks don't happen in a vacuum. They are shaped by geopolitical tensions, economic competition, and broad cultural shifts. Tracing the history of major cyber incidents over the last several decades reveals a menagerie of events. Surprisingly, each one can be tied to the social, political, or economic realities of its time.

For example, in periods of heightened political conflict, we observe a surge in espionage-linked attacks targeting governmental agencies or critical infrastructure. During economic downturns, financially motivated cyberattacks often escalate as organizations become more prone to identity threats and malicious actors targeting sources of revenue. Observing these large-scale patterns allows us to contextualize cyber threats as part of a broader system, rather than as isolated occurrences.

Moreover, examining how organizations, governments, and consumers responded—or failed to respond—to these attacks provides us with a blueprint for our current endeavors. No one should think going to the moon today is solely based on new technology. Everything we do today is built on knowledge (not wisdom) from the past. Retrospective criticism can illuminate missed opportunities for collaboration and help ensure future initiatives truly learn from the lessons of the past. Reviewing past endeavors can highlight inadequate or outdated defenses and faults in policies and procedures.

When placing cyberattacks in their broader historical and geopolitical context, we discover that the most resilient defense strategies stem from collaboration, shared intelligence, crowdsourcing, and allowing information to transcend the boundaries of competition between market rivals, as well as diplomatic friction among nations.

Another vital insight gained by studying past attacks is the close relationship between adversity and innovation. Many of the cybersecurity technologies we rely on today—intrusion detection systems, antivirus software, firewalls, privileged access management (PAM), and encryption protocols—were created in response to ongoing, real-world threats.

Groundbreaking incidents, from the Morris Worm[5] to the largest distributed denial-of-service attacks, like the Mirai Botnet,[6] have spurred rapid leaps in technology and practice. From these attacks, we can easily see why security experts, cornered by a novel exploit, rallied to develop new frameworks, standards, and, ultimately, new vendor solutions to combat these attacks. Everyone studying cybersecurity history should be aware that, at one time, organizations used to purchase anti-spyware and operating system firewalls as separate products. This was because modern threats of the time required new defensive technology that wasn't yet integrated into existing offerings.

In subsequent chapters of this book, we will explore a curated analysis of some of the most significant cyber breaches in modern history. We will dissect the technical methods used, analyze their financial impact, and explore the resulting innovations that emerged from the postmortem reviews. By observing how the cybersecurity community adapted to these attacks, you will gain a deeper understanding of the resilience and tenacity that underpins our modern cybersecurity landscape. Finally, you will see the innovation that emerges when a crisis demands an immediate response to a new threat—a critical moment that directly shaped the protective tools and methodologies we rely on today.

---

[5] https://www.fbi.gov/news/stories/morris-worm-30-years-since-first-major-attack-on-internet-110218

[6] https://www.cisecurity.org/insights/blog/the-mirai-botnet-threats-and-mitigations

## INTRODUCTION: PART I

While the history of cyberattacks can be fascinating from a purely academic standpoint, the ultimate goal of this book is practical application: learning how to defend better today and in the future. As I've argued in previous "Attack Vectors" volumes, the best defense is one that recognizes the fluid and cyclical nature of threats.

History teaches us that threat actors rarely rest on their laurels (or for a modern analogy—they don't retire the keyboard and log off after a breach); they adapt and transform. Each victory for the defenders is countered with new lines of malicious code and new cybersecurity bypass methods. It's a continuous game of cat and mouse that rarely slows down.

The true power of a historical perspective lies in fueling this ongoing cycle of anticipation and response that provides a backdrop for this cat and mouse game that we will revisit throughout this book. By studying how infiltration techniques have evolved—from SQL injections to advanced supply chain compromises—we can pivot faster and anticipate the shape of tomorrow's attacks. By analyzing how disinformation and social media manipulations emerged as potent tools, we can develop stronger resilience strategies for an era when public perception can be weaponized at scale. To reiterate, history is not merely a record of old cyber battles won or lost; it's the foundation of the next wave of confrontations.

Finally, an overarching theme throughout the "Attack Vectors" series has been the shared responsibility of all stakeholders: governments, corporations, educational institutions, and individual users. In analyzing historical breaches, we find that too often a failure in organizational culture or an oversight at a governmental policy level left the proverbial door wide open for threat actors. This brings an odd revelation to the table. Rarely does a breach postmortem end with the dissection of a sophisticated exploit, but rather it points back to a missed patch, a disregarded security warning, a stolen password, or a mismanaged privilege escalation. This highlights flaws in shared responsibilities, bringing the human equation into the light for the vast majority of cyberattacks.

It's my hope that this installment not only illuminates how historical attacks continue to reshape our current cybersecurity landscape but also reminds every reader—from corporate CISOs and policymakers to small business owners and individual smartphone users—of the vital role they play. When we expand our vision to see cyberattacks as the sum of human, technological, and historical factors, we begin to comprehend why a culture of security is paramount and should never be an afterthought. The most advanced systems in the world can still be undone by one careless mistake.

In an era defined by unprecedented connectivity, our digital footprints grow larger with each passing day. The threat landscape adapts alongside that expansion. Artificial intelligence, quantum computing, and the Internet of Things (IoT) push us into new frontiers of both opportunity and risk. Indeed, the sheer variety of digital platforms and devices, plus the explosion of machine identities, means our potential vulnerabilities and attack surface are multiplying. Looking back at how we arrived here is not merely a scholarly exercise; it is a practical necessity for understanding the best way to navigate the future.

As you continue your reading, I encourage you to adopt a stance of curiosity and reflection. The chapters ahead serve not merely as cautionary tales, but as templates for better governance, design, and strategy. They demonstrate how repeated oversight can be transformed into collective wisdom, how each breach can catalyze a breakthrough in security methodology, and how individual vigilance can protect an entire network. Whether you are new to the series or a longtime reader, you will find that the real power of this historical overview lies in its ability to inform your next steps.

We live in extraordinary times. The lines between physical and virtual realities are blurring. Economic stability, national security, and personal privacy all hinge on our ability to anticipate and repel digital assaults. We must understand that, while zero-day exploits and intricate phishing schemes may evolve, the bedrock principles of cyber defense remain rooted in awareness, collaboration, and continuous adaptation.

# Introduction: Part II

Cybersecurity doesn't demand a huge investment from an organization to be successful; it demands consistency. Much like a steady drumbeat from your favorite song, improving your security posture by just 1% at a time (based on James Clear's book, *Atomic Habits*[1]) can yield massive transformative results over time. Realistically, no business can guarantee immunity from a threat actor, but incremental, actionable improvements can significantly reduce risk and minimize dwell time.

As we enter the second half of the roaring 2020s (and yes, I like that expression), businesses should adopt a pragmatic, step-by-step approach to cybersecurity that is consistent, as opposed to one where improvement is largely tied to bursts of energy, money, or reactive projects.

To enhance cybersecurity for everyone in the 2020s, consider adopting these simple yet powerful recommendations to gradually improve your security posture by a meager 1% at a time. The reasons for these recommendations will become apparent as we explore the history of cybersecurity.

1. **Regularly Update and Patch Your Systems:** The first 1% improvement starts with embracing the mundane: patching and updating. Cybercriminals exploit known vulnerabilities in outdated software, a risk that's entirely avoidable if you consistently patch environments on a regular basis.

---
[1] https://jamesclear.com/atomic-habits

*Why it matters:* Unpatched systems are like unlocked windows and doors in your digital assets. Patching ensures you're protected against the latest vulnerabilities, reducing attack surfaces from exploitation by threat actors, regardless of whether the threat is targeted or opportunistic.

Actions:

- Schedule automatic updates for operating systems and applications, whether they're on-premise or in the cloud. Expect that some of these updates will require downtime to be successful.

- Create a patch management plan to track and apply updates consistently, with a policy and documentation to match. (This will help with many initiatives, such as cyber insurance cost-reduction, etc.)

- Prioritize critical patches for software tied to sensitive business functions, with a service level agreement that the business can measure and effectively own.

2. **Enforce Strong Password Policies, Least Privilege, and Use Multifactor Authentication (MFA):** Poor identity and access management have long plagued organizations as a major cybersecurity weak spot. However, these are truly issues that organizations can cost-effectively address to a significant degree. If your business can prioritize unique and complex passwords and passkeys, you will mitigate a significant amount of identity-based attacks. If you bundle in MFA, the simple theft of a credential will

mitigate the bulk of attacks based on username and password theft. Removing administrative rights and enforcing least privilege also vastly minimizes the attack surface and can even help proactively mitigate a large percentage of zero-day software vulnerabilities. While these three disciplines are distinctly different, identity hygiene and strong identity confidence for authentication form the basis for mitigating most modern identity attack vectors.

*Why it matters:* Insecure passwords are often the attack vector for a breach. If these passwords have administrative or root privileges, the threat actor has unrestricted access into your environment. Making passwords unique and complex is key to partially mitigating this threat. Adding MFA as a second verification mechanism ensures that, even if a password is compromised, your assets will not fall victim to unauthorized authentication attempts.

Actions:

- Require passwords to be complex with a mix of letters, numbers, and symbols, and ensure passwords are unique for every system and not reused. This can be performed manually or using technology defined in the next few bullets.

- Deploy a privileged access management (PAM) solution to store and generate complex passwords that are obfuscated from end-user access and rotated on a periodic basis. When users no longer know the password to a system but still have access via automation or single sign-on, a 1% improvement can easily be obtained by preventing a simple leakage of sensitive credentials.

- For small businesses and personal use within an organization, users should consider a personal password manager to create, store, inject, and obfuscate personal passwords. This ensures uniqueness and complexity but does not include the robustness of session management and automatic password rotation found in PAM solutions. This 1% improvement can help ensure personal passwords are not leaked or stored insecurely on paper or clear text files.

- Remove excessive privileges from accounts to ensure no one is logging on as administrator or root by default, especially on their local systems for daily activities.

- Implement MFA for all business systems, including email, customer databases, financial accounts, etc. Essentially, MFA should be used everywhere technically possible, and exceptions should be well known and documented.

This 1% improvement is a cybersecurity best practice that can make the biggest difference in protecting your business from an identity-based attack.

3. **Train Employees to Recognize and Respond to Cyber Threats:** Your employees are your first line of defense, but they're often considered the weakest link. Cybersecurity awareness training is a cost-effective way to reduce human error, raise risk

awareness, and improve your organization's overall security by empowering everyone to be vigilant about cyber threats.

*Why it matters:* Phishing, social engineering, and ignorant clicks on links and emails remain a leading cause of cybersecurity incidents. An educated employee base can generally spot and stop these attacks before they escalate into a cybersecurity breach.

Actions:

- Conduct regular training sessions for all employees on recognizing phishing emails and malicious links. These sessions should occur at least annually and be documented for compliance and cyber insurance initiatives.
- Use simulated phishing tests to reinforce lessons and to identify employees who need additional training or coaching.
- Create a culture of accountability by encouraging employees to report suspicious activity, not a culture that penalizes them for simple mistakes.

This 1% improvement in awareness typically is enough to stop even the latest zero-day phishing attack.

4. **Implement Segmentation:** Not every part of your network needs to be visible to every other part of the environment (flat network), and not every device needs access by every employee. By segmenting your network and using role-based access, you limit

the spread of malware and potentially unauthorized access. This segmentation concept is the foundation of a zero trust environment.

*Why it matters:* If a cybersecurity incident—or worse, a breach—occurs, segmentation ensures a threat actor cannot easily execute lateral movement across your network. With a strong segmentation model in place, even after exploitation has occurred and an attacker has gained a beachhead in your environment, they may still struggle to connect to any other endpoint, asset, application, or database. Segmentation keeps these resources electronically isolated to prevent threat actors from hopping between electronically connected systems.

Actions:

- Separate critical business systems (e.g., payroll, accounting, medical data, etc.) from less secure networks using network segmentation (e.g., guest Wi-Fi, IoT networks, etc.).

- Use firewalls, VLANs (virtual local area network), and access control lists (ACLs) to create logical boundaries between network segments.

- Assign access to network segments following the principle of least privilege (PoLP).

- Regularly review segmentation of networks and people to ensure access is appropriate.

Simply by making broad areas of your network environment (targets) inaccessible from one to the next, network segmentation can easily improve your defenses by another 1%. This simple act can stop or slow a wide range of threats, even after a compromise has occurred.

5. **Back Up Data and Test Recovery/Restoration Plans:** When all else fails, your backups are literally your safety net. Respectfully, they are only useful if they are current, secure, and recoverable in a timely manner. The backup and recovery process should be tested periodically to ensure success. Anything short of complete success can lead to excessive downtime and loss of critical business data.

    *Why it matters:* Ransomware payouts are typically made by victimized organizations when they lack reliable backups. Frequent backups and rehearsed recovery plans ensure your operations can continue with minimal disruption, even if a threat actor compromises an environment.

    Actions:

    - Schedule automated backups of critical data and key systems and store the backups securely in multiple locations, including offsite and in the cloud.

    - Encrypt backups to protect them from unauthorized access (regardless of location) and potential physical theft (if you are using removable media for backups).

- Test your recovery process at least quarterly to ensure backups are functional and accessible. Be sure to measure the time it takes to restore your systems. This is crucial to avoid excessive downtime when a recovery is required.

The time it takes to perform these tests periodically will easily justify a 1% improvement in downtime costs once the process is optimized but hopefully never used as a ransomware recovery technique.

Finally, if you implement all of these recommendations with simply a 1% improvement for each, the cumulative effect will decrease the risk surface for the organization. This is crucial for our history discussion because any improvements can potentially mitigate the next breach. Figure 2 illustrates this concept.

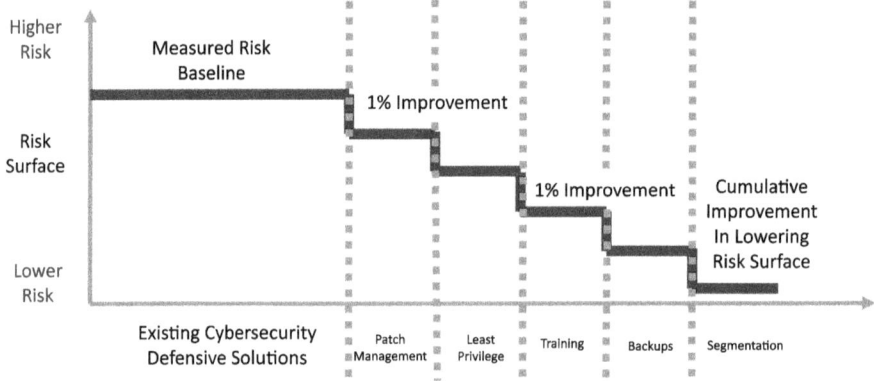

***Figure 2.*** *One percent improvement per discipline to lower an organization's overall risk surface*

The beauty of the 1% improvement strategy lies in its simplicity and consistency. These small steps don't require a massive investment of time or money, but their cumulative impact is significant. Cybersecurity is not about perfection; it's about persistence. By consistently focusing on incremental improvements, businesses can outpace threat actors, one step (or percent) at a time.

As my final recommendation, start with one tip, then tackle the next. Over time, these 1% gains will compound into a robust defense strategy, ensuring your business is better prepared for the evolving cybersecurity landscape of the 2020s and beyond. All of these recommendations are from a history lesson we will begin to explore.

## Attack Vectors: The History of Cybersecurity

From early worms to AI-powered deepfakes, *Attack Vectors* chronicles the relentless battle between hackers and defenders. This deep dive into cybersecurity's evolution unpacks the rise of malware from the Morris Worm to Stuxnet and the cyber syndicates that turned hacking into a billion-dollar underground industry. This book explores devastating exploits like Code Red and Heartbleed, revealing how vulnerabilities become weapons. Meet the visionaries who built the Internet's defenses and the adversaries who found ways to break them. Governments, corporations, and rogue actors all play a role in this ongoing digital war, where data is power and deception is an art.

As cyberattacks grow more sophisticated, understanding the past is crucial to securing the future. *Attack Vectors* is essential reading for anyone navigating today's high-stakes cyber landscape who wants to learn lessons from the past and discover how solutions today address the most pressing attack vectors predicted for the future.

**Start reading today to:**

- Understand the history of cybersecurity, from the early 1950s through today.

- Explore the history of terminology that defines the modern threat landscape.

- Examine the history of malware, exploits, breaches, syndicates, and people throughout the last 25 years.

- Learn how modern cybersecurity solutions have been developed to address the evolution of attack vectors.

- Explore best practices for what to do after a breach and how to manage some of the biggest risks, including human beings themselves.

# Who Is This Book For?

This book is intended for new security management professionals, information technology staff, information security students, governance teams, and anyone seeking to understand the history of cybersecurity, and where it is taking us, so we can be better prepared for the future.

# CHAPTER 1

# The History of Attack Vectors

## Foundations

When we think about cybersecurity, many imagine malicious hackers typing furiously in dark, smelly rooms, multinational organizations reviewing dashboards and logs scattered across war room screens, or security professionals staring deeply into their monitors as they try to identify the next attack vector. While there may be some elements of truth to these notions, they vastly oversimplify the cybersecurity playing field of today.

Cybersecurity is a crazy quilt evolving from decades of innovation, oversight, ambition, and trial and error. Like any great technological undertaking, it is shaped by human nature and the irresistible drive to do more, to move faster, and to expand the frontiers of what is possible. These concepts are as old as human history, but when it comes to cybersecurity (not security itself), we are only dealing with concepts that are less than a century old.

In the 1950s, computers were a rare sight. Few individuals knew how to operate one, and even fewer had any vision of the interconnected, digitized world we live in today. Security, if it was even considered at all, revolved around physical locks on doors and the near impossibility of accessing these expensive and specialized machines. Virtual threats were not on the radar, because the "virtual" world simply did not exist. Any electronic security was always an afterthought after an incident occurred. Simply put, concepts like passwords to your computer simply didn't exist.

That aside, the seeds for cybersecurity development were planted early. With the birth of the transistor and the subsequent development of integrated circuits, computing technology evolved at an exponential pace. Advancements in communications, ranging from telephone lines to satellite transmissions, also foreshadowed a world where data could flow freely across borders, regardless of whether it was analog or digital. With that free flow of data came the first glimmers of risk, from eavesdropping to data corruption (early denial of service, a.k.a. jamming).

As already stated, this book's goal is to provide context, depth, and a fresh perspective on cybersecurity's evolution. Too often, we treat modern threats as though they appeared overnight. In reality, everything we wrestle with today—viruses, worms, ransomware, zero-day exploits, identity theft, supply chain attacks, etc.–represents the culmination of years of parallel developments in technology, criminal enterprise, and global connectivity.

By understanding the long arc of cybersecurity's story, we better appreciate our present state. This foundation is vital, whether you're a business leader, technologist, enthusiast, or student. Knowing how we got here is the first step in figuring out where we need to go. The story begins in a time when the word "cybersecurity" didn't even exist (and when it first came into existence, we referred to it by two words, "cyber security," before it became a portmanteau, "cybersecurity," as commonly occurs over time with frequent usage of a term). So, let's time travel back to the 1950s.

CHAPTER 1    THE HISTORY OF ATTACK VECTORS

# Vacuum Tubes to Transistors (1950s–1960s)

In the 1950s, the word "computer" generally referred to a colossal machine filling entire rooms with racks of vacuum tubes and tangles of wiring. Often, these were housed in academic or government research labs. The cost of such a machine was astronomical, the knowledge required to operate it highly specialized, and the day-to-day usage tightly controlled. These early computers, such as the UNIVAC[1] (UNIVersal Automatic Computer) and the ENIAC[2] (Electronic Numerical Integrator and Computer), were milestones of human achievement. But in these times, "cybersecurity" would have sounded like science fiction and probably would have been dismissed by system operators.

To be clear, if you wanted access to an early computer, you had to walk into a locked facility, sign a logbook, and wear appropriate identification, like a name badge. Physical security was the gatekeeper for all access. Organizations that owned these expensive systems employed guards, more for asset protection than data protection. The concept of someone "hacking" the machine from an outside location was inconceivable. Indeed, the term "hacker" itself was rooted not in illegal activities, but rather in the idea of creative problem-solving and out-of-the-box thinking, often at institutions like the Massachusetts Institute of Technology (MIT).

While these early computers gained popularity, a quieter revolution was unfolding in parallel: the birth of information and data theory. At Bell Labs, mathematician Claude Shannon[3] laid foundational work that would later shape data encryption and cybersecurity as a discipline. In his 1948 paper, "A Mathematical Theory of Communication," Shannon introduced concepts that deeply influenced how data could be transmitted and secured.

---

[1] https://www.britannica.com/technology/UNIVAC
[2] https://www.britannica.com/technology/ENIAC
[3] https://www.britannica.com/biography/Claude-Shannon

CHAPTER 1    THE HISTORY OF ATTACK VECTORS

Though the term "cybersecurity" was not in anyone's dictionary yet, Shannon's theories seeded the intellectual groundwork for encryption and data error correction. This formed the bedrock upon which secure communications would stand for decades to come.

As we think about these theoretical advancements, we need to be reminded of the geopolitical climate in the 1950s and the role it played. The United States and U.S.S.R. (Union of Soviet Socialist Republics[4]–what is now largely Russia) Cold War demanded the secure exchange of military and diplomatic messages among allies. Cryptography, of course, was not new; it had been employed for centuries and was a critical tool in World War II. Governments understood the importance of encryption, and computers introduced a new dimension to making it unbreakable. The United States and the Soviet Union both invested heavily in technology that could encode and decode transmissions more efficiently. The tension of potential espionage and sabotage made secure communication a paramount goal and an early cyberattack vector.

We can see echoes of this era today in the never-ending cyber arms race of offense and defense, including planned red team and blue team simulated attacks. Back then (circa 1950s), the focus was on cryptographic machines like the SIGABA[5] (used by the United States) or the post-World War II versions of the Enigma[6] machine. The secrecy was tangible and physical, with entire intelligence agencies devoted to code-making and codebreaking (defensive and offensive cybersecurity).

One of the underappreciated evolutions of the late 1950s and early 1960s was the concept of time-sharing in computing. Instead of a single user monopolizing an expensive mainframe, time-sharing allowed

---

[4] https://www.history.com/topics/european-history/history-of-the-soviet-union
[5] https://www.nsa.gov/History/National-Cryptologic-Museum/Exhibits-Artifacts/Exhibit-View/Article/2719165/sigabaecm/
[6] https://www.britannica.com/topic/Enigma-German-code-device

multiple users to access the same machine through "dumb" terminals. This innovation brought with it the first semblance of "remote access," albeit within the same building or campus. It also was the basis for monetizing computer time based on the computing cycles used and business concepts like departmental chargeback for time used by a computer. These early concepts also helped to determine when computing time (cycles) was being used appropriately or inappropriately.

Time-sharing also introduced the first potential vulnerability. When multiple users accessed the same hardware, the question arose: how do we ensure one user's data remains private and inaccessible to others? Access control mechanisms and rudimentary segmentation, authentication, and permissions began to emerge. Password-protected accounts and user groups emerged shortly after to appropriately share information, sowing the seeds for more sophisticated security protocols that developed in subsequent years.

During this period, security was still an afterthought. The emphasis was on innovation and maximizing computational potential. Most individuals involved in these projects were colleagues or students, more interested in pushing the boundaries of what machines could do rather than how to "hack" them in modern terms. It's important to understand that the earliest pioneers of computing were not security experts, but they recognized that shared computing environments presented risks that needed a solution. Nonetheless, they laid the intellectual groundwork for everything that followed. Consider these individuals for their unique contributions, and note: later chapters will explore additional individuals for their specific contributions.

- **John von Neumann:**[7] A mathematician whose work on self-replicating automata foreshadowed the concept of computer viruses, decades before the term existed.

---

[7] https://www.britannica.com/biography/John-von-Neumann

## CHAPTER 1   THE HISTORY OF ATTACK VECTORS

- **Norbert Wiener:**[8] Coined the term "cybernetics" in the 1940s, which influenced how we think about information systems, feedback loops, and control mechanisms.

- **Grace Hopper:**[9] A trailblazer who invented the compiler and championed machine-independent programming languages. While she did not directly work on security, her drive to make computing more accessible contributed to the broader adoption and, ultimately, the exposure of risk to computerized assets.

Although these luminaries didn't see themselves as cybersecurity specialists, their legacies underpin the entire industry. The interweaving of mathematics, engineering, and computational theory sets the stage for future revelations about security and privacy.

As the 1960s approached, the Cold War waned, and computing technology advanced past the stage of exclusivity. More universities acquired mainframes. Government agencies recognized the strategic advantages of data processing. Corporations began to experiment with automation and the calculation power of early mainframe designs. All of this signaled that computing would not remain a scientific curiosity or an exclusive technology for only the organizations that could afford it.

The next section focuses on how these early systems evolved, the birth of new threats, and the growing awareness that digital resources needed protection beyond locked doors. From vacuum tubes and rotor machines, we will move to integrated circuits and multi-user mainframes. The stage for the cybersecurity conversation was about to become more intense, more relevant, and, eventually, global.

---

[8] https://www.britannica.com/biography/Norbert-Wiener
[9] https://www.britannica.com/biography/Grace-Hopper

CHAPTER 1   THE HISTORY OF ATTACK VECTORS

# Mainframes and Early Cybersecurity (1970s–Early 1980s)

The 1970s ushered in a wave of innovation that shrank computers from room-filling behemoths to relatively smaller and more economical systems. The transition from vacuum tubes to transistors, and then to integrated circuits, paved the way for more efficient machines. At this time, IBM (International Business Machines) dominated the decade with systems like the IBM System/370.[10] Governments, universities, and large corporations adopted mainframes for tasks like data processing, payroll, inventory management, and scientific research.

It's important to note that these mainframes were not yet connected in any meaningful sense as we understand networks today. Access was obtained through terminals that essentially could not function without the mainframe itself. Visionaries saw that shipping vast amounts of magnetic tape from one location to another was inefficient and time-consuming, and the seeds of interconnectivity were sprouting in places like the Advanced Research Projects Agency Network (ARPANET[11]). This project would define the next big leap in communication and the early model for what is the Internet today.

With more users relying on mainframes, the need for robust access control became clearer with each new use case and user request. Multi-user systems demanded separation of privileges, basic identity management, and audits and reporting.

Early cybersecurity technology was rudimentary, yet it quickly evolved to address the inherent risks of burgeoning computing environments. For example, IBM introduced the Resource Access Control Facility (RACF) in 1976 to manage user authentication and control specific resource access.

---

[10] https://www.ibm.com/history/system-370
[11] https://www.britannica.com/topic/ARPANET

Other vendors, such as Computer Associates (the first software vendor to reach $1 billion in annual revenue, now owned by Broadcom), entered the market with their own solutions. These offerings competed with IBM by addressing vulnerabilities in time-sharing, billing, and broader system protection within IBM's mainframe and mid-range hardware ecosystem.

Meanwhile, operating systems like Multics[12] (Multiplexed Information and Computing Service) at MIT served as testbeds for security features that would build foundational components for years to come. Multics is particularly noteworthy for pioneering concepts such as ring-based architecture, dynamic linking, and access control lists (ACLs). Much of modern cybersecurity architecture owes a debt to Multics' security-based design, whose influence remains visible in even the most modern solutions today.

As previously discussed, "security" mostly meant preventing curious insiders from reading, copying, printing, or deleting each other's data. The realm of unauthorized external threats still seemed farfetched, partly because these massive machines weren't broadly interconnected, and access was physically limited, even with terminals in an office environment.

Circling back, ARPANET was born in 1969 under the auspices of the US Department of Defense's Advanced Research Projects Agency (DARPA[13]). Initially linking four computing nodes, UCLA, Stanford, UC Santa Barbara, and the University of Utah, ARPANET aimed to explore new forms of communication by sharing computing data in real time across geographical locations. Early adopters were academic researchers, engineers, and scientists who shared data and ideas across thousands of miles without the need for physical tape transfers.

---

[12] https://web.mit.edu/multics-history/
[13] https://www.darpa.mil

Security for ARPANET, as typical in those days, was low on the priority list. Their focus was on ensuring data could be passed between different types of machines. Trust was implicit among the community of ARPANET users, who were mostly well-known researchers and students. Protocols, such as the Network Control Protocol (NCP), and later the Transmission Control Protocol (TCP), were designed with functionality in mind rather than robust authentication or encryption. For example, if you could "sniff" the wire for communications, you could reassemble the entire communications from clear text and "read" what was being transmitted.

As ARPANET grew, so did the possibility for remote exploitation. The first known "hack" was less an act of malicious intent and more a demonstration of vulnerabilities. In 1971, a programmer named Ray Tomlinson[14] (who famously invented email) discovered ways to send data to unauthorized locations. Incidents like this hinted that, while the network was groundbreaking, it could also be exploited in unforeseen ways.

By the late 1970s, forward-thinking malicious individuals began to wonder if computer systems could be used for criminal activity. Cases emerged of employees exploiting insider access to embezzle and launder money. Because mainframes ran financial and inventory systems, a knowledgeable user could manipulate data to funnel resources for personal gain. Investigations were often difficult.

In this era, computer forensics was in its infancy. Logging was minimal due to the high cost of processing time and storage, evidence was ephemeral when it was stored, and legal frameworks for prosecuting computer crimes were nearly nonexistent. Law enforcement and organizations began to realize that digital theft could be more profitable and less risky than traditional forms of physical crime, like breaking into a bank vault. This awareness triggered the development of stronger access controls, more comprehensive logging, and the earliest forms of data encryption in commercial settings.

---

[14] https://www.internethalloffame.org/official-biography-raymond-tomlinson/

CHAPTER 1   THE HISTORY OF ATTACK VECTORS

Simultaneously, a different phenomenon was developing among students and enthusiasts. "Hacker culture," initially synonymous with curiosity and innovation, gradually took on a darker and more malicious connotation. This shift accelerated when individuals discovered they could gain unauthorized access to systems simply by knowing how to navigate code, exploiting weak authentication (knowing someone's user ID and password), and even simply by sitting in front of someone else's terminal when they were away.

During the 1970s, phone phreaking,[15] a precursor to computer hacking, began to take shape, forming the foundation for groups like the 2600 Club. Hackers like John Draper[16] ("Captain Crunch") became minor celebrities by finding ways to manipulate telephone networks, often for free long-distance calls. Although phone phreaking wasn't strictly about computers, it highlighted a growing subculture devoted to studying and exploiting technological weaknesses. The techniques and attitudes of phone phreaking would later merge into a broader hacking milieu as computers became more interconnected via analog phone lines (modems).

Governments, primarily in the United States, started paying attention to these threats. The Federal Bureau of Investigation (FBI) and other agencies slowly developed specialized units to investigate crimes involving computer systems. Laws that would address computer misuse did not yet exist in any sort of tangible form. The first attempt to criminalize unauthorized access to government computers arrived with the US Comprehensive Crime Control Act of 1984,[17] laying the groundwork for future legislation based on unauthorized access or system abuse.

Despite these early efforts, the speed of innovation and the expanding curiosity of tech-savvy individuals often outpaced legal and policy

---

[15] https://www.britannica.com/topic/phreaking
[16] https://privacy-pc.com/articles/history-of-hacking-john-captain-crunch-drapers-perspective.html
[17] https://www.congress.gov/bill/98th-congress/senate-bill/1762

frameworks. Organizations struggled to keep up with the need for cybersecurity defense mechanisms, and many solution implementations remained reactive rather than proactive.

As we progressed into the early 1980s, businesses and consumers began to embrace personal computing (PC), with hobbyist kits like the MITS Altair 8800[18] and commercial successes such as the Apple II[19] and IBM XT.[20] Although mainframes retained their dominance in large-scale data processing, a massive paradigm shift was on the horizon. Personal computers would soon bring computing power to the masses, along with security headaches that nobody could have predicted in the mainframe era.

The lessons from these years are crucial to modern cybersecurity thinking. Security has always lagged behind functionality in technology's development. The mainframe era forced us to wrestle with the complexities of multiuser access, insider threats, and the initial notion of interconnected systems. While early hacking incidents were often more about exploration than exploitation, they foreshadowed the battles that would soon unfold in personal computing regarding cybersecurity research and the broader topics yet to follow.

In the next section, we will examine the explosion of personal computers in the 1980s, the rise of hacking as both a pastime and a criminal enterprise, and the government's frantic efforts to catch up through legislation and law enforcement.

---

[18] https://americanhistory.si.edu/collections/object/nmah_334396
[19] https://americanhistory.si.edu/collections/object/nmah_334638
[20] https://www.ibm.com/history/personal-computer

CHAPTER 1   THE HISTORY OF ATTACK VECTORS

# Personal Computing (1980s)

By the early 1980s, personal computing was becoming a reality for the masses. Companies like Apple, Radio Shack, Atari, Commodore, and IBM were selling machines small enough (and affordable enough) for home use. Suddenly, high school students and hobbyists could experiment with coding, gaming, and connecting via electronic bulletin board systems (BBSs) using dial-up modems.

This new world of personal computing introduced an era of democratized technology. While mainframes were guarded behind corporate or university walls, personal computers offered everyday individuals an avenue into the digital frontier. This interconnection then created opportunities for both technological advancement and potential abuse. As a result, a new breed of "hackers" materialized, completely removed from the academic circles of the 1960s and 1970s.

The availability of personal computers and BBS networks enabled curious minds to find and exploit vulnerabilities, share bootlegged copies of software, and share ideas on a wide variety of technical and political topics. Self-taught programmers (often teenagers—which spawned the notion for "script kiddies"[21]) probed software and communication protocols looking for ways to take advantage of the system. They discovered that codes controlling everything from games to system utilities could be modified, circumvented, or even repurposed for "fun," bragging rights, or malicious intent.

Not all hacking in this era was malicious. The traditional hacker mentality of pushing boundaries, exploring systems, and learning how things worked remained firmly intact. But law enforcement and the media

---

[21] https://www.techtarget.com/searchsecurity/definition/script-kiddy-or-script-kiddie

## CHAPTER 1   THE HISTORY OF ATTACK VECTORS

soon began lumping all manner of computer vulnerability research under the label of criminal hacking. High-profile cases in the early and mid-1980s made headlines, painting an image of hackers as "digital outlaws."

A defining moment occurred in 1983 with a group known as the "414s".[22] Named after their Milwaukee area code, these teenagers broke into a variety of high-profile systems, including the Los Alamos National Laboratory. Media coverage went into a frenzy, and the incident led to the first US Congressional hearing on computer security. During these hearings, lawmakers grappled with the question: "Is this a real threat or just teenage mischief?"

While the 414s claimed their activities were more curiosity-driven than malicious, the Los Alamos hacking event highlighted just how vulnerable interconnect computing technology was becoming. The hearing also underscored a theme that has persisted to this day: laws and regulations often significantly lag behind technological advancements. If you consider the cryptocurrency market today, generative artificial intelligence (AI) and agentic AI, you can see this premise still holds true.

In the same year, the movie *WarGames*[23] was released. The film stars Matthew Broderick, playing a young hacker who nearly starts World War III by inadvertently accessing a military supercomputer to play an unreleased computer game. The film introduced mainstream audiences to the concepts of hacking, phone phreaking, and their potential consequences, including a foreshadowing of artificial intelligence technology. At the time of the film's release, the plot seemed fantastical, but it rang true enough to spark public fear and intrigue, with some of the lessons and attack vectors potentially viable even today.

---

[22] https://www.discovermagazine.com/technology/the-story-of-the-414s-the-milwaukee-teenagers-who-became-hacking-pioneers
[23] https://www.imdb.com/title/tt0086567/

CHAPTER 1   THE HISTORY OF ATTACK VECTORS

Following *WarGames*, public perception of hackers crystallized into two camps: teenagers with incredible intelligence or criminals stealing data and causing all sorts of mayhem. This led to terminology like "script kiddies," which comes from the former perception of teenagers using content created by others and becoming dangerous enough to run malicious scripts for their own amusement. Either way, hacking captured the public imagination. It fueled a wave of legislative and corporate interest in computer security and sparked imagination of what was truly possible.

The mainstream impact of movies like *WarGames* included shedding light on the underground movement of BBSs. These systems became digital gathering places where like-minded tech enthusiasts could share software, information, and exploit code. Pirate bulletin boards offered cracked software, often accompanied by instructions on how to bypass copy protection. Unbeknownst to the user, some of this software might even contain a computer virus (I know, I ran one of these BBSs the early 1990s focusing on shareware).

"Phreaking" boards continued to thrive, teaching aspiring hackers to exploit telephone systems for inexpensive or free long-distance and local calls. As a matter of fact, some BBSs specialized in hacking and phreaking tutorials, forging a subculture that reveled in the outlaw mystique. Law enforcement, in turn, began to infiltrate these communities, posing as fellow hackers in an effort to identify and root out individuals engaged in criminal activity. The tension between privacy, freedom of information, and criminal intent became intense, foreshadowing broader debates about online rights that continue today.

Against this backdrop, in the early 1980s, lawmakers introduced new bills aimed at curbing unauthorized computer access. In the United States, this included amendments to the Comprehensive Crime Control Act of 1984 and the Computer Fraud and Abuse Act (CFAA) of 1986. While these laws provided legal frameworks for prosecuting hackers, they simultaneously sparked complex questions about overreach. A significant concern was their potential to impede legitimate security research, which seeks to identify system weaknesses before malicious actors can exploit them.

Outside the United States, other countries began to draft similar legislation, although with a different sense of urgency. Governments recognized that digital communications presented unique challenges in that they could cross borders with ease, unlike a physically stolen item. This complicated enforcement. International cooperation would eventually become a necessity, but in the 1980s, almost all efforts were geolocation-based, confined to individual nations.

In 1986, a significant event in cybersecurity history occurred at the Lawrence Berkeley Labs. An astronomer named Clifford Stoll,[24] who later became a systems administrator, was investigating a tiny accounting discrepancy in one of their computer systems. Financial data was off by a mere 75 cents, but what he discovered changed cybersecurity forever. His investigation into a minor accounting error led him to determine that a hacker had infiltrated networks operated by the US government and various universities. The threat actors' mission was to quietly steal military secrets and sell them to Soviet KGB agents. How Stoll figured this out is a legend in the industry.

With no incident response plans to follow and no formal governing body for these types of attacks, Stoll engineered methods to prove his findings. He set up digital traps, monitored keystrokes on key systems, logged access times, and tracked the hacker across a global web of dial-up lines all from a terminal in his office.

---

[24] https://www.chaintech.network/blog/year-1986-dr-cliff-stoll-the-cuckoos-egg/

CHAPTER 1   THE HISTORY OF ATTACK VECTORS

His understanding of computer systems and pursuit of the truth culminated in the first documented case of cyber espionage. The hacker, Markus Hess,[25] working out of West Germany, was eventually arrested based on a homemade alarm connected to Stoll's printer. Stoll wrote all about it in *The Cuckoo's Egg (1989)*,[26] a now-classic cybersecurity memoir that rivals fictional movies like *Mission Impossible*.[27]

Notwithstanding all the drama from these events, by the late 1980s, a fledgling security software industry began to take root. Antivirus (AV) software emerged in response to the first computer viruses, which were spreading largely through floppy disks that typically contained bootlegged (illegally licensed or copied) software.

One of the earliest known viruses, "Elk Cloner,"[28] appeared on the Apple II in 1982. This virus was created more as a prank than as a destructive tool. Companies like McAfee, Norton, and others introduced tools to detect and remove viruses based on a signature approach. While these early AV programs were rudimentary and prone to false positives, they established an important precedent: cybersecurity could be a commercial, profitable industry, one that also supported emerging legislation and compliance initiatives.

The 1980s cemented the notion that computers were here to stay, and their widespread adoption brought with it real risks that could take many forms. For the first time, everyday individuals—from students to hobbyists—and small businesses faced the possibility of having their data compromised. On one hand, the 1980s ushered in the democratization of computing, sparking waves of innovation. On the other, the decade also ignited a wave of security challenges that would only grow more complex with time. With that in mind, the 1980s provide some key teachable moments:

---

[25] https://www.guinnessworldrecords.com/world-records/612868-first-incident-of-cyber-espionage
[26] https://www.goodreads.com/book/show/18154.The_Cuckoo_s_Egg
[27] https://www.imdb.com/list/ls028479957/
[28] https://www.techtarget.com/searchsecurity/definition/Elk-Cloner

CHAPTER 1   THE HISTORY OF ATTACK VECTORS

- Personal computers propelled hacking from an academic niche into the mainstream consciousness.
- Early legislation laid the groundwork for prosecuting computer crimes, though legal definitions often struggled to keep pace.
- Public fascination with hacking soared, influenced by media portrayals, science fiction movies, and sensational news headlines.
- The seeds of the commercial cybersecurity industry were planted. Tools remained primitive but demonstrated that a profitable business could be formed.

Up next, the 1990s—a pivotal decade that saw the rise of the Internet, widespread adoption of email, and new forms of connectivity that made the world feel smaller and more vulnerable to cyberattacks than ever before.

## The Internet and Emerging Threats (1990s)

If the 1980s introduced personal computing to the masses, the 1990s propelled us into a hyper-connected era with the advent of the World Wide Web[29] (a.k.a. Internet, InterWeb, and a plethora of other terms that thankfully have faded in popularity). In 1989, Tim Berners-Lee,[30] working at CERN,[31] proposed what we now know as the Internet, before launching it publicly in 1991. Within just a few years, services like Mosaic[32] (the first

---

[29] https://www.britannica.com/topic/World-Wide-Web
[30] https://www.w3.org/People/Berners-Lee/
[31] https://home.web.cern.ch/science/computing/birth-web
[32] https://www.britannica.com/technology/Mosaic-computer-program

popular web browser), Netscape Navigator,[33] and eventually Microsoft's Internet Explorer[34] brought the Internet into households around the globe, even if their personal computers weren't always connected. Companies like Prodigy, CompuServe, and AOL (American Online) brought connectivity to everyone using phone lines and modems. The result was a semi-interconnected world piggybacked on a nondigital, analog phone system.

What started as a research-focused network, like ARPANET, and a handful of academic systems transformed into a commercial juggernaut of hardware, services, and information. Businesses rushed to establish an online presence, email became a standard communication tool, and ordinary people gained access to information and services at an unprecedented scale.

With the Internet's explosive growth, new attack vectors emerged. Malicious actors no longer needed physical access to a victim's computer; they could strike from anywhere in the world through services like email and chat. A new breed of hackers, motivated by profit, political ideology, or simple malicious intent, became widespread.

One of the earliest and most notorious examples of online maliciousness was the Morris Worm (1988), created by Robert Tappan Morris,[35] a graduate student at Cornell. Although it predates the widespread adoption of the web by a couple of years, the Morris Worm was a harbinger of the kinds of large-scale disruptions the Internet would soon face. It infected thousands of machines across ARPANET, clogging systems and demonstrating the fragility of network security. Throughout the remainder of the 1990s, viruses, worms, and Trojan horses

---

[33] https://www.slashgear.com/1353587/history-netscape-navigator-web-browser-explained/
[34] https://www.britannica.com/technology/Internet-Explorer
[35] https://www.crimemuseum.org/crime-library/white-collar-crime/robert-tappan-morris/#google_vignette

CHAPTER 1   THE HISTORY OF ATTACK VECTORS

proliferated. The Melissa virus[36] in 1999 spread via email attachments and foreshadowed countless email-borne threats. Macro viruses, which exploited Microsoft Office documents, became a favorite among threat actors due to widespread use of the legitimate software in business environments.

Hackers didn't stop there. The open frontier of the Internet unleashed a new ecosystem: online marketplaces where stolen data, hacking tools, and compromised systems were traded or sold. Some individuals pivoted from hacking for intellectual curiosity to hacking for profit. Identity theft, credit card fraud, and intellectual property theft became disturbingly common. Groups like the "Legion of Doom"[37] and "Masters of Deception"[38] in the late 1980s and early 1990s set the stage for more structured organizations of cybercriminals. Law enforcement found itself on unfamiliar turf, chasing elusive targets who operated across international borders, jumping from system to system to cover their digital tracks.

Corporations and government agencies scrambled to adopt defensive measures. Firewalls emerged as a first line of defense against external intruders. Marcus Ranum, William Cheswick, and others pioneered firewall[39] technologies that filtered network traffic based on predefined inbound and outbound rules. Early commercial firewalls included products from companies like Check Point, Cisco, and Juniper Networks to respond to these emerging threats.

---

[36] https://www.fbi.gov/news/stories/melissa-virus-20th-anniversary-032519
[37] https://dbpedia.org/page/Legion_of_Doom_(hacker_group)
[38] https://www.cybersecurityeducationguides.org/legion-of-doom-vs-the-masters-of-deception/
[39] https://www.paloaltonetworks.com/cyberpedia/history-of-firewalls#:~:text=There%20is%20not%20one%20inventor,Fred%20Avolio%2C%20and%20Brent%20Chapman

CHAPTER 1    THE HISTORY OF ATTACK VECTORS

Alongside firewalls, intrusion detection systems (IDS) began to appear, scanning network traffic for suspicious patterns, since traffic at this time was rarely encrypted. These tools were rudimentary by modern standards, but they marked an important shift toward proactive defense and detection technologies.

As e-commerce became the new marketplace for everything, secure online transactions became a necessity. The 1990s saw the standardization of cryptographic protocols like Secure Sockets Layer (SSL), which protected data in transit between web browsers and servers. This allowed people to enter credit card information on websites with greater confidence and without the fear of information being "sniffed"[40] off the wire. However, the US government initially classified strong cryptography as a munition. This resulted in restricting its export via US ECCN[41] (Export Control Classification Number) based on the weaponization of cryptography during World War II. This led to the "crypto wars," a period of intense debate over whether private citizens and foreign entities should have access to strong encryption. Eventually, these restrictions eased, recognizing that strong encryption was integral to global commerce and privacy.

In response to mounting cyber threats, governments around the world passed more stringent computer crime laws. The United States updated the Computer Fraud and Abuse Act multiple times, while other nations introduced comparable legislation. Law enforcement agencies, such as the FBI and Secret Service, expanded their cybercrime units to handle the escalation of attacks. Globally, Interpol and other agencies recognized that cybercrime required international cooperation and began forming protocols for multinational communications. Despite these efforts, universal standards for prosecuting cybercrime remain elusive.

---

[40] https://www.avg.com/en/signal/what-is-sniffer
[41] https://www.trade.gov/how-do-i-determine-my-export-control-classification-number-eccn

CHAPTER 1   THE HISTORY OF ATTACK VECTORS

Some nations, for instance, may consider hacking another country's infrastructure acceptable, as long as their own citizens or government isn't targeted.

While legal concepts for crimes like murder are global (though the penalties may vary from place to place), cybercrimes do not share the same threshold of severity in every nation.

This can be demonstrated best with high-profile arrests, like that of Kevin Mitnick[42] in 1995. His activities made headlines and underscored the seriousness of computer crime when critical infrastructure can be compromised. Mitnick, once labeled the "most wanted computer criminal in US history," had a reputation for social engineering and breaching corporate networks and telecom systems. His arrest signaled that US law enforcement was beginning to approach computer hacking with more seriousness and enforce laws against cybercriminals.

By the late 1990s, the dot-com boom was in full swing. Venture capitalists poured millions of dollars into Internet-based startups, fueling a frenzy of innovation, but also creating a frenzy of shortcuts for misguided, quick profits. The hype of the Internet was truly deafening, much like AI is today. Looking back, it is easy to postulate that development cycles were rushed, and security and data privacy were frequently an afterthought. Companies focused on growth and user acquisition, rather than on building robust defenses. The results would pave the way for breaches for years to come.

Meanwhile, savvy hackers exploited poorly secured web applications, hacked databases with SQL injections, performed cross-site scripting, and exploited vulnerabilities with buffer overflows to infiltrate systems. These attack vectors remain pervasive today, a testament to how fundamental coding errors and design oversight can persist even after decades of collective experience and best practices are applied.

---

[42] https://www.knowbe4.com/products/who-is-kevin-mitnick/

CHAPTER 1   THE HISTORY OF ATTACK VECTORS

Media coverage of cyber incidents continued to soar, driving home the message that online threats were not just the stuff of Hollywood. Movies like *Hackers*[43] (1995) glamorized the digital underground, while news reports of data breaches and virus outbreaks became increasingly common. This was when the conversations began to hit the board level of organizations.

During this time, public consciousness began to shift; the Internet was amazing but also potentially riddled with flaws, crime, and risk. By the end of the 1990s, it was clear that the Internet had reshaped modern life in profound ways, and that cybersecurity could not be simply solved with the flick of a switch or a single vendor's solution. The stage was set for the 21st century, where threats would only become more sophisticated and the stakes higher. Indeed, many core lessons from the 1990s remain relevant today:

- Security should never be an afterthought. It should be a part of all technology designs from day one and requires a good balance of usability and maintainability.

- Prevention from creating vulnerabilities in software is a balance of training, quality assurance, vulnerability management, code review, and testing to ensure risks are minimized.

- Technology, standards, frameworks, and models from over three decades ago are still powering the Internet today. Changing the foundation is hard and takes time and consensus to alter what still works, even if it carries risk. As an example, consider the pain and time that it has taken to transition from IPv4 to IPv6 and still maintain backward compatibility.

---

[43] https://www.imdb.com/title/tt0113243/

In the next section, we'll explore the early 2000s and how the challenges introduced in the 1990s evolved into a war against more advanced malware, cyberterrorism, and an accelerating cyber arms race between threat actors, defenders, and collateral damage within businesses, governments, and consumers.

## Cybersecurity and Dot-Com (Early 2000s)

The early 2000s were marked by the dot-com[44] bust, but the Internet did not vanish with the failing of startups, including those that failed to develop viable and secure solutions. Despite some setbacks, the Internet continued to grow more embedded in everyday life. Consider the dot-com bust a necessary course correction for businesses and investors. High-speed Internet connections, like early broadband (DSL and cable), became more common, e-commerce stabilized, and social media began emerging in primitive forms like Friendster (launched in 2002) and MySpace (launched in 2003).

With more people than ever online, cyberattacks evolved in scale and impact. Hackers didn't just target systems for curiosity anymore; large-scale theft, fraud, and disruption were on the rise. Malware authors capitalized on common user behaviors like clicking email attachments or visiting unsecure websites to propagate their attacks.

This period also saw the emergence of highly destructive worms that exploited network services on a massive scale. The Code Red worm[45] (2001) attacked Microsoft's Internet Information Services (IIS) web server, while Nimda[46] (also 2001) spread via multiple vectors, including

---

[44] https://www.investopedia.com/terms/d/dotcom.asp
[45] https://www.scientificamerican.com/article/code-red-worm-assault-on/
[46] https://www.techtarget.com/searchsecurity/definition/Nimda

email, web servers, and file shares. Slammer[47] (2003) hit Microsoft SQL database servers, infecting thousands of systems within minutes and causing widespread Internet slowdowns. These examples, and others, will be explored later in this book to provide a deeper understanding of the true motives and impact. These worms demonstrated that a single vulnerability could lead to a global incident, practically overnight, through self-propagation and code exploitation. The ease with which such attacks spread underscored that the Internet's interconnected nature left no system immune.

After the events of September 11, 2001[48] (the World Trade Center attacks in New York City), the idea of cyberterrorism and a physical attack being combined into real-world warfare captured headlines. In fact, confirmed acts of cyberterrorism (loosely defined by DHS/NIST) were virtually nonexistent after 9/11, despite government predictions. This helped emphasize the difference between cybercrime, cyberwarfare, and cyberterrorism as unique definitions within the industry. Unfortunately, at the time, government agencies worried that terrorist groups could exploit digital vulnerabilities to launch attacks on critical infrastructure, like power grids, water systems, and transportation networks. While actual occurrences of cyberterrorism remain rare even today, the threat at the time influenced both legislation and funding for research and defense. Cybersecurity suddenly became a national security priority, with budget allocations from defense and intelligence agencies becoming mainstream and visible to all. Nations across the globe began to take a more focused approach to the risks.

Businesses also recognized that poor cybersecurity could lead to disastrous consequences, both financially and reputationally. An unmitigated cyber incident had the potential to become a game-over event.

---

[47] https://www.caida.org/catalog/papers/2003_sapphire/
[48] https://www.911memorial.org/911-faqs

Regulatory frameworks, such as the Health Insurance Portability and Accountability Act (HIPAA[49]) and Gramm-Leach-Bliley Act (GLBA[50]) in the United States, mandated better protection of sensitive data, especially in healthcare and finance. Sarbanes-Oxley (SOX[51]), enacted in 2002 in response to corporate scandals like Enron,[52] imposed stricter accounting and data retention controls to ensure accountability of both technological systems and human processes in preventing potential abuse.

While these regulations were not exclusively about cybersecurity, they catalyzed a shift toward more robust corporate security policies and procedures. Companies invested more in firewalls, intrusion detection systems, secure gateways, and employee training. More mature risk management practices emerged, treating cybersecurity as a business priority rather than a mere IT concern. Again, this was an afterthought, but the risks to the business from a cyberattack, regardless of insider or external threat, proved that investments in cybersecurity technology were warranted as a mitigation strategy.

Unfortunately, the early 2000s also saw the rise of botnets as a new technology and attack vector. Botnets[53] evolved to infiltrate networks and leverage compromised machines under the control of a single entity for some nefarious missions. Botnet owners used these infected computers to launch distributed denial-of-service (DDoS[54]) attacks, send spam emails, or conduct click fraud. Infected users were often unaware their computers were part of a criminal enterprise. Botnets operated with advanced

---

[49] https://www.hhs.gov/hipaa/for-professionals/privacy/laws-regulations/index.html
[50] https://www.ftc.gov/business-guidance/privacy-security/gramm-leach-bliley-act
[51] https://sarbanes-oxley-act.com
[52] https://www.britannica.com/event/Enron-scandal
[53] https://www.techtarget.com/searchsecurity/definition/botnet
[54] https://www.cisa.gov/news-events/news/understanding-denial-service-attacks

CHAPTER 1   THE HISTORY OF ATTACK VECTORS

techniques to obfuscate their behaviors even from the most advanced antivirus solutions. This included sophisticated Command and Control[55] (C2) technology that could use communications like IRC channels[56] or encrypted communications over trusted TCP ports, like 80 or 443[57] (HTTP or HTTPs).

Botnets became another important vehicle for organized crime rings to form beachheads within businesses. Using this type of technology, bot masters could electronically steal credit card numbers, create new phishing scams, and monitor systems for other forms of valuable data. Cybercriminals took advantage of online payment systems and unregulated cryptocurrency exchanges (though Bitcoin[58] had not yet appeared; that would come in 2009) to launder money, all through malware installed as bots.

In response to the accelerating threats posed by botnets, law enforcement agencies across the globe ramped up collaborations. High-profile arrests continued to make headlines, but for every cybercriminal busted, new ones emerged, often in locations where law enforcement lacked jurisdiction. The game of cat and mouse had escalated and now included geolocations that were simply off limits for an arrest. In many modern cases today, threat actors may vacation in regions within a legal jurisdiction and then find themselves apprehended by local enforcement. Arresting a Russian cybercriminal in France is a perfect example of a cat's patience to wait out a roaming mouse.[59]

---

[55] https://csrc.nist.gov/glossary/term/c2
[56] https://www.zscaler.com/blogs/security-research/irc-botnets-alive-effective-evolving
[57] https://security.stackexchange.com/questions/107387/detecting-botnets-that-use-http-instead-of-irc
[58] https://bitcoin.org/en/
[59] https://www.bitdefender.com/en-us/blog/hotforsecurity/french-authorities-arrest-russian-national-allegedly-connected-to-hive-ransomware

CHAPTER 1   THE HISTORY OF ATTACK VECTORS

As these threats evolved, a new cybersecurity services industry blossomed. Companies like eEye Digital Security (now BeyondTrust), Metasploit (now Rapid 7), ISS (end-of-life by IBM), Core Impact (Core Security), and many more developed specialized technologies—from vulnerability management to penetration testing—to detect if vulnerabilities existed and if they could actually be exploited. Penetration testing services, once the domain of a niche subset of hackers, became mainstream commercial technology, despite ethical concerns. At the executive level, CISOs (Chief Information Security Officers) emerged as key figures in large organizations, advocating for security within the organization to prevent the business from becoming the next victim.

With the commercialization of cybersecurity tools that could detect vulnerabilities and exploit them, companies and individuals wanted to provide proof they understood the risks and that the business applications were being appropriately managed. Certifications such as the Certified Information Systems Security Professional[60] (CISSP) gained popularity, signaling a professionalization of the cybersecurity workforce. Training programs and university courses multiplied, recognizing that cybersecurity expertise was now critical across multiple industry sectors and a requirement to prove your expertise and qualifications for a cybersecurity role.

By the mid-2000s, the Internet had fundamentally changed business, communication, and daily lives. It had also changed the nature of crime and warfare. Some key takeaways and lessons from the 2000s include the following:

- Threats are global, sophisticated, and often financially or politically motivated, rather than being driven by bragging rights or "fun."

---

[60] https://www.isc2.org/certifications/cissp

CHAPTER 1   THE HISTORY OF ATTACK VECTORS

- Technology often responds to a threat, but like anything else, it may wane or prove obsolete based on the changing threat landscape. Cybersecurity is very dynamic in response, and so is the technology.

- Regulatory compliance can be viewed as the checks and balances for cybersecurity but should never be considered a burden to the business. It exists for a reason and provides guardrails for known attack vectors.

- Physical and electronic attack vectors are very real, and the convergence of cyberattacks with threats to physical assets, such as critical infrastructure, demands serious attention at all organizational levels. Later on, this theory would be proven true.

The next section will explore how these trends escalated in the mid-to-late 2000s and beyond. Some subtopics covered include the proliferation of advanced persistent threats[61] (APTs), the explosion of social media vulnerabilities, and the wave of data breaches that reshaped public perception of digital security.

# Risk Management (Mid-2000s–2010s)

Around the mid-2000s, the cybersecurity lexicon gained a new term: advanced persistent threat (APT). APTs refer to stealthy, prolonged cyberattacks—often orchestrated by nation-states or well-funded criminal organizations—that gain advantage by having a long-standing electronic presence that goes undetected. Unlike "smash-and-grab" style attacks

---

[61] https://www.techtarget.com/searchsecurity/definition/advanced-persistent-threat-APT

seeking immediate profit, APTs aim to remain undetected for extended periods. APT attacks involve infiltrating deep into networks to gather intelligence or intellectual property using a variety of malware, bots, and other advanced techniques to perform command, control, and reconnaissance.

One of the early, widely publicized APT examples was Operation Aurora in 2009,[62] where hackers targeted major corporations, like Google, Adobe, and others, exploiting zero-day vulnerabilities. The level of coordination and resources implied nation-state involvement, highlighting how cyber espionage had become a sophisticated game of infiltration rather than merely disruptive attacks.

Next, in 2010, the WikiLeaks[63] breach was not just a sensitive data dump; it was a rupture in the way nations secure their secrets. A US Army intelligence analyst Chelsea Manning[64] exfiltrated over 700,000 classified military and diplomatic documents, which were later published by WikiLeaks (next topic). The breach exposed war logs, embassy cables, and Guantanamo Bay files, unmasking operations, allies, and vulnerabilities in one of the most significant intelligence leaks in modern history.

But this was not just another story about a hacker bypassing firewalls; Manning had authorized access. The failure? Excessive trust, weak segmentation, and a lack of behavioral auditing within privileged systems. Like Snowden (covered later), Manning didn't exploit a system weakness; she exploited a policy weakness: the assumption that someone on the inside would never turn. The breach laid bare how government systems were over-permissive with data access and under-protective of context-aware monitoring. When one person can download hundreds of

---

[62] https://www.sciencedirect.com/topics/computer-science/operation-aurora
[63] https://www.bbc.com/news/technology-47907890
[64] https://www.justiceinitiative.org/litigation/united-states-v-private-first-class-chelsea-manning

## CHAPTER 1   THE HISTORY OF ATTACK VECTORS

thousands of sensitive files without setting off alarms, it's not just a user issue, it is a workflow flaw. No least privilege. No session monitoring. No alerts. Just open access in a closed system.

WikiLeaks may have been the publisher, but the real story was about internal blind spots. It pushed agencies to rethink access controls, reevaluate segmentation, and implement stronger data loss prevention (DLP) tools. It also marked the beginning of a new threat model: the insider with ideological motivation. Manning exposed the cost of unmonitored trust. The history lesson? Assume breach—it can come from within. Trust is not a security control, but verification is.

In addition, the discovery of Stuxnet[65] in 2010 sent shockwaves through the cybersecurity community. A complex worm that targeted specific Industrial Control Systems[66] (ICS) at Iranian nuclear facilities, Stuxnet was the first known example of code engineered to damage physical infrastructure. It infected Windows machines but only activated within configurations linked to Siemens Step 7[67] software controlling high-speed centrifuges. Stuxnet demonstrated a terrifying possibility: software could be weaponized to destroy or sabotage critical infrastructure without direct military action. While its origins remain shrouded in secrecy, it's often rumored the United States and Israeli governments coordinated its development. Stuxnet was a watershed moment that redefined the global threat landscape, proving early theories that cybersecurity breaches could indeed pose tangible, real-world consequences of putting lives in jeopardy.

---

[65] https://www.wired.com/2014/11/countdown-to-zero-day-stuxnet/
[66] https://www.cisa.gov/topics/industrial-control-systems
[67] https://www.siemens.com/global/en/products/automation/systems/industrial/controller-sw.html

CHAPTER 1   THE HISTORY OF ATTACK VECTORS

In 2013, the cybersecurity world was blindsided not by malware or phishing, but by an insider with a flash drive and an agenda. Edward Snowden,[68] a former NSA contractor working through Booz Allen Hamilton, exfiltrated an estimated 1.7 million classified files, exposing the scope and scale of US global surveillance programs. It was not a sophisticated zero-day exploit that compromised national security. It was a failure of identity governance, privilege management, and enforcing oversight.

Snowden's access wasn't anomalous; it was systemic. He had legitimate credentials, elevated privileges, and a trusted role in the intelligence ecosystem. But he also had a hidden intent, and therein lies the real breach: trust without verification. What Snowden revealed, through leaks to journalists like Glenn Greenwald,[69] wasn't just about bulk data collection. It was about how the digital surveillance machine lacked checks on its own people.

The Snowden affair didn't just shake the intelligence community. It rewrote the playbook on insider threats. It forced governments and enterprises alike to rethink how they monitor administrative access, segment data, and detect anomalous behavior. Snowden became the cautionary tale in every privileged access management (PAM) and insider threat training program worldwide.

In the end, the Snowden breach taught us that the enemy doesn't always hack in; they log in. And if you're not auditing your most trusted users with the same scrutiny you apply to external threats, then you've already lost control of your security perimeter because the perimeter now lives inside your network.

---

[68] https://www.britannica.com/biography/Edward-Snowden
[69] https://www.rollingstone.com/culture/culture-news/snowden-and-greenwald-the-men-who-leaked-the-secrets-104970/

CHAPTER 1    THE HISTORY OF ATTACK VECTORS

The late 2000s ushered in a new era of interconnectedness with the widespread adoption of mobile devices (smartphones, etc.) and cloud services. The launch of Apple's iPhone in 2007 and Google's Android OS in 2008 revolutionized mobile computing and always-on connectivity but simultaneously introduced a host of new attack vectors. While these computing trends offered unprecedented convenience and cost-savings, they also unveiled significant vulnerabilities. Mobile malware emerged as a growing threat, while cloud-based breaches highlighted issues of data isolation, multitenant risk, and shared resource responsibility. Threat actors capitalized on these developments, exploiting misconfigured servers, weak API security, and human errors in cloud administration, which in turn broadened the scope for criminal syndicates and their exploitation methods.

With the emergence of social media platforms like Facebook, Twitter, and LinkedIn, threat actors gained new avenues to exploit human nature—a tactic now widely known as social engineering. They rapidly adopted phishing emails, which grew more convincing by sometimes blending personal information scraped from social media profiles to target specific victims. This highly targeted approach is referred to as "spear phishing."

Today, social engineering has become a dark art that pits an attacker's acting skills against human weaknesses. Threat actors skillfully impersonate co-workers, relatives, or friends online, tricking unsuspecting individuals into revealing sensitive information, downloading malicious payloads, or submitting unwarranted payments via gift cards, cryptocurrency, or even credit cards. These deceptions are often facilitated by clever watering hole websites and other socially engineered lures. Despite technical security measures, human gullibility or a lack of awareness remains a significant weak link, a topic we will explore in greater detail later.

CHAPTER 1   THE HISTORY OF ATTACK VECTORS

The 2010s were marred by a series of massive data breaches affecting major organizations. From Yahoo's breach[70] of three billion accounts to the Equifax breach[71] exposing sensitive credit data from over 140 million people, these incidents underscored the potential scale of compromise. Retail giants like Target and Home Depot suffered breaches via third-party vulnerabilities, while banks, healthcare providers, and even dating services fell victim to sophisticated attacks. These incidents often led to staggering consequences, including lawsuits, hefty regulatory fines, and severe reputational damage. Tragically, some breaches resulted in the worst possible outcomes for individuals, as seen in the 2015 Ashley Madison[71] fallout where exposed sensitive data led to suicides. For victims, personal hardship was compounded as their information surfaced on dark web marketplaces with, at the time, little recourse to mitigate the risks.

While these attacks focused on raw data theft and release, a new threat was appearing on the horizon, too. Originally surfacing in the mid-2000s, ransomware[72] exploded in prevalence during the 2010s. Threat actors found they could lock victims out of their own systems or encrypt data and demand payment, often in Bitcoin, for decryption keys to retrieve information that had been hijacked.

High-profile attacks like the WannaCry[73] outbreak (2017) and NotPetya[74] (2017–which initially started as ransomware but later was categorized as a wiper) impacted thousands of organizations worldwide, from hospitals to shipping companies, and encrypted all forms of data at

---

[70] https://www.nytimes.com/2017/10/03/technology/yahoo-hack-3-billion-users.html
[71] https://krebsonsecurity.com/2022/07/a-retrospective-on-the-2015-ashley-madison-breach/
[72] https://www.fbi.gov/how-we-can-help-you/scams-and-safety/common-frauds-and-scams/ransomware
[73] https://www.cisa.gov/news-events/alerts/2017/05/12/indicators-associated-wannacry-ransomware
[74] https://attack.mitre.org/software/S0368/

scale, preventing legitimate business operations from functioning without this information. Ransomware's profitability triggered a "gold rush" for cybercriminals, who began offering ransomware-as-a-service (RaaS) tools on the dark web. Some affiliates specialized in double extortion, threatening to leak sensitive data if ransoms weren't paid. Making matters worse, paying the ransom offered no guarantee of receiving a working decryption key, depending on the malware's nuances or the cybercriminal organization's sophistication. This grim reality spurred new markets for cyber insurance, remote data backup technologies, and a greater emphasis on preventing ransomware infections in the first place.

In response to these escalating threats, regulatory frameworks evolved, and like all legislation, it lagged what was already occurring at a rapid pace and broad scale. The European Union introduced the General Data Protection Regulation[75] (GDPR) in 2016, enforcing strict data protection measures and granting significant enforcement powers to privacy regulators. Other nations subsequently passed analogous laws, compelling organizations to prioritize data security and disclose security incidents in a timely manner.

In addition, verticalized cybersecurity standards, such as the Payment Card Industry Data Security Standard[76] (PCI DSS), became mandatory for businesses handling credit card data to prevent data breaches. Sectors like healthcare and finance continued to face additional scrutiny, with compliance playing an ever-increasing role in shaping risk mitigation strategies both physically (as an example, ATM and white card/plastic[77]) and electronically.

The scale and sophistication of newer attacks forced security professionals to collaborate more closely. Sharing threat intelligence information on emerging malware, phishing campaigns, or zero-day

---

[75] https://gdpr.eu/what-is-gdpr/
[76] https://www.pcisecuritystandards.org/standards/
[77] https://www.firstfcu.org/images/ThievesUsing.pdf

CHAPTER 1   THE HISTORY OF ATTACK VECTORS

vulnerabilities has become essential. Without such collaboration, new cyberattacks are managed reactively, with inconsistent expertise on a per-incident basis. This fragmented approach severely hampers scalability and effective defensive strategies.

To counter the escalating threats, organizations, government agencies, and security vendors formed alliances and information-sharing groups such as ISC2, MITRE, and CISA to ensure threat information is communicated accurately and promptly. The commercial industry also began bug bounty[78] programs with companies such as Google, Microsoft, Oracle, and Facebook paying ethical hackers to responsibly find and report vulnerabilities before an incident could occur. This critical shift encouraged responsible disclosure over illicit black-market exploitation.

By the end of the 2010s, cybersecurity had truly become an arms race. Threat actors continually adapted techniques and leveraged automation, AI-driven tools, and advanced social engineering to breach defenses. Defenders responded with threat intelligence, machine learning-powered detection tools, and zero trust architectures, but the cat and mouse games still continue today.

The challenges from the last decade have grown more complex: supply chain attacks, state-sponsored espionage, and massive-scale vulnerabilities like Heartbleed[79] and Shellshock[80] highlighted systemic weaknesses across all our technology. The era was a testament to both the resilience and fragility of our interconnected world, and from it, we gathered some concrete lessons learned:

- Threat actors focus primarily on two goals: monetization or disruption, regardless of their attack vectors.

---

[78] https://www.techtarget.com/whatis/definition/bug-bounty-program
[79] https://heartbleed.com
[80] https://www.cisa.gov/news-events/alerts/2014/09/25/gnu-bourne-again-shell-bash-shellshock-vulnerability-cve-2014-6271

- Attack vectors like ransomware demonstrate the creativity of threat actors. Never underestimate the ingenuity of a motivated threat actor.

- Attack vectors are not limited to one technology, application, vendor, or service. Any asset or resource can be compromised—it's just a matter of how and when.

In the next section, we'll move into the modern era, from the late 2010s to the present, where we will explore how emerging technologies, like artificial intelligence, the Internet of Things[81] (IoT), and quantum computing, are reshaping the cybersecurity landscape. We will also examine the continued evolution of ransomware, data privacy battles, and the tightening interplay between geopolitical tensions and cyberwarfare operations.

# Modern Threat Landscape (Late 2010s–Today)

As we entered the mid-2010s, the Internet of Things (IoT) took center stage. Suddenly, more than just computers and smartphones were connected to the Internet: refrigerators, thermostats, security cameras, medical devices, and even cars were going online. This surge brought convenience and efficiency but opened a literal Pandora's box of vulnerabilities due to poor coding, design, and ill-conceived features. Once again, cybersecurity was an afterthought as these new technologies materialized, and attacks ramped up.

---

[81] https://www.techtarget.com/iotagenda/definition/Internet-of-Things-IoT

CHAPTER 1   THE HISTORY OF ATTACK VECTORS

The truth is, manufacturers, eager to release innovative "smart" products, often neglected security best practices. Default passwords, unpatched and unpatchable firmware, and limited encryption became the norm, rendering these devices vulnerable even to unsophisticated attacks. Threat actors quickly capitalized on these poor implementations, creating IoT botnets like Mirai (2016) that commandeered thousands of devices to launch devastating distributed denial-of-service (DDoS) attacks.

The concept of compromising suppliers to undermine an organization's security has become a paramount concern, now widely characterized as supply chain attacks. The 2020 SolarWinds[82] attack stands out as a prime example of this threat. Threat actors inserted malicious code into a routine software update of the SolarWinds Orion Network Management product, subsequently affecting thousands of organizations, including major government agencies. While we will discuss this event in detail later, it starkly illustrates how even well-intentioned systems can be compromised when a determined adversary, often state-sponsored, exploits vulnerabilities like an insecure auto-update mechanism

The SolarWinds supply chain attack laid bare that even companies with robust in-house security can be compromised through trusted third-party partners or vendors. Vetting and monitoring supply chains have thus become top priorities for security-conscious organizations.

As the 2010s ended and we entered the beginning of the roaring 2020s, privacy took center stage with incidents like the Cambridge Analytica scandal[03] (2018). This scandal revealed how Facebook user data was being misused for political profiling. This event, alongside other high-profile incidents, fueled demands for stronger privacy legislation and tighter controls over how companies collect, store, sell, and monetize user data.

---

[82] https://www.techtarget.com/whatis/feature/SolarWinds-hack-explained-Everything-you-need-to-know
[83] https://bipartisanpolicy.org/blog/cambridge-analytica-controversy/

37

CHAPTER 1   THE HISTORY OF ATTACK VECTORS

Regulatory frameworks like the California Consumer Privacy Act[84] (CCPA) and similar laws worldwide now offer consumers greater protection against these types of threats. Nonetheless, tensions remain between corporations seeking data-driven insights, governments wanting surveillance powers for national security, and individuals demanding privacy.

As the 2020s unfolded, the Internet increasingly became a battleground for nation-states, characterized by cyber espionage, misinformation campaigns, and the dissemination of fake news. Attacks targeting election systems, vaccine research, and critical infrastructure caused disruptions and widespread influence on an unprecedented scale. Countries openly accused each other of orchestrating these attacks, though definitive attribution remained elusive, often even when affecting election outcomes. While cybersecurity has become deeply entwined with global politics, trade negotiations, and international alliances, diplomatic efforts to establish "cyber norms" have seen mixed success, as states continue to balance cooperation with competitive interests.

As we embark forward from the middle of the decade (2025), new technology and threats continue to manifest. For example, quantum computing promises to break certain forms of encryption that underpin today's secure communications. National research labs, tech giants, and startups are racing to develop advanced quantum-resistant cybersecurity solutions to protect these systems and the computational capabilities they represent. Though mainstream quantum computing may be years away, the potential impact on cybersecurity is already prompting major shifts to encryption standards that are quantum resistant.

Another example is AI/ML technology. Artificial intelligence (AI) and machine learning (ML) have influenced every facet of technology, including cybersecurity. On the defensive side, AI-powered systems analyze vast datasets to detect unusual patterns, accelerate incident

---

[84] https://oag.ca.gov/privacy/ccpa

CHAPTER 1   THE HISTORY OF ATTACK VECTORS

response, and predict novel threats. However, threat actors also leverage AI to craft more convincing phishing emails; create deepfake photos, video, and audio, and adapt malicious code on the fly.

To combat these initiatives—and remember: it's always a cat and mouse game with a response pending—there's been a major philosophical shift in cybersecurity. This centers on the concept of "zero trust," which assumes that all users, devices, and network traffic are inherently untrustworthy. Instead of a single perimeter defense, zero trust employs continuous verification and strict access controls, improving resilience against external attacks and insider threats alike. And, if an incident is detected, automation allows quick containment so threats like ransomware simply cannot propagate, limiting the attack's blast radius.

Large organizations and government entities have begun adopting zero trust architectures. Cloud-native technologies, containerization, and microservices all support this approach, offering granular segmentation to limit the damage when an attacker breaches one component. In compliment to this approach, a just-in-time (JIT) access model removes standing privileges and provides access dynamically, only for the finite moments needed. A JIT model is a key facet of modern least privilege and drastically mitigates the growing risk from identity-based attacks. And, as we approach the back end of the roaring 2020s, we've come to realize it's often easier for a threat actor to simply log in rather than hack in, thus making an identity-first security approach more important than ever to an organization's cyber defenses.

As we stand in the mid-2020s, the lessons from the past remain relevant: neglecting cybersecurity until after a breach is a costly mistake. The initiatives implemented today are crucial for addressing both historical vulnerabilities and anticipating future threats.

From the vacuum-tube leviathans of the 1950s to the ubiquitous connectivity of today, cybersecurity has continually adapted to new technologies, social shifts, and global pressures. The narrative of each decade reveals an interplay of ambition, oversight, triumph, and crisis.

CHAPTER 1   THE HISTORY OF ATTACK VECTORS

As we move deeper into a century being defined by artificial intelligence, quantum computing, and hyper-connected IoT ecosystems, the stakes will only rise.

Therefore, in the next few chapters, we will delve into more nuanced topics regarding cybersecurity:

- In-depth explorations of specific threat actors, their motivations, and modus operandi.
- Detailed breakdowns of various malware and exploits that have wreaked havoc over time.
- Brief case studies on landmark breaches and what they teach us about the real-world impact.
- A detailed look at the people who've shaped modern cybersecurity and their contribution to the industry.
- Cybersecurity solutions that have been developed over the years to address various attack vectors and a few insights into what the future potentially holds for new solutions.

But before we begin, let's quickly revisit what we have learned:

- Understanding history is crucial because it provides context for the challenges we face today.
- The same fundamental questions have persisted since the mainframe era:
  - How do we balance innovation with security?
  - How do we ensure the systems we rely on remain resilient against exploitation?
  - How can we foster collaboration between corporations, governments, and citizens to address threats that know no borders?

- New technology will always be exploitable; it's just a matter of how. Yet, threat actors' broader motives and goals remain largely unchanged.

Make no mistake, the journey is ongoing. New vulnerabilities surface daily, and threat actors are constantly honing their craft. But so too are the defenders. Each wave of attacks sparks fresh innovations in detection, prevention, and response. The story of cybersecurity is the story of an evolving frontier, one that remains as much about people as it is about technology. This continuous evolution means effective cybersecurity requires sustained investment. Thus, a compelling business justification is crucial for securing necessary budgetary funding and for framing cybersecurity as a critical, preemptive strategy rather than merely a reactive cost. Now, let's explore what this actually means.

# CHAPTER 2

# Business Justification

One cannot overstate the critical importance of cybersecurity. From small ventures, multinational conglomerates, and nation-states, the threats related to data protection, risk management, and reputation are universal. Every organization must keep pace with threat actors who develop increasingly sophisticated methods of breaching electronic defenses.

While the potential cost of a robust cybersecurity strategy may cause initial hesitation, investing in reliable technologies is more than a precaution; it should be a business requirement for safeguarding assets, improving competitive advantage, and ensuring long-term sustainability.

To understand the importance of cybersecurity, one must first recognize the cyber threat landscape. Threat actors target organizations of all sizes, seeking financial gain, intellectual property, personal data, or operational disruption. As we've touched on earlier, threat actors come in many forms—from nation-state-sponsored entities all the way through "script kiddies" using utilities created by someone else.

In the last two decades, the world has witnessed a plethora of high-profile cyber breaches that have dominated headlines for weeks and caused distress for businesses and consumers alike. Some of these attacks compromised critical infrastructures, like healthcare and energy, while others set their sights on financial institutions and social media. Such attacks underscored the modern reality that cybersecurity breaches are a universal truth: no entity is immune.

CHAPTER 2    BUSINESS JUSTIFICATION

Moreover, threat actors are utilizing an ever-evolving toolkit. Ransomware, distributed denial-of-service (DDoS) attacks, phishing campaigns, supply chain attacks, and advanced persistent threats (APTs) are just a few methods in their attack vector arsenal. The compounding risk and distributed nature of cyberattacks make it evident that no single defense is sufficient in itself to mitigate the risks of a breach. Constant vigilance, ongoing investment, periodic system evaluations, and regular updates to security policies and procedures must become normal business operations, if they are not already so. It's this evolving context that supports the value of a licensed cybersecurity solution to mitigate modern risk and attempt to stay ahead of the latest threats. The word "license" is key to this discussion since every solution needs updates, patches, and modifications to address the evolving threat landscape.

If we indulge ourselves and look back at the history of cyber breaches, one observation becomes painfully clear: the cost of responding to an attack often exceeds the price of preventing it. When a data breach occurs, organizations face a myriad of unforeseen expenses. While some immediate costs—like incident response, forensic investigations, and system downtime—are typically anticipated and outlined in incident response[1] (IR) plans, these represent only a fraction of the true financial burden.

However, the long-term repercussions of a breach often extend far beyond immediate costs, including reputational damage, lost customer trust, legal penalties, and increased regulatory scrutiny. These impacts, which can be difficult to quantify, may significantly affect an organization's overall revenue. The final expenditure can be staggering, sometimes reaching tens of millions of dollars, and in the worst cases delivering a fatal blow to the business.

---

[1] https://www.cisa.gov/topics/cybersecurity-best-practices/organizations-and-cyber-safety/cybersecurity-incident-response

CHAPTER 2    BUSINESS JUSTIFICATION

Consider the fallout from a massive data breach experienced by a premier cybersecurity firm several years ago. The direct aftermath involved notifications to customers, lawsuits, loss of contracts, and a profound erosion of business confidence. This entity, which was supposed to represent the pinnacle of security for cybersecurity solutions and forensic capabilities, saw its reputation severely damaged. As of this writing, it still has not fully recovered. While not every breach is as public or devastating, one lesson stands true: the lack of a structured cybersecurity program can lead to significantly worse and longer-lasting breach.

From a business justification perspective, licensed cybersecurity solutions are crucial for mitigating breach-related costs and minimizing threat actor dwell time. By selecting appropriate cybersecurity solutions, businesses gain access to proven technologies and authoritative support to address both issues.

Earmarking budget for cybersecurity might not easily demonstrate tangible returns in the same sense as a marketing campaign or product launch. However, the return on investment[2] (ROI) is often realized in intangible but critical ways, much like having business insurance. For every breach thwarted, every regulatory penalty avoided, and every customer retained, the investment in a cybersecurity solution pays for itself by ensuring business continuity. Over time, consistent cybersecurity investments build a foundation of trust with clients, governments, regulators, and partners, creating an environment where businesses are trusted—even if the worst-case scenario occurs.

This is where historical trends become a lesson for the path forward. As regulations like the General Data Protection Regulation (GDPR) and the California Consumer Privacy Act (CCPA) gain momentum, data protection and breach notification requirements have become top of mind for every business. There are now legal requirements for public disclosure that cannot, and should not, be ignored. To put it bluntly, cybersecurity

---

[2] https://councils.forbes.com/blog/roi-of-cybersecurity

solutions are no longer discretionary spending; they have become an essential component of regulatory compliance, cyber insurance requirements, and truly mitigate legal and financial risks that demonstrate best effort to secure the organization if the worst occurs. Inadequate investment in cybersecurity can now expose CxO executives to personal liability, particularly if they were aware of the risks but failed to implement mitigating actions. The CISO of SolarWinds[3] is a notable example of this litigation.

For all business stakeholders, the decision to license cybersecurity solutions goes far beyond signing a purchase order or balancing departmental budgets. It's a strategic requirement that reflects a commitment to protecting financial assets, preserving brand reputation, and cultivating customer trust. Lessons learned from decades of escalating cyberattacks demonstrate that underestimating the importance of a proactive, well-funded cybersecurity program can result in your organization becoming a case study about "what not to do." For organizations seeking to stay ahead of threat actors, the business justification for cybersecurity solutions is clear.

Finally, as artificial intelligence (AI) becomes increasingly integrated into our daily lives, it helps us distill complex challenges into clear imperatives. For instance, AI could succinctly summarize the core message for any cybersecurity project: "In a world of heightened scrutiny, rapidly evolving threats, and rising expectations from consumers and regulators alike, licensing cybersecurity solutions provides more than a shield against bad actors; it offers a pathway to continuous improvement, strategic risk mitigation, and sustained business growth." (Note: this summary was generated by ChatGPT.) AI is becoming a solution to augment our intelligence, just as the emergence of search engines opened the world to vast amounts of information and WiFi allowed ubiquitous connectivity virtually anywhere and anytime. The business

---

[3] https://www.sec.gov/newsroom/press-releases/2023-227

justification of AI and its risks warrant organizations to think about the future and not just what is a threat today.

In today's modern threat landscape, natural language-based attacks can now be created with just a keystroke, leveraging the power of both human and machine capabilities, even by someone with the most trivial of malicious intent. However, by integrating cybersecurity into the fabric of organizational planning and operations, businesses can confidently forge ahead into the digital frontier, embrace the latest technologies like AI, and know their most valuable assets remain under vigilant protection. This provides the business justification in licensing cybersecurity solutions that we should all embrace and recognize as a part of business operations.

## CHAPTER 3

# Definitions

As we peer back across the history of cybersecurity, we see that words can hold different meanings across decades and generations. We've discussed a few already, like "hacker." Something that was "hip" yesterday is "cool" today and may be "sweet" or even "fire" tomorrow. "Of course, of course" as Gen Z might say.

A foundational aspect of learning from cybersecurity's past is the consistent application of terms such as "bug," "vulnerability," "identity," and "exploit." To ensure a shared and precise understanding as we proceed, establishing common definitions is paramount. While these terms are readily searchable, their consistent interpretation across historical contexts is what allows for meaningful analysis. Therefore, let us now clarify these key concepts.

## Bugs

The modern definition of a software bug is an error, flaw, failure, or fault in a computer program or system that causes it to produce an incorrect or unexpected result, or to behave in unintended ways. This definition encompasses a broad range of issues, from minor glitches that slightly affect user experience to severe faults that can cause a system to crash or become vulnerable to security breaches.

We choose to say "modern definition" because the historical origin of the term "bug" is quite different. In the context of engineering, the term "bug" predates computer software, originally used to describe a defect or problem

CHAPTER 3   DEFINITIONS

with electrical or mechanical systems. The most famous anecdote attributing the term's origin in computing comes from Grace Hopper, a pioneering computer scientist. While working on the Harvard Mark II[1] computer in 1947, her team discovered an actual moth causing a malfunction by short-circuiting the mechanism. They removed the moth and taped it in their logbook, humorously annotating it as the "first actual case of bug being found." This incident popularized, but did not originate, the term in computing.

Today, software bugs are not merely mistakes, oversights, or unexpected glitches. They are symptomatic of deeper issues in the software development process, including:

- **Complexity of Software Systems:** Modern software is incredibly complex, integrating multiple subsystems and third-party components. This complexity can breed bugs as different parts of the system interact in unforeseen ways, stemming from issues like timing discrepancies or case sensitivity.

- **Human Error:** Developers are human and prone to error when code is unchecked. Misunderstandings of specifications, oversight, or lack of experience can lead to unexpected bugs.

- **Changing Requirements:** As software evolves to meet new user needs, changes can introduce unintended side effects in existing code, especially when new code is introduced.

- **Environmental Factors:** Software might behave differently in various environments or under different configurations, leading to bugs that are hard to predict or replicate when hardware or processing differences exist.

---

[1] https://americanhistory.si.edu/collections/object/nmah_334663

A key aspect of software bugs is their potential to become vulnerabilities. A vulnerability is a weakness in the system that can be exploited by a threat actor, such as a hacker, to perform unauthorized actions. When a bug is identified and exploited to compromise a system's security, it becomes an exploit. The process from bug to exploit is as follows (we will explore these definitions in detail further in a moment):

- **Identification:** A bug is discovered, either by developers, users, quality assurance, bug bounties, or malicious actors.

- **Analysis:** The bug is analyzed for its potential impact. If it can be used to bypass security measures, it becomes a security vulnerability.

- **Exploit Development:** Hackers and penetration testers develop exploits, code, or methods that take advantage of the vulnerability to gain unauthorized access or control.

- **Deployment:** The exploit is deployed against vulnerable systems, often as part of malware or hacking attacks, and it may be unknown and be classified as a zero-day vulnerability.

To mitigate and manage software bugs and their risks, organizations can embrace multiple strategies:

- **Preventive Measures:** Implementing robust software development practices, including thorough code reviews and comprehensive testing (such as penetration testing), helps prevent bugs.

- **Detection and Patching:** Regularly scanning software for vulnerabilities and releasing patches or updates to fix them, especially in open source code.

CHAPTER 3   DEFINITIONS

- **Incident Response:** Having plans in place for responding to security breaches resulting from exploited bugs.
- **Education and Awareness:** Training developers and users about common vulnerabilities and secure coding practices to prevent coding mistakes.

This leads us to a model for the lifecycle of a software vulnerability:

1. **Introduction:** A vulnerability is introduced during the software development process and is probably unknown to the developers or organization. The word "unknown" is key because poor software development practices will often allow the release of known vulnerable software, especially from open source components that haven't been updated or vetted during the development process.

2. **Exploitation:** Once a vulnerability is discovered, it can potentially be exploited by threat actors. If a vulnerability is exploited before it is identified and publicly documented, it is referred to as a zero-day vulnerability. Ideally, detection—the next crucial step—should occur before exploitation.

3. **Detection:** When a vulnerability is detected—either through active security testing, user reports, or after an incident—the findings are typically presented to the vendor. Unfortunately, some vendors ignore these findings.

4. **Patch Development:** Normally, the software developer creates and releases a patch or update to fix the vulnerability based on the data provide to research, incident, or based on bug bounty.

5. **Disclosure:** The vulnerability is publicly disclosed to the community. By this stage, a patch or instructions for mitigation would have typically been disseminated, with sensitivity, to all impacted or concerned parties. Rarely does disclosure occur in the absence of mitigation tactics unless the vulnerability is a zero-day or cannot be remediated at all.

6. **Deployment of Patch:** Finally, organizations should deploy the patch to mitigate the risk based on the severity and their own service level agreements (SLAs). In some instances, it may be inadvisable to implement a patch due to the potential for disruption, or because it may lead to noncompliance. This is why it's important to have a defense-in-depth approach in place, with the principle of least privilege (PoLP) as the centerpiece. With least privilege and defense-in-depth implemented, many vulnerabilities can be mitigated outright, or at least the blast radius minimized, even in the absence of patching. Today, this is a part of a zero trust strategy which will be discussed in more detail later on.

In summary, software bugs represent a critical challenge in the field of computer science and cybersecurity. They shouldn't be viewed merely as coding errors, but as symptomatic of broader issues in software development, detection, and management. The potential for bugs to transform into security vulnerabilities with exploits necessitates a vigilant and proactive approach to software design, testing, and maintenance. Understanding the nature and implications of software bugs is essential for developers, users, defenders, and organizations to safeguard against the myriad risks they represent.

CHAPTER 3   DEFINITIONS

# Vulnerability

As previously stated, it's a good time to understand software vulnerabilities and their potential exploitation by threat actors. A software vulnerability is a flaw, weakness, or error based on a bug in a software application or operating system that can be exploited by threat actors to gain unauthorized access, cause harm, or disrupt services.

Vulnerabilities can arise from a variety of sources, including programming errors, lack of security features, or configuration mistakes. The exploitation of vulnerabilities poses significant risks to individuals, organizations, and even national security, as history has shown us. Not all vulnerabilities have exploits. Some are purely theoretical, others only have proof-of-concepts, and some are so complex that their exploitation is statistically unlikely. It's the vulnerabilities with working and reliable exploits that generally make the news.

Some of the most common types of vulnerabilities arising from bugs in applications and websites include:

- **Buffer Overflows:** Occurs when a program writes more data to a buffer than it can hold, potentially allowing threat actors to overwrite memory locations and execute malicious code.

- **Injection Flaws:** Such as SQL injection, where threat actors can inject malicious code into a program, often through input fields to compromise resources supporting the application, like a database.

- **Cross-Site Scripting (XSS):** Where web applications allow malicious scripts to be injected into web pages viewed by other users.

CHAPTER 3  DEFINITIONS

- **Authentication and Authorization:** These include weak login mechanisms or faulty access controls that can be bypassed or exploited to gain unauthorized access.

- **Misconfigurations:** Improperly configured entitlements, permissions, rights, or privileges that can expose sensitive information, or unnecessary services running on a system that can be exploited due to errant settings (like a default password, etc.)

**Note** This list is meant to be illustrative of the range of vulnerabilities that can occur, but it is nowhere near an exhaustive one.

The security industry has multiple security standards to document the risk, threat, and relevance of all vulnerabilities. The most common standards are:

- **Common Vulnerabilities and Exposure[2] (CVE):** A standard for information security vulnerability names and descriptions.

- **European Union Vulnerability Database[3] (EUVD):** A standard for information security vulnerabilities developed or implemented within the European Union. These entries occur after CVEs are published in order to avoid conflicts in reporting or disclosure.

---

[2] https://cve.mitre.org
[3] https://euvd.enisa.europa.eu/

55

CHAPTER 3   DEFINITIONS

- **Common Vulnerability Scoring System[4] (CVSS):** A mathematical system for scoring the risk of information technology vulnerabilities.

- **The Extensible Configuration Checklist Description Format[5] (XCCDF):** A specification language for writing security checklists, benchmarks, and related kinds of documents.

- **Open Vulnerability Assessment Language[6] (OVAL):** An information security community effort to standardize how to assess and report upon the machine state of computer systems.

- **Common Configuration Enumeration[7] (CCE):** Provides unique identifiers to system configuration issues to facilitate fast and accurate correlation of configuration data across multiple information sources and tools.

- **Common Weakness Enumeration[8] (CWE):** Provides a common language for discussing, finding, and addressing the causes of software security vulnerabilities within the code.

- **Security Content Automation Protocol[9] (SCAP):** A synthesis of interoperable specifications based on existing standards. For example, ratified version 1.2

---

[4] https://nvd.nist.gov/vuln-metrics/cvss
[5] https://csrc.nist.gov/projects/security-content-automation-protocol/specifications/xccdf
[6] https://github.com/OVAL-Community/OVAL
[7] https://ncp.nist.gov/cce
[8] https://cwe.mitre.org
[9] https://csrc.nist.gov/projects/security-content-automation-protocol

of SCAP is comprised of multiple standards—such as XCCDF, OVAL, OCIL, ARF, CCE, CPE, CVE, CVSS, and CCSS—each at specific, frozen versions. This design allows individual standards to evolve independently while ensuring stable collections for communication. Note that while some of these standards have been deprecated, they continue to be used in the latest SCAP standard.

- **Open Web Application Security Project[10] (OWASP):** An online community that provides a not-for-profit approach to developing secure web applications by providing methodologies, tools, technology, and an assessment approach for vendors, organizations, and end users.

With this information, security professionals and management teams can effectively discuss and prioritize risks from software vulnerabilities. In the end, the vulnerabilities must be remediated to prevent exploitation, or the business must accept the risk as a part of operations and, if possible, implement mitigating security controls. A common language and structured approach are crucial for communicating these vulnerabilities across vendors, companies, and government bodies. Without this, assessments would lack comparability, especially given that a critical risk for one company might be irrelevant for another due to differing contexts and environments. Standards like CVE, CVSS, and EUVD, among others, ensure that risk can be clearly conveyed to all stakeholders.

---

[10] https://owasp.org

CHAPTER 3   DEFINITIONS

# Exploitation

Threat actors, ranging from individual hackers to organized crime syndicates and state-sponsored groups, exploit software vulnerabilities to achieve various malicious objectives. The process of developing and deploying an exploit typically involves several steps:

1. **Discovery:** Finding a vulnerability, either through their own research, shared information in hacker communities, or purchasing details about vulnerabilities from sources like the dark web.

2. **Development of Exploit:** Creating a method or tool to take advantage of the vulnerability. This could be a piece of software, a script, or a set of commands that provides a working exploit.

3. **Delivery:** Deploying the exploit against the target. This can be done through various means like phishing emails, infected websites, or direct attacks on exposed network services.

4. **Execution:** The exploit performs its intended action, which could be stealing data, installing malware (like ransomware), or creating a backdoor for future access.

5. **Propagation:** In some cases, the exploit can propagate itself, as seen in worms, bots, and certain types of malwares, to spread the attack to other systems or networks.

The exploitation of software vulnerabilities can lead to various negative outcomes and real-world implications, including:

- **Data Breaches:** Unauthorized access to sensitive data such as personal information, intellectual property, or financial records.

- **System Damage:** Corruption of systems, disruption of services, or complete system takeovers.

- **Financial Losses:** Direct financial losses through theft, or indirect costs associated with recovery and reputational damage.

- **National Security Threats:** Vulnerabilities in critical infrastructure or government systems can pose significant national security risks.

Similar to bugs and vulnerabilities, there are high-level steps and best practices for mitigating systems with known exploits. Note: there are entire books and cybersecurity frameworks dedicated to this topic. This list is simplified to keep the discussion going:

1. **Regular Updates and Patch Management:** Keeping all software and systems updated with the latest patches is crucial.

2. **Security Testing:** Regular security audits, vulnerability assessments, and penetration testing can help identify and address vulnerabilities.

3. **Secure Coding Practices:** Developers should follow secure coding guidelines to minimize the introduction of new vulnerabilities.

CHAPTER 3   DEFINITIONS

4. **Awareness and Training:** Educating staff and users about common threats and safe practices can reduce the risk of successful attacks.

5. **Incident Response Planning:** Having a plan in place for responding to security incidents can help mitigate the damage and accelerate recovery.

Software vulnerabilities and their corresponding exploits pose a significant risk in the digital world, offering threat actors a gateway to compromise systems and cause harm. The exploitation of vulnerabilities can have far-reaching consequences, from personal data theft to large-scale security breaches affecting critical infrastructure. Addressing the risk from exploits requires a combination of technical measures, like regular patching and security testing, and human factors, such as awareness and training.

# Obfuscation

Obfuscation is a technique used in software development to make the source code or binaries difficult to understand, reverse engineer, and perform security assessments on. It's a form of "security through obscurity," which, while not foolproof, can be an effective strategy. By transforming the code into a form that is challenging to read and analyze, obfuscation can help hide vulnerabilities from potential threat actors and delay or prevent exploitation.

Some of the common principles and techniques of software obfuscation include:

- **Code Complexity:** Obfuscation involves increasing the complexity of the code. This can be accomplished through various means such as changing variable names to meaningless labels, altering program structures, or inserting redundant or misleading code.

- **Control Flow Alteration:** Altering the control flow of the application, making the execution path less predictable and harder to follow.

- **Data Obfuscation:** Encrypting or otherwise altering data structures and storage formats to obscure the data's true nature or purpose.

- **Antidebugging and Antitampering Techniques:** Implementing features that make it harder for an attacker to debug, reverse engineer, or modify the code.

One of the potential goals of obfuscation is to hide vulnerabilities or make them harder to find by researchers or threat actors in compiled code. Obfuscation can hide vulnerabilities in several ways:

- **Complicating Exploit Development:** By making the codebase less comprehensible, it becomes more challenging for a threat actor to identify vulnerabilities and develop exploits.

- **Masking Known Vulnerabilities:** In cases where immediate patching of a known vulnerability is not feasible, obfuscation can help hide these weaknesses, at least temporarily.

- **Protecting Sensitive Code Paths:** Key algorithms or security-related code can be specifically targeted for obfuscation to protect them from being easily analyzed and exploited.

Obfuscation can provide additional security for software, but it has some limitations and technical considerations:

- **Deterrence:** While not making code invulnerable, obfuscation raises the effort and skill level required to analyze and attack the software, thereby deterring some threat actors.

CHAPTER 3   DEFINITIONS

- **Protecting Intellectual Property:** Obfuscation helps protect the intellectual property contained in software by making reverse engineering more difficult.

- **Compliance and Protection of Sensitive Data:** In some industries, obfuscation can help meet compliance standards that require protection of sensitive data, such as encryption keys or personal data.

Limitations and considerations:

- **Not Foolproof:** Skilled threat actors with sufficient resources may still be able to reverse engineer obfuscated code. Therefore, obfuscation should be part of a broader security strategy and not the only component.

- **Performance Impact:** Obfuscation can impact the performance and functionality of the software, which needs to be balanced against security benefits.

- **Maintenance Challenges:** Obfuscated code can be more difficult to maintain, update, and debug since complexity is essentially designed in.

Obfuscation serves as an additional layer of defense for protecting software. Intentionally making code less intelligible helps mask vulnerabilities, protect sensitive parts of the code, and deter less skilled threat actors. However, it's crucial to remember that obfuscation is not a silver bullet and should be used in conjunction with other security practices, such as regular patching, secure coding practices, and thorough testing. It's a part of a comprehensive security strategy that can significantly enhance the overall protection of software systems. As stated commonly in the industry: "security through obscurity."

CHAPTER 3   DEFINITIONS

# Virus

A computer virus is a type of malicious software (malware) designed to perform a malicious task and can be coded to automatically spread from one computer to another. Viruses can alter how a computer operates, with the potential to cause varying degrees of damage to data, operations, and software. Understanding the evolution of computer viruses is crucial in grasping their complexity and how their history shows what they can become in the future.

At its core, a computer virus is a piece of code that attaches itself to other operating systems and applications, often containing self-replicating components. Like biological viruses, a computer virus spreads from host to host, frequently capable of mutating and evading detection. Its primary characteristics include replication, the need for a host software or firmware, and the activation of a payload—the detrimental effect or objective of the virus.

The concept of a self-replicating program is traceable to theoretical discussions as early as the 1950s. However, it wasn't until the early 1980s did the first actual computer viruses appear.

1. **Beginning (1980s):** The first viruses were relatively benign and often limited to specific computing environments. One of the first notable viruses was the "Elk Cloner," which infected Apple II systems. These early viruses spread through floppy disks, from one computer to another, dependent on humans as the carrier.

2. **Evolution (1990s):** In the 1990s, viruses made significant leaps in variety and complexity. The advent of the Internet and email dramatically accelerated their spread. Notable early examples

include the "Melissa" virus and the "ILOVEYOU"[11] worm, which caused widespread damage and highlighted the potential for serious impact. We'll discuss these in detail in later chapters.

3. **Sophistication (2000s):** From a simple annoyance to persistence, viruses evolved into rootkits and ransomware that could survive operating system reinstallation. Notable examples from this era include the Sony Rootkit[12] (2005), delivered via Music CDs, and Lockbit[13] (2022), which holds the dubious title of being the most prolific ransomware ever.

As technology advanced, so did computer viruses, growing in sophistication and potency. Some of the most notable types, without creating an exhaustive list, include:

- **Polymorphic and Metamorphic Viruses:** These types of viruses can change their code and employ automatic obfuscation techniques as they propagate, making detection and removal more difficult via traditional antivirus software.

- **Macro Viruses:** Exploiting macros in software like Microsoft Word, these viruses proliferate through documents and were a dominant form in the late 1990s. Macro viruses operate at the application layer and can be transmitted any way office files are shared.

---

[11] https://www.techtarget.com/searchsecurity/definition/ILOVEYOU-virus
[12] https://www.theregister.com/2021/12/10/autorunning_away/
[13] https://www.state.gov/reward-for-information-lockbit-ransomware-as-a-service/

- **File Infectors and Boot Sector Viruses:** Targeting specific types of files or the boot sector of a hard drive, these viruses could be particularly damaging to system operations and are notoriously difficult to remove.

We come to a startling conclusion based on this summary. The 21st century witnessed the transformation of computer viruses from mere nuisances to sophisticated tools used in cyberwarfare, espionage, and for financial gain. This evolution supports our history lesson by allowing us to classify the most important viruses into these four high-level categories:

- **Ransomware:** Perhaps the most notorious modern form, ransomware encrypts the victim's files and demands payment for the decryption key. Examples include WannaCry and CryptoLocker.

- **State-Sponsored and Espionage-Driven Viruses:** Some viruses are developed for political, military, or espionage purposes. Stuxnet, a notable example, targeted Iranian nuclear facilities.

- **Botnets:** Infected computers can be corralled into botnets, used for coordinated attacks or for sending spam emails.

- **Zero-Day Exploits:** Viruses exploiting unknown vulnerabilities (zero days) in software can cause significant damage before being detected and patched.

When we review the most popular and noteworthy viruses in future chapters, we will also attempt to document the known impact and implications from their widespread infection. Keep these data points in mind when reviewing them and what the mission may be for any new infections:

- **Economic Damage:** The cost of virus-induced damages can be in the billions, including data loss, productivity loss, and recovery costs.

- **Security and Privacy Violations:** Viruses can compromise personal and corporate data, leading to significant privacy breaches.

- **Social and Psychological Impact:** Beyond tangible damage, the threat of viruses can create a climate of fear and mistrust in technology.

And, like any other cybersecurity threat, there are recommended mitigation and defense strategies against viruses (malware):

- **Antivirus, Antimalware, or Endpoint Detection and Response (EDR) Software:** Continuously evolving to detect and remove viruses and other malicious software, including those that employ behavioral abuse.

- **Regular Software Updates:** Patching known vulnerabilities to prevent exploitation by viruses.

- **Backup and Recovery Plans:** Regular backups can mitigate the damage caused by viruses, particularly ransomware.

- **User Education:** Teaching users to recognize and avoid potential threats that could deliver viruses via the web, email, macros, or files.

- **Least Privilege:** Implementing a security principle that ensures users, applications, and systems are granted the minimum access necessary to perform their legitimate functions by removing unnecessary administrative privileges.

The journey from the simple, often harmless, viruses of the early 1980s to the complex, multifaceted threats of today illustrates the dynamic nature of computer viruses. They have evolved in step with technological advancements, leveraging new platforms and methods to spread and inflict damage.

# Worms

A computer worm is a type of malware (virus) that self-replicates to spread to other computers, often utilizing network services to reproduce. Unlike a traditional virus, a worm doesn't need to attach itself to an existing program. A worm typically exploits vulnerabilities in network security and applications or utilizes social engineering to proliferate. The primary intent of a worm can range from a harmless prank to serious destructive activities, including stealing data, overloading systems (denial of service), ransomware, creating botnets, and installing backdoors.

The first computer worms date back to the 1970s, predating the modern Internet. The first known worm emerged in the early 1970s and was called The Creeper System.[14] It was an experimental self-replicating program developed by Bob Thomas[15] at BBN Technologies and ran on the ARPANET—the precursor to the modern Internet. Creeper was relatively benign; it simply replicated itself and displayed a message saying, "I'm the creeper, catch me if you can!" Shortly after this proof-of-concept worm, The Reaper, a rudimentary antivirus program, was specifically designed to seek out and delete Creeper.

---

[14] https://www.historyofinformation.com/detail.php?entryid=2860
[15] http://www.computer-timeline.com/timeline/bob-thomas/

CHAPTER 3    DEFINITIONS

Ultimately, this led to an evolution of worms, and some were more notable and destructive than others. While we will explore some of these in more detail later, a few stand out as history lessons for our discussion in this chapter:

- **The Morris Worm (1988):** Created by Robert Tappan Morris, a graduate student at Cornell University, the Morris Worm was one of the first worms distributed via the Internet. As such, it gained significant media attention. It exploited vulnerabilities in UNIX systems and caused considerable disruption by consuming system resources, leading to slower systems, and even crashes. This incident highlighted the need for network security and led to the foundation of the Computer Emergency Response Team (CERT).

- **ILOVEYOU/Love Letter (2000):** This worm was a standalone program that spread through email, masquerading as a love letter. It overwrote files, including documents and images, and sent itself to all contacts in the victim's Microsoft Outlook address book. The ILOVEYOU worm caused billions of dollars in damage globally.

- **Code Red (2001):** Targeting machines running Microsoft's IIS web server, Code Red exploited a buffer overflow vulnerability. It performed a distributed DDoS on the White House's web servers and significantly slowed down Internet traffic.

- **Conficker**[16] **(2008):** Conficker, also known as Downup or Downadup, infected millions of computers worldwide, including government, business, and home computers. It used a flaw in Windows OS to create a botnet.

---

[16] https://attack.mitre.org/software/S0608/

CHAPTER 3   DEFINITIONS

- **Stuxnet (2010):** Considered one of the most sophisticated worms, Stuxnet was designed to target and damage Iran's nuclear program. It's believed to be a state-sponsored worm developed by the United States and Israel. Stuxnet specifically targeted Programmable Logic Controllers (PLCs) used in industrial control systems.

Computer worms have caused significant economic damage, loss of productivity, and security breaches. Their ability to propagate quickly and widely makes them particularly dangerous. Responses to worms include developing more robust security protocols, regular software updates, network monitoring, and public awareness about cybersecurity, including the introduction of concepts like zero trust[17] and least privilege[18] to prevent their propagation.

From the Creeper to Stuxnet, computer worms have evolved significantly, both in terms of technology and impact. They continue to represent a major challenge in cybersecurity, capable of causing widespread disruption and damage.

# Bots

A software bot (short for robot) is an automated software program designed to perform specific tasks autonomously or with minimal human intervention. Bots can be used for legitimate purposes and for nefarious ones. Tasks performed by software bots range from simple, repetitive actions like indexing web content for search engines to complex activities

---

[17] https://www.cisa.gov/zero-trust-maturity-model
[18] https://www.techtarget.com/searchsecurity/definition/principle-of-least-privilege-POLP

CHAPTER 3   DEFINITIONS

like simulating human interactions in customer service. Bots can also be wielded by threat actors to wage distributed DDoS attacks, perform keystroke logging, exfiltrate data, and more.

Bots operate across various platforms, including web servers, social media platforms, and personal computing devices. Software bots distinguish themselves from viruses and other malware due to their autonomous nature. They are programmed to execute predefined tasks or respond to certain triggers without direct human control. With this in mind, there are several primary types of bots (good and bad):

- **AI Bots:** Also called AI agents[19] that perform AI-related tasks locally, without the need for a heavy computational footprint or continuous communication with a Command and Control server.

- **Chatbots:** Simulate human conversation, used in customer service or information retrieval.

- **Crawlers:** Used by search engines to systematically browse the web and index content.

- **Transactional Bots:** Perform automated transactions, like stock trading or online purchases.

- **Malicious Bots:** A wide variety of bots that execute cyberattacks, spread malware, or carry out other harmful activities in an automated fashion.

One of the earliest and most significant automated programs in the context of cybersecurity was the Morris Worm, which we have previously discussed. Though not a bot in the modern sense, it was an early example

---

[19] https://www.ibm.com/think/topics/ai-agents

CHAPTER 3   DEFINITIONS

of an automated program that had a profound impact on the basic understanding of cybersecurity. Consider some of the Morris Worm's bot-like functions:

- **Purpose:** Designed to gauge the size of the Internet, the Morris Worm was a self-replicating program that exploited known vulnerabilities in UNIX systems. This function alone is why it classifies as an early bot.

- **Propagation:** It spread across networks by exploiting vulnerabilities in the UNIX operating system, using a few different attack vectors, including a buffer overflow in the fingerd network service and a trusted-host authentication flaw in the rsh/rexec suite of programs. This is why it's classified as a worm.

- **Impact:** Contrary to Morris's expectations, the worm replicated excessively, causing buffer overflows that led to system crashes and significant slowdowns. An estimated 6,000 computers were affected, which was a significant portion of the Internet-connected computers at the time.

- **Response:** The incident prompted a reevaluation of network security practices and led to the formation of the first Computer Emergency Response Team[20] (CERT).

Today, bots have evolved significantly, both in complexity and in the roles they play. They are integral to many benign applications but are also used in malicious activities like DDoS attacks, spam, and spreading

---

[20] https://www.cisa.gov/sites/default/files/publications/infosheet_US-CERT_v2.pdf

71

CHAPTER 3   DEFINITIONS

misinformation on social media. The challenge for cybersecurity is distinguishing malicious bot activity from legitimate automated processes and effectively countering bot-based threats.

Software bots, as demonstrated by the legacy of the Morris Worm, have had a lasting impact on the landscape of cybersecurity. While they offer immense benefits in automating tasks and analyzing data, their capacity for widespread disruption has necessitated the development of sophisticated cybersecurity measures. The evolving nature of bot technology continues to pose unique challenges, making continuous innovation and vigilance crucial in formulating cybersecurity defenses.

# Rootkits

Rootkits are a type of malicious software designed to gain unauthorized root or administrative access to an operating system while simultaneously hiding their presence by leveraging the boot up process of a system. Rootkit installation typically occurs before any defensive solutions are enabled (e.g., the boot sector of a hard disk before the operating system loads). The primary goal of this malware type is to evade detection, making them particularly insidious threats. By masking themselves and other malware, rootkits can maintain persistent presence on infected systems, allowing threat actors to remotely control the system, steal sensitive information, and perform other malicious activities over time.

In addition, due to the location of rootkits on the asset, reloading the operating system is often insufficient to remove the malware. A rootkit is typically composed of a collection of software tools that provide unauthorized access and control to a system. Once installed, a rootkit can intercept and manipulate system calls, alter system files and processes, and hide its existence from standard monitoring tools at the lowest levels of the system possible. In summary, the key functionality of a rootkit is as follows:

- **Concealment:** Rootkits hide files, processes, and system data, making them invisible to both the system's users and its defense mechanisms.

- **Privilege Escalation:** They often grant threat actors administrative privileges, bypassing normal authentication and authorization processes.

- **Persistence:** Designed to survive reboots and maintain continuous control, rootkits can be particularly challenging to remove.

- **Backdoor Access:** Providing threat actors with backdoor access, rootkits facilitate ongoing exploitation of the compromised system.

The concept of rootkits dates back to the early days of computer systems. However, one of the first documented malicious rootkits in the context of computer security was the UNIX Rootkit,[21] which appeared in the early 1990s. These early rootkits targeted UNIX systems and were primarily a collection of tools and scripts designed to replace critical system binaries with compromised versions. This substitution allowed threat actors to maintain administrative-level access, while concealing their activities in code that was designed to operate as normal business functions. The emergence of rootkits marked a significant shift in the landscape of cybersecurity for several reasons:

- **Stealthy Nature:** The ability of rootkits to hide themselves and their activities challenged existing security paradigms, requiring more sophisticated detection methods.

---

[21] https://terokarvinen.com/otherauthors/eliimatt-wordpress-org-puppet-liimatta-2013/www.rootsecure.net/content/downloads/pdf/unix_rootkits_overview.pdf

CHAPTER 3   DEFINITIONS

- **Deep System Integration:** Rootkits often operate at a low level within the operating system, making detection and removal difficult without specialized tools.

- **Prolonged Access:** By granting threat actors persistent access to systems, rootkits increase the risk and potential impact of data breaches and espionage.

- **Evasion of Traditional Defenses:** Standard antivirus and security software, especially in the early days, were ill-equipped to detect or remove rootkits.

To combat rootkits, both technology and strategy had to evolve for detection and removal. Modern techniques rootkit defense and mitigation techniques include:

- **Behavioral Detection:** Implementing security systems that detect anomalous behavior rather than relying solely on signature-based detection.

- **Secure Boot Mechanisms:** Ensuring the integrity of the system's boot process to prevent rootkit installation at the boot level.

- **Kernel Integrity Checks:** Regular checks of the kernel and critical system files for unauthorized modifications.

- **Privilege Management:** Limiting administrative privileges and employing least privilege principles to minimize the risk and impact of rootkits.

Rootkits represent one of the more covert and dangerous types of malware. Mainstream awareness started with ill-advised usage by Sony[22] (2015), with a real business need, but a subverse implementation that left millions of systems compromised. It was revealed that the implementation

---

[22] https://fsfe.org/activities/drm/sony-rootkit-fiasco.en.html

of copy protection measures on about 22 million (Compact Discs) CDs distributed by Sony BMG installed one of two pieces of software that provided a form of digital rights management by modifying the operating system to interfere with CD ripping and copying.

## Configuration

Software configuration mistakes can be significant vulnerabilities that expose an organization's many cybersecurity risks, but they are often overlooked. These mistakes can vary from improper settings in software, use of default usernames and passwords, to misconfigured network equipment—all of which leave an organization susceptible to compromise. Such errors create openings that can be exploited by threat actors to gain unauthorized access, steal data, or disrupt services.

The most common misconfigurations that can lead to a system compromise include:

- **Improper Security Settings:** This can include weak encryption, open ports, and unnecessary services running on a system. Threat actors can exploit these to gain access or escalate privileges.

- **Default Credentials:** Many systems and applications come with default usernames and passwords that are easily guessable. Failure to change these credentials is a common vulnerability.

- **Inadequate Access Controls:** Improperly configured user permissions can allow unauthorized access to sensitive data or critical functions.

- **Misconfigured Network Devices:** Routers, switches, and firewalls with incorrect settings can expose internal networks to the public Internet.

- **Lack of Regular Updates:** Not configuring software to update automatically can lead to outdated systems vulnerable to known exploits.

When systems are misconfigured, the consequences can be costly and include:

- **Data Breaches:** Unauthorized access to data due to misconfigurations can lead to theft of sensitive personal and corporate information.
- **System Compromise:** Threat actors can exploit configuration weaknesses to install malware, create backdoors, or take over systems.
- **Service Disruption:** Misconfigurations can be exploited in denial-of-service attacks, disrupting business operations and services.
- **Compliance Violations:** Failing to configure systems securely can lead to violations of regulatory standards, resulting in legal and financial penalties.

One of the earliest and most notable examples of a major cyberattack exploiting a configuration flaw can also be attributed to the Morris Worm. The worm exploited configuration vulnerabilities in the UNIX operating system, particularly in the `sendmail` program, a widely used email utility, and an exploit in the `finger` daemon, a service for locating users on other systems. The worm was intended to gauge the size of the Internet, but due to a programming error, it replicated excessively, causing buffer overflows and significantly slowing down infected systems to the point of them becoming unusable.

Software configuration mistakes can lead to significant cybersecurity vulnerabilities. They highlight the need for vigilant management of software settings, regular updates, and adherence to best security practices, especially for settings and system hardening. As technology evolves, the challenge of maintaining secure configurations becomes more complex, necessitating ongoing efforts in education, tool development, and policy formation to safeguard against potential attacks.

# Attack Vectors

While we have been discussing vulnerabilities and exploits, the actual methods and models used by a threat actor are normally not defined in standards like CVE or CVSS. Therefore, as we begin to look at attacks throughout history, we need to define and consider what the definition of an attack vector actually is.

A cyberattack vector is the path or method threat actors exploit to breach an organization's security perimeter, gain unauthorized access, and compromise systems, data, or users. Attack vectors range from exploitable vulnerabilities, such as unpatched software, misconfigured cloud assets, and zero-day vulnerabilities all the way through human tactics like social engineering and credential theft. The rise of AI-driven threats, deepfake-based impersonation, and supply chain vulnerabilities is driving a significant increase in attack vectors.

Effective cybersecurity strategies focus on reducing the number of attack vectors through zero trust principles, continuous monitoring, and robust identity security. Organizations that fail to holistically address attack vectors risk falling victim to ransomware, data exfiltration, operational disruptions, as well as regulatory and legal consequences.

Next, let's break down an attack vector into its components:

- **Techniques:** Specific ways threat actors attempt to carry out their tactics.
- **Subtechniques:** More specific actions that break down techniques and tools used to conduct the attack.

CHAPTER 3   DEFINITIONS

- **Tactics:** Categorized behaviors that threat actors use to achieve their goal—social engineering and brute force password attacks are some key examples.

The MITRE ATT&CK[23] framework helps define and measure the techniques and tactics used by threat actors. The MITRE ATT&CK framework provides:

- A model for threat actors' tactics and techniques.
- A technical path to demonstrate how to detect or stop cybercriminals.
- A classification model to help threat detection and prevention strategies.
- A methodology for identifying security gaps in existing processes, procedures, and solutions that could lead to a breach.
- Guidance to prioritize defenses based on exposure.
- Guidance on how to monitor and improve security controls throughout an organization.
- A community to share information and collaborate with others in the industry.

MITRE has created multiple living categories to describe each attack vector. There are also multiple subcategories (techniques) that describe the attack by name, unique identification code, methods for detection, and, when possible, mitigation methods. The tactics provided by MITRE are divided into three categories: enterprise, mobile, and ICS. For the sake of our conversation, let's focus on enterprise assets:

---

[23] https://attack.mitre.org

CHAPTER 3   DEFINITIONS

- **Reconnaissance:** Consists of techniques that involve threat actors actively or passively gathering information that can be used to support targeting. Such information may include details of the victim's organization, infrastructure, or human identities. This information can be leveraged by the threat actor to aid in other phases of the attack chain, such as using gathered information to plan and execute initial access, to scope and prioritize postcompromise objectives, or to push and advance further reconnaissance efforts.

- **Resource Development:** Consists of techniques that involve threat actors creating, purchasing, or obtaining resources that can be used to support future targeting. Such resources include infrastructure, accounts, or capabilities. These resources can be leveraged by the threat actor to aid in other phases of the threat actor kill chain, such as using purchased domains to support Command and Control, email accounts for phishing as a part of initial access, or stealing API keys to help with defense evasion.

- **Initial Access:** Consists of techniques that use various infiltration methods to gain their initial beachhead within an environment. Techniques used to gain initial access include targeted spear phishing and exploiting weaknesses on public-facing web servers.

- **Execution:** Consists of techniques that result in threat actor-controlled code running on a local or remote system. Techniques that run malicious code are often paired with techniques from all other tactics to achieve broader goals, like mapping a network or stealing data.

- **Persistence:** Consists of techniques threat actors use to maintain access to systems across restarts, changed credentials, and other interruptions that could terminate their access. Techniques used for persistence include any access, action, or configuration changes that allow them to maintain their presence on systems, such as replacing or hijacking legitimate code or modifying startup routines.

- **Privilege Escalation:** Consists of techniques threat actors use to gain higher-level permissions on a system, network, or environment. Threat actors can often enter and explore a network with unprivileged access but require elevated permissions to follow through on their goals. Common approaches include taking advantage of system weaknesses, misconfigurations, and vulnerabilities.

- **Defense Evasion:** Consists of techniques threat actors leverage to avoid detection throughout their compromise. Techniques used for defense evasion include uninstalling, removing, reconfiguring, disabling security software, obfuscating, or encrypting data and scripts. Threat actors also leverage and abuse trusted processes to hide and obfuscate their malware.

- **Credential Access:** Consists of techniques for stealing credentials, such as account names and passwords. Techniques used to steal credentials include keylogging, pass-the-hash, or credential dumping. Using legitimate, albeit stolen, credentials can enable threat actors to access systems while making their presence and actions harder to detect, since it may mimic normal behavior.

- **Discovery:** Consists of techniques a threat actor may use to gain knowledge about the system, network, or environment. These techniques help threat actors observe the environment and orient themselves before deciding how to act.

- **Lateral Movement:** Consists of techniques threat actors use to enter and control remote systems in an environment and move across assets, network zones, and even through firewalls to complete their mission. Threat actors might install their own remote access tools to accomplish lateral movement or use legitimate credentials with native network and operating system tools.

- **Collection:** Consists of techniques threat actors may use to gather information and the sources of information relevant to their mission. Frequently, the next goal after collecting data is to either steal (exfiltrate) the data or to use the data to gain more information about the target environment.

- **Command and Control:** Consists of techniques threat actors may use to communicate with systems under their control within the target network. Threat actors commonly attempt to mimic normal, expected traffic to avoid detection while conducting discovery, lateral movement, or data exfiltration.

- **Exfiltration:** Consists of techniques threat actors may use to steal data from your network. Once they have collected data, threat actors often package it to avoid detection while removing it. Tactics used to accomplish this can include compression and encryption.

CHAPTER 3   DEFINITIONS

- **Impact:** Consists of techniques threat actors use to disrupt availability, cause a denial of service, or compromise integrity by manipulating business and operational processes. Multiple techniques can be leveraged, including destroying or tampering with data, applications, or configurations.

***Figure 3-1.*** *MITRE ATT&CK framework (https://attack.mitre.org), illustrating known attack vectors*

The MITRE ATT&CK® framework (Figure 3-1) is a relatively new classification system (developed around 2015), especially when compared to the long history of cyberattacks. MITRE, a US nonprofit organization, created this framework to provide a common language and reference for all defenders as attack vectors evolve. It's a living framework, constantly updated with new techniques observed in real-world attacks, or when there's sufficient evidence a theoretical technique should be included. Many cybersecurity concepts covered in the following pages can be mapped directly into the MITRE ATT&CK framework.

## CHAPTER 4

# Malware

In the late 1990s, personal computers were already becoming a mainstream tool, and the year 2000 (after the Y2K[1] software bug) demonstrated how a simple inconvenience could have long-standing business and personal effects. For better or worse, that prediction has come true. However, with that promise came darkness (not Darth Vader[2]-ish, but close). An underworld of clever code, cheeky pranks, and malicious intent shrouded the positive intentions of personal computers everywhere and for everyone. Initiatives like the One Laptop per Child (OLPC)[3] XO project attempted to make the best intentions free to everyone, but hardware and software limitations curtailed these ambitious goals.

Over the last 25 years, computer viruses and other forms of malware have grown from simple annoyances spread by floppy disks into sophisticated, automated global threats capable of crippling entire economies. It's a continued story of cat and mouse played between security experts and threat actors, of governments facing off against state-sponsored cybercriminal syndicates, and organized crime hellbent on profiting off foreign assets.

---

[1] https://americanhistory.si.edu/collections/object-groups/y2k
[2] https://www.starwars.com/databank/darth-vader
[3] https://www.engineeringforchange.org/solutions/product/xo-laptop/

## CHAPTER 4  MALWARE

If you'll indulge me, let's take a walk through that shadowy digital past in the next few chapters. We'll add a dash of storytelling, bad humor and puns, and the earnest desire to teach everyone a thing or two about how we got to today's state of cybersecurity.

To kick things off, in the year 2000, the ILOVEYOU[4] worm (often called the "Love Bug") swept across the Internet like an unstoppable flurry of chain letters. If you are unfamiliar with chain mail,[5] follow this link in the footnotes. As a child, not following up on a chain letter was a guaranteed way to have years of bad luck; at least, that's what we naively feared. But I digress.

ILOVEYOU was a computer virus that arrived via email with a subject line no one could resist: "I Love You." Clicking on it triggered a script (malware) that overwrote files, stole passwords, and spread to one's entire email contact and address book faster than you could reach behind your personal computer and pull out the plug. The ILOVEYOU worm, believed to have originated in the Philippines, showcased a critical truth about computer security: even the best technical defenses can be undone by human curiosity and the desire to be loved. People just had to open that "love letter," and in doing so, they ushered in a new era of social engineering and denial-of-service attacks.

Shortly thereafter, in 2001, the Code Red[6] worm (identified by Marc Maiffret from eEye Digital Security) rampaged through web servers worldwide with a dubious outcome. Code Red exploited a vulnerability in Microsoft's Internet Information Services (IIS) and defaced websites with the phrase "Hacked by Chinese!" That same year, another worm, Nimda[7] (that's

---

[4] https://www.forbes.com/sites/daveywinder/2020/05/04/this-20-year-old-virus-infected-50-million-windows-computers-in-10-days-why-the-iloveyou-pandemic-matters-in-2020/

[5] https://www.volusiasheriff.gov/news/dont-respond-to-a-chain-letter.stml

[6] https://www.cybereason.com/blog/what-is-code-red-worm

[7] https://www.giac.org/paper/gsec/1542/nimda-worm/102853

CHAPTER 4   MALWARE

"admin" spelled backward, by the way), piggybacked on the chaos. Nimda spread via email, infected shared network drives, and even compromised websites. If Code Red was akin to a malicious party crasher, Nimda was that opportunistic agitator who saw the front door open and barged right in to the party. Together, they underlined how deeply interwoven our systems had become and how a single worm could wreak havoc on businesses, government agencies, and everyday personal computer users, all at once.

Moving forward into the mid-2000s, the Internet experienced the emergence of large botnets compromised of "zombie" computers. These were infected with malware and controlled by organized syndicates for nefarious goals. One of the big headliners was the Blaster[8] worm in 2003. Blaster exploited a DCOM RPC vulnerability in Windows to spread far and wide, famously causing infected machines to repeatedly crash with an ominous system shutdown message. While the initial malware was allegedly written in China, at least one of the variations was traced back to Jeffrey Lee Parson, an 18-year-old from Hopkins, Minnesota. He was arrested for creating the B variant of the Blaster worm. Parson admitted responsibility and was sentenced to an 18-month prison term. The damage wrought by this malware forced Microsoft to scramble to patch the vulnerability. The entire event underscored how quickly an unprotected system could be overwhelmed, if exploited. In fairness, this event provided awareness to the entire business community regarding the linkage between vulnerabilities, exploits, and malware.

It only took one more year for things to escalate again. In 2004, the world experienced the Sasser[9] worm, which exploited the LSASS service in Windows XP and 2000. Sasser was authored by a German teenager. If you experienced a computer perpetually restarting during the 2004 timeframe, you might have been one of Sasser's victims.

---

[8] https://www.cybereason.com/blog/what-is-the-blaster-worm
[9] https://www.xenonstack.com/insights/sasser-virus/

CHAPTER 4    MALWARE

Remarkably, as fast as this type of malware can spread, antivirus firms and vendors like Microsoft raced to provide patches and antivirus signatures to detect, remove, and block future infections. But for many, by the time the patch arrived, Sasser had already done its damage, leaving entire organizations in perpetual reboots. As painful as it was, the fix necessitated physically visiting every affected computer one by one to resolve the issue. This spawned the need for more advanced antivirus solutions and better automated patch management solutions.

The next big wave was Mydoom,[10] which demonstrated in the most painful ways possible that malware could launch massive denial-of-service attacks. Mydoom established a model where threat actors could harness thousands, if not millions, of infected machines to flood a target site or server with garbage traffic. This effectively knocked targets offline due to the sheer volume of unmanaged traffic. This incident raised awareness that any web site could be a target and that advanced firewalls and other solutions would be needed to mitigate malicious Internet traffic. We will talk more about the evolution of cybersecurity solutions in later chapters.

After 2005, an uptick in Trojan horse malware signaled a shift in threat actor strategy. Instead of attacking systems with a "big bang" and "shock and awe" mentality, which forced users and information technology staff to apply immediate attention, threat actors adopted a stealthier approach.

Threat actors began designing programs that masqueraded as legitimate software including games, utilities, and add-ons to existing solutions. Some were disguised as free antivirus tools, others as fake rumors regarding holiday pranks like Elf Bowling[11] (1999). Their goal? To slip past security defenses and linger quietly in the background, logging keystrokes or stealing banking credentials. These Trojan horses thrived

---

[10] https://www.radware.com/security/ddos-knowledge-center/ddospedia/mydoom/

[11] https://www.deccanchronicle.com/technology/in-other-news/281217/how-devastating-is-fake-news-it-destroyed-this-fun-christmas-game.html

CHAPTER 4  MALWARE

because users were now accustomed to downloading software from websites, shared floppies, or even email. If a pop-up promised a free screensaver or an essential security fix, many folks just clicked "run" or "install" without a second thought about cybersecurity.

One notable Trojan horse from this period was Zeus[12] (also known as Zbot), first identified around 2007. Zeus became infamous for its skill at keylogging, an attack vector that recorded everything a user typed, including sensitive passwords. By secretly collecting online banking credentials, it enabled its operators via Command and Control (CnC) to siphon millions of dollars from unwitting victims. Zeus's success was a cold reminder that the focus of cybercrime had shifted from showy vandalism to profit-driven theft, proving that the employment of stealthy malware could be very lucrative.

As more and more corporate and governmental operations embraced racks of servers and personal computers for everyone, malware took a turn toward corporate espionage. The late 2000s and early 2010s saw a dramatic escalation in targeted attacks, with carefully crafted malware aimed at specific organizations. These weren't just random viruses bouncing around email servers; these were tailor-made pieces of malware, like advanced persistent threats (APTs), designed to infiltrate a company's or a government's network, steal secrets, and remain undetected for as long as possible.

The poster child for this era was Stuxnet,[13] discovered in 2010. As we covered earlier in the "Risk Management (Mid-2000s–2010s)" section, Stuxnet was no ordinary computer virus. It was developed as a sophisticated cyber weapon, believed to be crafted by a partner of multiple nation-states (allegedly the United States and Israel), that specifically targeted Iran's nuclear facilities. By cleverly exploiting four separate

---

[12] https://www.proofpoint.com/us/threat-reference/zeus-trojan-zbot
[13] https://spectrum.ieee.org/the-real-story-of-stuxnet

zero-day[14] vulnerabilities in Microsoft Windows, Stuxnet caused physical centrifuges to spin out of control while sending false feedback to operators. This ultimately delayed Iran's ambitions of purifying uranium for their nuclear program. This was a watershed moment, proving malware could be used as a cyber weapon to inflict damage on industrial infrastructure. It also marked a turning point in public awareness, demonstrating how nations could engage in covert sabotage without ever firing a conventional weapon.

In the mid-2010s, ransomware raised the bar for denial of service and extortion attack vectors. While earlier forms of ransomware were known, it wasn't until CryptoLocker[15] in 2013 that the world realized just how devastating—and profitable—this type of malware could be. CryptoLocker worked by encrypting victims' files and demanding payment, typically in Bitcoin, to unlock them. Businesses, individuals, and even police departments found themselves at the mercy of anonymous hackers. Pay the ransom, or your files would never be accessible again. As with many crimes, copycat threat actors recognized the success of this attack, and countless strains emerged, each deadlier than the last, but all demanding ransom. Security experts extorted businesses and individuals to keep robust backups, but many organizations were not prepared financially or technically.

Then came WannaCry[16] in 2017. While we have discussed this in detail already, it is worth restating again in this section. WannaCry exploited a leaked NSA tool to infect Windows machines on a massive scale, based on a library of weaponized cyberattacks known to the United States government. Within days, WannaCry had paralyzed parts of the United Kingdom's

---

[14] https://www.ibm.com/think/topics/zero-day
[15] https://www.cisa.gov/news-events/alerts/2013/11/05/cryptolocker-ransomware-infections
[16] https://www.cloudflare.com/learning/security/ransomware/wannacry-ransomware/

CHAPTER 4  MALWARE

National Health Service, forced car manufacturers to halt production, and left countless victims worldwide staring at a pop-up demanding ransom in cryptocurrency. The fiasco gained worldwide notoriety, proving that modern malware attacks were far beyond a mere annoyance; they could truly impact anyone and everyone, worldwide. Malware had multibillion-dollar cybercriminal enterprise that required a new approach to mitigate the potential risks.

Not long after WannaCry, the NotPetya[17] attack rolled out, initially disguised as ransomware, but harboring a darker secret that morphed into a wiper (data destruction malware). Its real purpose seemed to be a denial of service for data access by targeting Ukraine's infrastructure, and it quickly leaped beyond intended targets. Multinational companies, from shipping conglomerates to pharmaceutical giants, were crippled by NotPetya, sustaining billions of dollars in damages. The end results offered no simple path to recovery (outside of data backup and recovery solutions), and this incident blurred the distinction between criminal and state-sponsored malware more than ever.

As we moved into the 2020s, the COVID-19 pandemic accelerated digital transformation worldwide. Remote work became the business response to the human health pandemic, and video conferencing replaced office cooler banter. With this abrupt shift in working environments, cybercriminals immediately saw opportunity.

Phishing emails mentioning medical updates, vaccine registrations, and job furlough notices found their way into countless inboxes. Unpatched home routers and personal devices provided fresh attack vectors, since they fell outside of corporate management and government. In addition, ransomware groups became more organized, evolving into professionalized operations with customer support lines and negotiation

---

[17] https://www.wired.com/story/notpetya-cyberattack-ukraine-russia-code-crashed-the-world/

playbooks. Attacks now targeted people working from home (remotely) and all their devices, especially the consumer-oriented ones that lacked the built-in security that would be expected of enterprise endpoints.

At the same time, organizations witnessed targeted supply chain attacks, most infamously the 2020 SolarWinds[18] breach. However, this was not a unicorn breach. In 2023, the MOVEit[19] supply chain attack was executed, targeting users of the MOVEit Transfer tool, owned by the US organization Progress Software. MOVEit is designed to transfer sensitive files in a secure manner, and it is popular in the United States. The ransomware syndicate, C10p, was credited with the attack. The attackers used EWIs (exposed web interfaces) to cause significant damage. The web-facing MOVEit app was infected with a web shell called LEMURLOOT, which was then used to steal data from MOVEit Transfer databases affecting the companies installed customer base. In addition, the MOVEit solution was licensed as an embedded application and was included in other software that needed to move files as a part of normal business operations.

So, where does all of this leave us after 25 years of malware-laden history? In one sense, we are smarter than ever and definitely not as gullible. Cybersecurity research has advanced exponentially, antivirus programs use machine learning to detect threats, and companies employ skilled information security professions to hunt for suspicious activity in real time. But this cat and mouse game is always like a good episode of Tom and Jerry,[20] and malware authors are equally as inventive in trying to catch their prey. Figure 4-1 illustrates this evolution in a basic timeline for your reference.

---

[18] https://www.cisa.gov/news-events/alerts/2020/12/13/active-exploitation-solarwinds-software
[19] https://www.encryptionconsulting.com/top-10-supply-chain-attacks-that-shook-the-world/
[20] https://www.britannica.com/topic/Tom-and-Jerry

CHAPTER 4   MALWARE

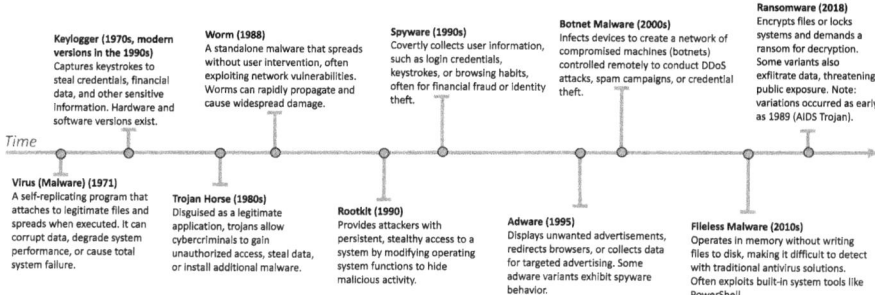

***Figure 4-1.*** *Illustration of the evolution of malware from simple viruses to advance ransomware*

While threat actors attempt to hide behind layers of encryption and exploit emerging technologies, like deepfakes and artificial intelligence, they always continue to exploit the most vulnerable link in the chain: humans.

From the ILOVEYOU worm to the cutting-edge supply chain attacks, the last quarter century of malware evolution presents a grim testament to both the resilience of the Internet and the boundless creativity of threat actors. We've progressed from simple worms that spread through naive curiosity to complex networks of criminals leveraging zero-day vulnerabilities, espionage tactics, and mass-scale ransoms. The boundary between everyday malware and cyberwarfare is becoming vanishingly small, leaving governments, businesses, and individuals to fend off threats that can feel as invisible as they are inevitable.

Yet, hope remains. Cybersecurity is a booming field, brimming with brilliant minds and innovative technologies. Every breach and data dump is a lesson learned, even if it's painful, expensive, or worse. If the past 25 years have taught us anything, it's that staying vigilant is nonnegotiable. Updating software, practicing good password and identity security hygiene, and cultivating a healthy skepticism toward every link and

CHAPTER 4   MALWARE

attachment is the digital equivalent of wearing a seatbelt while driving down the road. Malware and speed bumps can be anywhere, and an accident can occur at any time. For those readers who want to dig deeper into the history of malware, please visit a curated list in Appendix A. Now, we will explore how exploits can lead to malware infections.

# CHAPTER 5

# Exploits

Over the past quarter century, software exploits have evolved from rudimentary script-based attacks to sophisticated, multilayered processes orchestrated by cybercrime syndicates and nation-states. These exploits have shaped the way we build, distribute, and protect software, from development through quality assurance and public release. From the modest beginnings of the Internet in the late 1990s, when the world was coming "online" and becoming connected, security practitioners and threat actors raced to discover, disclose, and patch vulnerabilities. This chapter will trace the major milestones in software exploitation over the last 40 years, showing how vulnerabilities have grown into complex exploits and how the security community has adapted.

However, before we begin, sometimes the most significant threat isn't the external threat actor or the potential for an insider threat. It's a trusted and approved application, like an administrative tool, a privileged process, or an automation script that gets manipulated into doing something it was never intended to do. This is the foundational definition for the "confused deputy problem," a classic privileged escalation exploit with very modern consequences, particularly in the realm of agentic AI technology and least privilege enforcement. It forms the basis for many of the exploits we experience today and is worthy of our discussion as a history lesson.

The confused deputy problem arises when a program or application (the "deputy"), which has legitimate authority to access certain resources, is tricked into misusing its established privileges by another, less-privileged program, application, or user. This vulnerability occurs when deputy

CHAPTER 5  EXPLOITS

program lacks sufficient context or safeguards to distinguish between requests it should honor and those that it should reject based on behavior, context, or sensitivity, including the data that may be requested. In fairness, this problem is not new. The term comes from a 1988 paper by Norm Hardy,[1] where a compiler (the deputy) was allowed to overwrite billing files because it trusted the file paths given to it by end-user applications. These programs lacked the authority to access these files directly, but the compiler had the appropriate entitlements to do so and ultimately overwrote them on the end user's behalf exploiting the system. In essence, the deputy had more power than the end user and was compromised into overwriting files based on inappropriate requests.

Today, we commonly refer to this as privileged escalation vulnerability, but when it is program to program, it is the confused deputy problem. And, in the world of machine identities, automation, and agentic AI, the confused deputy problem is the source of many modern exploits based on an old concept. In fact, it is a common source of trouble in many cloud IAM misconfigurations, misused APIs, OAuth scopes, and SuDo commands, and it drives on as one of the primary use cases for embracing least privilege and content filtering for machine identities. It then begs the question: How do you prevent privileged escalation between programs and applications? Sometimes a program is exploited directly to execute unauthorized code (traditional vulnerabilities and exploits), and sometimes another program does it due to unmitigated boundary conditions.

The confused deputy problem is much more than just a technical footnote. With emerging agentic AI, it has become a strategic challenge. It reminds us that power without discernment is a vulnerability, and that least privilege is not just about access; it is about intent, control, and mitigating exploitation due to poor coding and application designs. With AI appearing everywhere and a part of every conversation, your most trusted tool can become your most dangerous adversary. All it takes is the right

---

[1] https://css.csail.mit.edu/6.858/2015/readings/confused-deputy.html

CHAPTER 5   EXPLOITS

level of confusion to make a good program behave badly, or a vulnerability and exploit to compromise it directly. Now, with this foundation, let's step back into our time machine and consider exploitation for the last few decades.

In the late 1990s and early 2000s, the Internet was expanding rapidly, bringing millions of new users online every day with every personal computer and modem sold. Commercial operating systems, like Microsoft Windows 95, Windows 98, and eventually Windows XP, were becoming household names, while lesser names like GeoWorks[2] and IBM OS/2[3] were being swallowed by the competition, eventually disappearing from the consumer and business landscape.

During this time, threat actors began to take advantage of code flaws in Windows, since it commanded the lion's share of the market. Buffer overflows, which occur when a program attempts to write more data to a buffer than it can hold, became a common exploit. Infamous examples include the "Ping of Death[4]" attack, which exploited a vulnerability in how systems handled oversized ICMP packets. Threat actors discovered they could crash systems simply by sending specially crafted network packets to a host. This seemingly simple assault devastated many organizations, catching them flat-footed.

A major turning point for the advancement of exploits was the rise of self-propagating worms. As discussed in Chapter 4, the Code Red and Nimda worms rapidly spread through vulnerabilities in Microsoft's solutions. The cybersecurity community became highly tuned to the fact that vulnerabilities didn't just represent theoretical risk, but that many could be exploited in the wild to launch malware payloads.

---

[2] https://winworldpc.com/product/geos/2x
[3] https://www.britannica.com/technology/IBM-OS-2
[4] https://www.cloudflare.com/learning/ddos/ping-of-death-ddos-attack/

CHAPTER 5  EXPLOITS

Large-scale incidents also demonstrated how rapidly malware could spread across the globe, highlighting the dangers of network-connected systems that lacked robust defenses and could be targeted with reliable exploits. Software vendors and governments realized they could no longer ignore vulnerabilities, and the exploitation of software flaws became a headline issue for remediation, testing, and a basis for the investment in cybersecurity solutions.

The mid-2000s saw the proliferation of more advanced exploit types. The emergence of rootkits and kernel mode driver malware was especially notable as previously discussed. These malicious programs aimed to maintain persistent access to compromised systems by hiding themselves deep within an asset, even before the operating system potentially loads.

During this time, exploit writers also began to target user applications, such as web browsers, office productivity suites, and media players, due to the rise of peer-to-peer media sharing programs like Napster[5] and LimeWire.[6] Browser-based attacks, for instance, took advantage of vulnerabilities in ActiveX controls (a technology deprecated with the end of Microsoft Internet Explorer), Sun Java, search tools, and other plugins. These flaws allowed threat actors to run code remotely on unsuspecting users' machines simply by getting them to visit a malicious web page. Exploitation could then occur without a vulnerability, simply by coercing the user to run a program under the guise of a legitimate application. This proved that even simply renaming an application could socially engineer an end user into executing malware unintentionally. The mitigation for these attacks cemented the need for least privilege and checking an application's digital signature.

By the late 2000s, threat actors had further refined their craft, focusing on zero-day vulnerabilities. By definition, a zero-day vulnerability is based on unknown flaws with no available patch. It may have a working exploit

---

[5] https://www.theguardian.com/music/2013/feb/24/napster-music-free-file-sharing
[6] https://www.kraken.com/learn/what-is-limewire-lmwr

in the wild. One high-profile case was the Aurora[7] operation (2009–2010), a series of cyberattacks that targeted major corporations, including Google and Adobe. In this instance, the threat actors exploited a zero-day flaw in Internet Explorer to gain access to critical corporate data. This served as an early example of how state-aligned actors and APTs could leverage undisclosed vulnerabilities and working exploits to conduct espionage. Around this time, more sophisticated exploitation techniques also emerged, such as Return-Oriented Programming[8] (ROP), which allowed threat actors to bypass traditional exploit mitigations, like Data Execution Prevention[9] (DEP), by chaining existing code fragments in memory after initial code execution.

In the early 2010s, exploits became increasingly stealthy and targeted in their missions. The notorious Stuxnet worm, discovered in 2010, highlighted a new era of cyberwarfare, demonstrating how multiple zero-day vulnerabilities could be exploited simultaneously for a highly targeted attack. Rather than focusing purely on IT infrastructure, Stuxnet specifically targeted industrial control systems (ICS) within Iran's nuclear facilities. It showcased how software exploits could have real-world, physical impacts, as discussed in Chapter 4. However, as an exploit, Stuxnet demonstrates that the value of a working exploit diminishes significantly once a software patch becomes available. After that point, there's a diminishing return as more and more systems are patched, leaving the exploit relatively unusable. Only organizations and consumers who fail to patch, or have end-of-life systems, remain vulnerable to such exploitation. This serves as a quick history lesson as we move forward.

---

[7] https://www.darkreading.com/cyberattacks-data-breaches/google-aurora-hack-was-chinese-counterespionage-operation
[8] https://www.infosecinstitute.com/resources/hacking/return-oriented-programming-rop-attacks/
[9] https://heimdalsecurity.com/blog/dep-data-execution-prevention-windows/

CHAPTER 5   EXPLOITS

Around the same time, the commercial vulnerability market emerged. Bug bounties and vulnerability brokers, such as Zerodium[10] (which later went out of business), began offering significant sums of money for zero-day exploits in popular systems like iOS, Android, and Windows. Many of these bounties became the subject of news articles by Forbes[11] and the likes later in the decade. Such incentives drove high-stakes competition in discovering and weaponizing exploits, with prices rising into the hundreds of thousands of dollars, especially for reliable, working exploits.

Meanwhile, many legitimate software companies, including Facebook, Google, and Microsoft, launched their own bug bounty programs, encouraging ethical hackers to disclose vulnerabilities responsibly. By compensating ethical hackers to discover vulnerabilities, these enterprises hoped to proactively address these flaws, preventing them from being found and exploited in the wild by threat actors. This evolution helped funnel some research efforts into more controlled disclosure processes. Yet, the black market for undisclosed exploits remained lively, with cybercriminals and state-sponsored actors continuing to purchase zero-day exploits for offensive operations.

As the 2010s progressed, exploit mitigation strategies and defense solutions continued to advance. Microsoft introduced technologies like Address Space Layout Randomization[12] (ASLR) and Control Flow Guard[13] (CFG), while Apple strengthened iOS security with native application

---

[10] https://www.intelligenceonline.com/surveillance--interception/2024/05/21/iconic-american-vulnerability-trader-zerodium-to-close-its-doors,110228370-art

[11] https://www.forbes.com/sites/jeanbaptiste/2019/09/04/why-zerodium-will-pay-2-5-million-for-anyone-who-can-hack-android-but-only-2-million-for-an-iphone/

[12] https://www.techtarget.com/searchsecurity/definition/address-space-layout-randomization-ASLR

[13] https://learn.microsoft.com/en-us/windows/win32/secbp/control-flow-guard

sandboxing and code-signing requirements. Concurrently, the industry saw a surge in mobile exploits targeting smartphone operating systems and applications, including those properly vetted through vendor Application Stores. Threat actors found new opportunities by exploiting weaknesses in application submission ecosystems, SMS protocols, and baseband firmware, leading to a myriad of new attack vectors.

Meanwhile, threat actors began to favor web application exploits, including SQL injection and cross-site scripting, which became the decade's primary entry points for data breaches. High-profile incidents like the 2013 Target[14] breach, made possible by network segmentation deficiencies and stolen credentials, demonstrated how organizational security practices could fail under the relentless probing of cybercriminals, even after initial exploitation occurred.

The late 2010s to early 2020s brought some of the most impactful exploits to date, like EternalBlue[15]. This original exploit, believed to have been developed by the US National Security Agency (NSA) for an unknown purpose, was initially used to compromise Windows systems on an unprecedented scale and speed. EternalBlue eerily demonstrated the value of an exploit to governments in an all-out cyberwar; however, based on its leakage, it became the weaponized foundation for ransomware like WannaCry.

In 2018, a different class of vulnerabilities gained attention, including Spectre and Meltdown.[16] Rather than targeting traditional software flaws, these exploits leveraged design flaws in modern CPU architectures (microcode), enabling threat actors to read sensitive data from memory using speculative execution. This took the security world by surprise,

---

[14] https://www.commerce.senate.gov/services/files/24d3c229-4f2f-405d-b8db-a3a67f183883
[15] https://www.sentinelone.com/blog/eternalblue-nsa-developed-exploit-just-wont-die/
[16] https://meltdownattack.com

CHAPTER 5    EXPLOITS

demonstrating that even hardware-level design choices could be vulnerable. In response to these vulnerabilities, organizations scrambled to patch both operating systems and microcode to prevent exploitation.

Around the same time, the world saw the emergence of supply chain attacks. These attacks, as described earlier, focus on compromising a trusted software vendor, library, or update mechanism to inject malicious code directly at the source. This includes open source code as well as proprietary vendor solutions. The 2020 SolarWinds supply chain attack and breach (detailed previously in Chapter 4) became the poster child for such attacks.

In 2021, the emergence of the Log4Shell vulnerability (CVE-2021-44228[17]) in Apache Log4j stirred a worldwide panic due to the open source library's widespread use for logging in to countless Java applications. Threat actors could trigger remote code execution simply by logging a specially crafted string that interacts with the embedded library. Given the adoption of Log4j in enterprise environments, this vulnerability and its well-documented public exploit led to a global rush to identify and patch affected systems. In many cases, organizations didn't even know where all of the libraries existed, or which vendors had them embedded in their solutions. Log4Shell underscored how a single open source library flaw could introduce systemic risk, affecting everything from cloud services to consumer devices.

Today, we are in an era of heightened threat awareness and advanced security research. State-sponsored threat groups employ sophisticated toolkits that include zero-day exploits, sophisticated phishing campaigns (discussed in a later chapter), and supply chain compromises. In response, security professionals deploy layers of defense: firewalls, intrusion detection systems, endpoint detection and response (EDR) solutions, privileged access management (PAM), and real-time identity and vulnerability threat intelligence. Companies are more transparent about

---

[17] https://cve.mitre.org/cgi-bin/cvename.cgi?name=cve-2021-44228

disclosures, with coordinated vulnerability disclosure programs and bug bounties becoming industry standards. Nevertheless, the cat and mouse game continues. As exploit mitigations improve, threat actors, too, discover new angles for attacks. What started with exploitations on personal computers expanded to exploits on Internet of Things (IoT) devices, and then to penetrating cloud infrastructures and containerized environments. What began with relatively simple exploits like buffer overflows has given way to complex, multipronged zero-day strategies. Nation-state actors, exploit brokers, and bug bounty platforms have reshaped the vulnerability ecosystem, blurring the lines between gray and white markets for security research and the purchase of exploits. On the defenders' side, layered security, the principle of least privilege, patch management, and responsible disclosure practices have become fundamental. Unfortunately, history shows that every new technology introduces new weaknesses for a wide variety of reasons. As the world becomes ever more interconnected, vigilance, collaboration, and continuous cybersecurity innovation remain critical to keeping software safe from exploit-driven threats.

To learn about some of the top exploits, please review Appendix B, which covers some of the exploits we've discussed, as well as many others that have shaped the history of cybersecurity.

# CHAPTER 6

# Breaches

It's time for a little more time travel. My muse (and my nightmare of reverse identity theft), John Titor,[1] helps take us back to the dawn of the new millennium. Consider a wide-eyed technology enthusiast excitedly ushering in the year 2000, absolutely certain that "Y2K" would wreak a catastrophic shutdown of computers across the world. Some heralded that this event would cause planes to fall from the sky, electrical power would cease to exist, and ATMs would spit free money at the first sign of trouble. But when the clock struck midnight, only a few notable events occurred, like glitches in payroll systems printing the wrong date on checks and some personal computer software that was incapable of correctly calculating future dates.

While the aftermath of Y2K amounted to minor inconveniences, our palpable relief was short-lived. Although we had prepared so diligently for a Y2K apocalypse, few of us were ready for the wave of cybersecurity breaches that would shape technology for the next quarter century. These breaches would reshape how we think about technology within businesses and governments for decades to come.

So how did this time travel exercise start? Let us go back 25 years again (John Titor style).

It was the year 2000 when we received our first collective wake-up call in the shape of the "ILOVEYOU" virus. What seemed like a sweet, innocuous email from a secret admirer turned out to be a computer worm that spread worldwide in record time by capitalizing on human traits.

---

[1] https://en.wikipedia.org/wiki/John_Titor

## CHAPTER 6  BREACHES

When you merge the underlining concepts of ILOVEYOU with Code Red (2001)—named by Marc Maiffret after a popular caffeinated beverage (Code Red Mountain Dew)—you have real-world proof-of-concept attacks that foreshadowed the breaches yet to come.

Code Red didn't just aim to inconvenience folks; it attempted to take down the US White House website by launching a DDoS attack. The worm never quite succeeded in that boastful plan, but it demonstrated how quickly malicious software could spread and cause widespread disruption. These two attacks paved the way for modern breaches by proving vulnerabilities, exploits, and malware could be used over the Internet for nefarious missions.

As Internet adoption soared in the early 2000s, threat actors embraced novel and downright awful methods to target organizations and consumers. Phishing,[2] a term that conjures images of cunning anglers reeling in unsuspecting fish looking for a quick meal on a hook, began to gain momentum and entered the common household lexicon. Threat actors would send emails masquerading as banks, credit card companies, princes with dowries, lost funds, or even the newly popular online auction sites, hoping to hook into personal details from unsuspecting users.

By 2003, the Slammer worm lived up to its name by "slamming" network services around the globe in mere minutes. It was truly one of the first breaches that inflicted notable business outcomes, including lost revenue and service downtime. One of Slammer's high-profile victims included a major bank whose ATM network[3] went offline due to infections. The outage left customers stuck in long lines at banks, their debit cards useless, and unable to access personal and business accounts. While damage control teams raced to restore services, the worm's lightning-fast

---

[2] https://consumer.ftc.gov/articles/how-recognize-and-avoid-phishing-scams
[3] https://www.cutimes.com/2003/02/04/sql-slammer-worm-races-through-internet-hits-online-banking-atms/

propagation left almost no vulnerable machine untouched, significantly heightening awareness of the potential impacts of breaches.

In 2005, the world experienced the infamous ChoicePoint[4] breach, which exposed the personal data of over 160,000 Americans. While small in comparison to modern breaches, this was not just a technical mishap; it was a wake-up call that storing huge troves of unencrypted sensitive data in centralized locations could be a recipe for disaster. In an age that began to recognize data was quickly becoming currency, threat actors discovered that breaching a data aggregator was like breaking into Fort Knox.[5] It presented a digital trove of valuable personally identifiable information (PII).

At the end of the 2000s, the stakes grew far more complex for cybersecurity breaches. Some of the largest breaches became less about quick money grabs and more about large-scale infiltration and sabotage. In 2007, Estonia[6] was hammered by a massive DDoS attack that crippled government websites, banks, and media outlets. While the motives weren't fully exposed by the threat actor during the attack itself, some speculated that this was an act of nation-state-sponsored cyberterrorism. Cyberspace was now a political battlefield.

This does not mean older-style attack vectors were over with. In 2008, Conficker[7] worm leveraged Windows vulnerabilities to construct a massive botnet, amassing tens of millions of compromised computers into an unwilling global cyber army. This army was commanded to commit targeted attacks for financial gain and corporate espionage. Even though security patches were released in a timely manner, patching alone

---

[4] https://www.csoonline.com/article/515029/compliance-the-five-most-shocking-things-about-the-choicepoint-data-security-breach.html
[5] https://www.usmint.gov/learn/tours-and-locations/fort-knox?srsltid=AfmBOopXUZ1LGasoxFO2W36fkWdVauUz47SxH7AI721intQU9A5CHwgo
[6] https://ccdcoe.org/uploads/2018/10/Ottis2008_AnalysisOf2007FromTheInformationWarfarePerspective.pdf
[7] https://www.cybereason.com/blog/what-is-the-conficker-worm

CHAPTER 6   BREACHES

wasn't enough to eradicate Conficker from an environment. Combating it required a multifaceted approach: blocking new infections, patching system images, and actively managing the threat on the network itself. This challenge helped spawn a wide variety of cybersecurity strategies we still use today.

In 2010, Stuxnet famously emerged, specifically targeting Iran's nuclear facilities. This was a breakpoint moment for cybersecurity breaches. The malware was unbelievably sophisticated, yet allegedly, deployed simply via a USB key to create the initial beach head. This threat demonstrated the vulnerability of critical infrastructure to digital sabotage, and proved breaches could be used to quietly stop a nation-state's ambition for banned munitions.

When one hears the phrase "breach," or as my CISO peers might call it, the dreaded "B Word," one might immediately think of a large organization issuing a legally required press release about a recent security event. This public announcement nearly always states that user data has been compromised. The early 2010s are littered with such big, splashy corporate breaches. For example, Sony experienced a now-infamous hack in 2011, resulting in the theft of personal data from 77 million PlayStation Network[8] users. Gamers worldwide spent weeks offline, outraged and furious as they waited for some information that Sony provided in drips. As many could imagine, lawsuits ensued, news headlines flared, and a new wave of cynicism about corporate cybersecurity measures took root. This provided a lesson to all organizations on how to communicate a breach and, candidly, what not to do.

In 2012, LinkedIn[9] users were among the next wave of victims, with millions of passwords posted to underground forums. Almost every user account on the platform was exposed. The hack raised urgent questions

---

[8] https://www.twingate.com/blog/tips/Sony%20PlayStation%20Network-data-breach
[9] https://www.bbc.com/news/technology-36320322

## CHAPTER 6  BREACHES

about password storage practices. It turns out that storing passwords in clear or weakly hashed formats is akin to handing your bank PIN over to a crook who already has your debit card in their possession. It took years for LinkedIn to convince users to change their passwords and even longer for attacks attributed to LinkedIn's breach to subside.

A year later, in 2013, Target[10] fell prey to a large-scale breach of tens of millions of credit card numbers, upping the ante for threat actors to commit instant fraud at scale. This fiasco cost the retailer hundreds of millions of dollars. It also caused countless headaches for customers who found suspicious charges on their statements. These breaches highlighted that repercussions could last for years, impacting personal identities and credit card accounts. It also reminds us that even an older breach (like stolen credentials) could still impact someone years later.

In 2014, the salacious Sony Pictures Entertainment hack[11] involved the leaking of company emails into the public domain for anyone to read. This was a different breach than the Sony PlayStation Network hack and unrelated to the Sony Music rootkit we have previously discussed. The breach's alleged ties to a nation-state once again illustrated the blurred lines between hacktivism, espionage, and sabotage. The breach leaked sensitive information about upcoming movies, including one that featured an assassination attempt on North Korea's leader in a warped comedy format, called *The Interview*.[12] The loss of revenue due to this movie's leak, combined with the controversy over its perceived poor taste, only deepened the divide between nations.

In parallel, new threat actors materialized, capitalizing on previously stolen personally identifiable information and engaging in early forms of ransomware. CryptoLocker, as previously discussed, and its successors

---

[10] https://krebsonsecurity.com/2014/02/target-hackers-broke-in-via-hvac-company/
[11] https://www.vox.com/2015/1/20/18089084/sony-hack-north-korea
[12] https://www.imdb.com/title/tt2788710/

spread rapidly, encrypting victims' files and then demanding a ransom payment, often in Bitcoin, to unlock them. Hospitals, schools, and small businesses were frequent victims, as these organizations tend to lack the security maturity present in larger entities. Using a simple analogy, this was the dark side of digital innovation. No matter how many patches or firewalls you deployed, an unwary click on an email attachment could reduce your life's work to a jumble of unreadable bytes, serving as a hard lesson for anyone that got compromised.

In 2015, the dating world was rocked by a devastating cyberattack that ruined lives. As we walked through in the history of cybersecurity earlier in the book, the Ashley Madison[13] breach laid bare the personal information of millions of users seeking extramarital connections. Consider the breach and website's intent as two intertwined issues; it became obvious that no platform, regardless of its moral or ethical focus, was beyond the reach of determined threat actors. The sensational nature of the data dump, in excess of 10GB at the time, overshadowed the underlying truth that personal privacy on the Internet is never truly private, and digital information can always be copied. There is never just one secure copy in one place at one time.

If the early 2010s taught us anything, it's that any organization could be hacked. In 2017, one of the darlings of credit ratings and models for cybersecurity themselves got hacked. The Equifax[14] breach in 2017 exposed the sensitive credit information of nearly 150 million Americans. Consider the theft of names, addresses, and US Social Security Numbers (SSN). These were all out in the open for anyone to download and abuse–if they knew where on the Internet to look. People were outraged and demanded a government and legal response to the breach. After all,

---

[13] https://www.trendmicro.com/vinfo/us/security/news/online-privacy/ashley-madison-breach-isnt-just-about-infidelity
[14] https://oversight.house.gov/wp-content/uploads/2018/12/Equifax-Report.pdf

this was a credit bureau that prided itself on its stewardship of personal information and now was breached itself, leaking data for everyone that they were supposed to protect and monitor.

That same year, WannaCry hammered computer networks worldwide as we have previously discussed. The linkage between vulnerabilities, exploits, malware, and breaches should now be more apparent than ever. Large healthcare systems, including the UK's National Health Service,[15] bore the brunt of the attack. Patients' appointments were canceled, surgeries postponed, and doctors resorted to manual methods to continue providing patient care. It was as if the world had woken up to discover that computers and electronic data no longer worked. If you are a science fiction fan, think of the backstory for *Blade Runner 2049*,[16] where all information before a certain point in time was just gone, or Netflix *Zero*,[17] where an hour-long digital blackout caused mass chaos.

The subsequent two years saw a relentless series of data exposures from social media giants, tech behemoths, and financial institutions. High-profile data leaks or information security breaches became almost weekly occurrences, fueling intense debates on data privacy, regulation, and the ethical obligation of organizations to protect entrusted personal information.

Now, let's fast forward a few years. When the COVID-19[18] pandemic forced a global shift to remote work in 2020, borderless networks presented an expanded opportunity for threat actors. While cybercriminals had always targeted remote workers, the pandemic enabled them to focus their efforts on entire remote workforces, scaling their attacks significantly.

During this time, organizations had to rapidly configure expanded virtual private network (VPN) access while employees had to juggle

---

[15] https://www.england.nhs.uk/long-read/case-study-wannacry-attack/
[16] https://www.imdb.com/title/tt1856101/
[17] https://www.imdb.com/title/tt23872886/
[18] https://www.who.int/europe/emergencies/situations/covid-19

CHAPTER 6   BREACHES

personal and professional commitments on the same devices. This all created a broader attack and risk surface. Phishing attacks began to surge, often disguised as pandemic updates, new remote work policies, or relief fund notifications. These attacks targeted individuals using personal and corporate devices that shared networks, email programs, and even operating systems. Threat actors capitalized on the pandemic-driven chaos, and organizations paid dearly as they struggled to maintain business continuity through hastily adopted changes that often lacked, or entirely bypassed, effective security controls.

The biggest bombshell arrived in December 2020 with the SolarWinds[19] attack. While we've covered this from a malware perspective, the breach itself was devastating. Threat actors inserted malicious code into a legitimate software update process, effectively sneaking into thousands of organizations, including top US government agencies, under the guise of a legitimate update. The duration, sophistication, and gall of this third-party attack vector were astonishing and truly only theoretical at this scale up until this point.

As details of the SolarWinds supply chain attack gradually emerged over months, one takeaway was immediate: blind trust in vendor supply chains could be as perilous as falling asleep at the wheel during a late-night drive. The urgent need for thorough assessments of vendors within one's supply chain became a top concern. It quickly became a best practice to identify, communicate, and secure any software developed by external organizations. After all, even if your organization maintains robust direct defenses, a breach within one of your vendors could still lead to a "game over" scenario for you. Furthermore, your supply chain itself has its own suppliers, creating a complex web of interconnected risk. Breaches occurring two or more vendors removed from your direct relationships

---

[19] https://www.fortinet.com/resources/cyberglossary/solarwinds-cyber-attack

## CHAPTER 6  BREACHES

could still ultimately compromise your organization (a reality I have witnessed firsthand).

As we approach the present, data breaches and large-scale cyberattacks remain a persistent challenge for organizations. Increasingly, cloud services, once hailed as a more secure alternative to on-premises infrastructure, have become prime targets for threat actors. While ransomware has evolved, threat actors now wage "double extortion" campaigns by not only encrypting data for ransom but also threatening to leak sensitive information if payment isn't made. Plus, there really is no guarantee you will get your data back, or prevent its leakage, even if you pay.

In addition, deepfake technology has introduced new layers of deception into social engineering attacks. In one audacious incident, scammers deepfaked the CFO of an engineering firm (Arup[20]) during a video conference call, successfully tricking a finance team member into transferring $25 million US dollars into a threat actor's bank account. Other call attendees were reportedly deepfaked as well, further enhancing the illusion of authenticity. This incident, while sounding like something out of a *Batman* villain's playbook, underscores a serious reality: the creation of sophisticated look-alikes has become far too easy, representing an attack vector we must all be highly concerned about in the future.

In response, governments worldwide are tightening regulations and pushing for better cybersecurity standards and overall accountability. Large multinational companies are scrambling to fortify their defenses with zero trust architectures and advanced threat intelligence platforms. Information security professionals champion encryption, decentralized solutions, and data loss prevention technologies. Yet, each new wave of security advancement seems to spark an equally inventive wave from threat actors.

---

[20] https://www.cfodive.com/news/scammers-siphon-25m-engineering-firm-arup-deepfake-cfo-ai/716501/

## CHAPTER 6  BREACHES

So here we are, 25 years or so after the turn of the century, having journeyed through a period marked by heartbreak, opportunism, cautionary tales, and an unrelenting pace of innovation. From the ILOVEYOU virus to the infiltration of major tech supply chains, our cybersecurity history lesson is a testament to our perseverance in the face of constantly evolving threats. Despite headlines that often convey disaster and doom, we have also seen incredible leaps in security technology. Encryption is stronger, public awareness is higher, and the cybersecurity domain now holds job security and positions of authority throughout organizations.

If there's one thing these past 25 years have taught us, it's that cybersecurity is not a destination, but an unending journey.

To learn more about key breaches throughout the history of cybersecurity, please review Appendix C, where we have curated a list with descriptions and impacts to further enrich our discussion.

# CHAPTER 7

# Regulations

Regardless of who the threat actors are and the crime syndicates that are present, governments worldwide have responded with legislation to manage these threats. In this chapter, we'll review the top ten countries by GDP (gross domestic product in trillions of USD based on data from the International Monetary Fund[1] (IMF) as of January 10, 2025) and provide a simple list of notable cybersecurity regulations. This list includes various laws that govern aspects of cybersecurity, data protection, and information security. It's important to note that this list does not include all legislation that might derive from individual states, such as the California Consumer Privacy Act (CCPA) or for specific vertical industries like payment card industry (PCI) or Health Information Portability and Accountability Act (HIPPA). Instead, this list represents individual government legislative initiatives that are the most relevant to the evolving history of cyber threats.

United States–GDP 30.34

- **Homeland Security Act (2002):** Establishes the Department of Homeland Security and sets forth measures to prevent terrorist attacks within the United States, including cybersecurity initiatives (https://www.dhs.gov/homeland-security-act-2002)

---

[1] https://www.imf.org/en/Home

CHAPTER 7   REGULATIONS

- **Federal Information Security Management Act (FISMA) (2002):** Requires federal agencies to develop, document, and implement an information security and protection program (https://www.cio.gov/handbook/it-laws/fisma/)
- **Cybersecurity Information Sharing Act (CISA) (2015):** Promotes the sharing of information related to cybersecurity threats between the government and private sector (https://www.cisa.gov/sites/default/files/publications/Cybersecurity%2520Information%2520Sharing%2520Act%2520of%25202015.pdf)

China–GDP 19.53

- **Cybersecurity Law (2017):** Encompasses network security, data protection, and cybersecurity governance. It emphasizes the protection of critical information infrastructure (https://assets.kpmg.com/content/dam/kpmg/cn/pdf/en/2017/02/overview-of-cybersecurity-law.pdf)
- **Data Security Law (2021):** Focuses on data processing and usage, establishing a comprehensive data security governance system across all sectors (https://www.chinalawtranslate.com/en/datasecuritylaw/)

Germany–GDP 4.92

- **IT Security Act (2015, Updated to 2.0 in 2021):** Enhances the level of cybersecurity in critical infrastructures and increases the responsibilities of federal offices for information security (https://www.vanta.com/resources/germany-it-security-act-2-0)

- **Federal Data Protection Act (BDSG):** Complements the GDPR and regulates the processing of personal data by private companies and federal government agencies (https://www.gesetze-im-internet.de/englisch_bdsg/)

Japan–GDP 4.39

- **Act on the Protection of Personal Information (APPI) (2003, Revised in 2017):** Governs the protection and use of personal data (https://www.japaneselawtranslation.go.jp/en/laws/view/4241/en)
- **Cybersecurity Basic Act (2014):** Establishes policies and a framework for promoting cybersecurity measures across both public and private sectors (https://www.japaneselawtranslation.go.jp/en/laws/view/3677/en)

India–GDP 4.27

- **Information Technology Act (2000, Amended in 2008):** Provides the legal framework for electronic governance by giving recognition to electronic records and digital signatures (https://www.indiacode.nic.in/bitstream/123456789/13116/1/it_act_2000_updated.pdf)
- **National Cybersecurity Policy (2013):** Aims to protect the public and private infrastructure from cyberattacks (https://www.geeksforgeeks.org/the-national-cyber-security-policy-2013/)

CHAPTER 7   REGULATIONS

UK–GDP 3.73

- **Data Protection Act (2018):** Updates the UK data protection laws, including the processing of personal data and enforcement of GDPR (https://www.legislation.gov.uk/ukpga/2018/12/contents)

- **Network and Information Systems Regulations (NIS) (2018):** Transposes the EU Directive on the security of network and information systems into UK law, focusing on critical infrastructure and digital service providers (https://www.gov.uk/government/collections/nis-directive-and-nis-regulations-2018)

France–GDP 3.28

- **Military Programming Law (2013, Updated Periodically):** Sets directives for the planning and programming of military equipment and infrastructure, including provisions for cybersecurity (https://www.lexology.com/library/detail.aspx?g=f043af92-82d2-4f81-b313-e864a1fc49f1)

- **Digital Republic Act (2016):** Strengthens data protection regulations and public access to digital data (https://www.kiteworks.com/risk-compliance-glossary/french-digital-republic-act/)

Italy–GDP 2.46

- **Cybersecurity National Framework (2017):** Establishes strategic objectives and governance models for cybersecurity, aligning with the National Cybersecurity Strategy (https://www.newstrategycenter.ro/wp-content/uploads/2019/07/Italian-Cybersecurity-Action-Plan-2017.pdf)

CHAPTER 7   REGULATIONS

- **Privacy Code (Amended in 2018 to Incorporate GDPR):** Governs the processing of personal data and ensures data protection (https://www.velotix.ai/privacy-regulations/italian-data-protection-code/)

Canada–GDP 2.33

- **Digital Privacy Act (2015):** Amends the Personal Information Protection and Electronic Documents Act (PIPEDA) to enhance online security (https://laws-lois.justice.gc.ca/eng/annualstatutes/2015_32/page-1.html)

- **Act Respecting Cybersecurity (ARCS) (2022):** Recent legislation aimed at strengthening cybersecurity across critical sectors and federal agencies (https://www.canada.ca/en/public-safety-canada/news/2022/06/protecting-critical-cyber-systems.html)

Brazil–GDP 2.31

- **General Data Protection Law (LGPD) (2020):** Regulates the use and processing of personal data by businesses and government agencies (https://iapp.org/resources/article/brazilian-data-protection-law-lgpd-english-translation/)

- **Brazilian Internet Act (Marco Civil da Internet) (2014):** Establishes principles, guarantees, rights, and duties for the use of the Internet in Brazil (https://www.cgi.br/pagina/marco-civil-law-of-the-internet-in-brazil/180)

117

CHAPTER 7   REGULATIONS

These laws represent the main regulatory frameworks for cybersecurity and data protection in each country. As a reminder, each country may have additional regulations or guidelines that complement these laws, particularly concerning sector-specific requirements like finance, health, or energy.

# CHAPTER 8

# People

In this chapter, I want to acknowledge and highlight some of the cybersecurity thought leaders who have shaped defense strategies and the underlying technologies over the last quarter century. These are the luminaries who advanced cryptography, pioneered ethical hacking, and ushered in new ways to protect data on a global scale. Like modern-day rock stars—and many of them truly are—they've risen to every challenge the digital realm has thrown at them. So, to start, here are a select few of those thought leaders who have made an indelible impression on my own journey.

First and foremost, there's Bruce Schneier.[1] He's a rock star in the world of encryption and cryptography. While his seminal book, *Applied Cryptography*, was published slightly before our 25-year window, his ongoing contributions, blog posts, and thought leadership have remained influential into the present day. Schneier, with his deep dives into encryption algorithms and public policy, showed us that security was as much about code and math as it was about people and cultures. He emphasized a holistic view of cybersecurity, one that stretched beyond one's personal firewall and into our collective global consciousness.

Next is Kevin Mitnick,[2] who was once the "most wanted" hacker in the United States. He turned his nefarious exploits into a cautionary tale that ultimately benefited the very industry he once challenged. Released

---

[1] https://www.schneier.com
[2] https://www.mitnicksecurity.com

CHAPTER 8   PEOPLE

from prison in the late 1990s, Mitnick transformed into a cybersecurity consultant and advocate for ethical hacking. He wrote books that exposed human vulnerabilities within systems and spotlighted social engineering as a powerful dimension of hacking. By converting his experiences into constructive advice, Mitnick proved that sometimes, the best way to beat a hacker is to think like one.

Our notable mentions wouldn't be complete without Peiter Zatko,[3] better known by his handle, "Mudge." Rising to fame in the 1990s as part of the L0pht hacking collective, Mudge testified before the US Senate on the state of computer security. While his earliest work also predates our 25-year marker, his sustained influence as a DARPA (US Defense Advanced Research Projects Agency) program manager and later a security lead at Twitter cemented his status as an incredibly influential luminary in the community. Mudge's research on buffer overflows and code vulnerabilities has been foundational for many modern security protocols. He proved that collaboration between hackers and government agencies, though sometimes rocky, is vital for progress and to solve real-world issues.

Dan Kaminsky[4] gave the world a startling wake-up call in 2008 by exposing a colossal domain name system (DNS) vulnerability. This flaw could have allowed threat actors to quietly and systematically reroute Internet traffic to other assets without any notification to the sender. Kaminsky's disclosure and subsequent coordination with industry giants demonstrated how swift collaboration could avert a crisis. His approach to responsible disclosure, where researchers alert software vendors before going public, became an enduring model for vulnerability reporting that is still honored today.

On the corporate and policy front, Window Snyder[5] stands out as a powerhouse. Having worked at Microsoft, Mozilla, Apple, and Fastly,

---

[3] https://www.darpa.mil/about/people/peiter-zatko
[4] https://dankaminsky.com
[5] https://en.wikipedia.org/wiki/Window_Snyder

she consistently pushed the conversation from mere security patches to proactive product security. Snyder authored *Threat Modeling* and advocated for baking security into software from the ground up—a key lesson we've emphasized repeatedly in this book. Her stance was that cybersecurity shouldn't be an afterthought but a fundamental step in the development pipeline, a significant shift in a technology culture that often-prioritized rapid release over robust defense.

Finally, Katie Moussouris[6] revolutionized the "bug bounty" process model. By championing Microsoft's first bug bounty initiative and later founding Luta Security, she created frameworks that encourage hackers to ethically report security flaws before public disclosure. Moussouris argued for compensating researchers in a fair and transparent way, giving them a legitimate path to confidentially disclose vulnerabilities. This shift not only bolstered the global patch culture but also recognized the important role good hackers play in fortifying our digital domains.

In many ways, these luminaries have helped shepherd us through an ever-evolving cyber wilderness, continuously adapting and innovating to stay one step ahead of the dark side of the digital realm. Their contributions demonstrate that cybersecurity is less about static defenses and more about living, breathing strategies. The Internet may have started as a virtual frontier without rules or guardrails, but thanks to their tireless efforts, our online world now has champions prepared to identify and mitigate the next threat before it becomes a catastrophe.

While we've highlighted only a few names that have truly stood out in the cybersecurity community in this chapter, there are many, many more. In fact, too many to actually cover in this book from researchers to solution innovators. Appendix D contains many more notable "rock stars" from my research who played instrumental roles in shaping modern cybersecurity.

---

[6] https://www.sans.org/profiles/katie-moussouris/

# CHAPTER 9

# Syndicates

At its inception, the Internet promised unlimited communication, knowledge, and boundless potential. While entrepreneurs and dreamers steadfastly believed the World Wide Web could usher in a new era of global enlightenment, commerce, and transparency, early traffic patterns soon revealed a darker side with the rise of pornography, malware, and scams. As with most human inventions, the Internet's possibilities were quickly exploited by threat actors and those with less lofty motives. Rogue coders, shadowy cartels, and entire criminal syndicates deeply explored the art of what was possible, leveraging the technology for their own gains. Therefore, with a heavy head, let us proceed with a gentle nod to the epochs and an acknowledgment to the known entities that have given the Internet a bad reputation.

Before we go further, let's first clearly define what we mean by cybercrime syndicate. A cybercrime syndicate is an organized group of threat actors that collaborates to conduct large-scale cyberattacks, including data theft, ransomware campaigns, financial fraud, and identity theft. These groups operate much like traditional criminal organizations but leverage advanced hacking techniques, malware, and social engineering to exploit digital vulnerabilities. Cybercrime syndicates are often highly structured—like many legitimate businesses or enterprises—and may feature dedicated roles for malware developers, money launderers, and ransomware operators. These syndicates represent a persistent and

CHAPTER 9  SYNDICATES

evolving threat to businesses, governments, and individuals worldwide. With that, let's time travel back and review how the world of cybercrime syndicates first took shape and then evolved.

The late 1990s were literally the construction phases of the Internet. It was a time of screeching dial-up modems, bustling text-based message boards, and early search engines attempting to index everything online. Cybersecurity barely existed, and clicking on the wrong link could lead to unpredictable and undesirable outcomes, regardless of the link's stated purpose. Large corporations and government agencies were just beginning to experiment with placing services online, often without fully understanding the vulnerabilities and potential risk exposure.

Early cybercriminals quickly grasped the risks—and opportunities—in this nascent but expanding connected environment. They honed their practices, adapting physical attack methods to target unsuspecting entities. For example, simply changing a physical mail address could reroute a new credit card to a threat actor. These earliest cybercrime groups were more akin to lose collectives of curious hackers than the professional syndicates we know today.

In the early days, cybercrime actors primarily sought bragging rights and easy, ill-gotten money. They relied on rudimentary tools like basic Trojan horses, code injection scripts, credential theft, and email spoofing tactics to breach systems or impersonate individuals. These threat actors, some hailing from high school computer labs or cramped college dorm rooms, took pride in defacing websites with cartoonish graphics or cryptic "handles," leaving their digital graffiti as a testament to their skill.

However, even in these formative years, there were glimpses of what was to come. Some cybercrime outfits started to trade compromised credit card numbers in Internet Relay Chat (IRC)[1] chat rooms, forging the first threads of an illicit dark web community. Payment systems were simpler, the Internet was more trusting, and major data heists were rare.

---

[1] https://www.geeksforgeeks.org/internet-relay-chat-irc/

Nevertheless, the attack vectors began to take root, and it wouldn't be long before these vulnerabilities matured into the sprawling criminal networks of the subsequent decades.

In the early 2000s, the PTSD (post-traumatic stress disorder) from the Y2K bug was absolutely real. I remember it well and had many conversations with clients at the time about "what's next?" Post-Y2K, organizations lacked the appetite for another big project for a few years, which left a strange tension in the air when discussing new solutions. However, the emergence of new cyberattacks promoted a thawing of this mindset, as organizations clearly needed to adapt to respond effectively.

No longer was the Internet largely a hobbyist's playground. By the mid-2000s, threats no longer stemmed from small groups of script kiddies testing their skills on government servers. It was the beginning of international organized crime conglomerates that had become well-versed in hacking techniques and were now putting those skills to use to serve a wide variety of nefarious missions.

Simultaneously, the Internet saw the emergence of specialized roles within cybercrime organizations. Malware authors crafted code designed to harvest financial credentials. Spammers refined the dark art of phishing, luring unsuspecting victims with promises of foreign lotteries or urgent messages seemingly from banks. Money mules helped launder illicit proceeds into legitimate financial institutions. Increasingly, cybercrime syndicates began to resemble small businesses, albeit with a mission focused squarely on organized crime.

At this point in time, law enforcement agencies struggled to keep up, hampered by jurisdictional boundaries, global geolocations, and the challenges of establishing reliable digital evidence for prosecution. Regardless, governments and corporations grew more reliant on the Internet for ecommerce and communication. Credit card companies launched online portals, banks encouraged customers to manage their finances digitally, online dating emerged as a way to find love, and email began to displace traditional postal mail for correspondence and advertising.

CHAPTER 9   SYNDICATES

The more connectivity expanded, the more doors opened for cybercriminals. The main challenge for these criminal actors became less about penetrating hardened systems and more about refining their social engineering tactics to dupe unsuspecting users. In fact, social engineering remains the top attack vector today, used to compromise individuals and employed by almost all cybercriminal organizations. SentinelOne reports that up to 98%[2] of modern attacks still involve some form of social engineering.

By the mid-2000s, cybercriminal syndicates had begun to mirror legitimate commerce in operational complexity. One of the most significant developments of this period was the proliferation of underground forums and markets, now known as the dark web.[3] While earlier syndicates relied on IRC or private message boards to monetize their stolen data, the mid-2000s witnessed a surge in sophisticated black-market websites that accepted payments for information.

To be truthful, these hidden forums catered to every conceivable illicit digital service. They sold zero-day exploits at premium prices, offered hacking-as-a-service for clients seeking industrial espionage, sold illegal and immoral pictures and videos, and traded in botnets that could be rented on an ephemeral basis. A sense of Net Promoter Score[4] (NPS) even developed among criminals, complete with ratings and reviews for sellers, mimicking the structure of legitimate ecommerce business. Cryptocurrencies (primarily Bitcoin), though still in their earliest stages of acceptance and adoption, teased the possibility of anonymous, borderless payments, further fueling the ease and speed of these untraceable and unaccountable transactions.

---

[2] https://www.sentinelone.com/cybersecurity-101/cybersecurity/cyber-security-statistics/
[3] https://www.csoonline.com/article/564313/what-is-the-dark-web-how-to-access-it-and-what-youll-find.html
[4] https://www.qualtrics.com/experience-management/customer/net-promoter-score/

Fast forward a few years, and major data breaches drew public attention to the magnitude of the threat. Household-name retail giants reported the theft of millions of credit card records, creating a news frenzy that forced the average citizen to acknowledge the risks of being online and the importance of embracing even basic cybersecurity. For example, simple dictionary-based passwords reused on every website raised awareness to the basic risks of the Internet. Once an organized crime syndicate had one password, they could potentially use it everywhere. This is the concept of a password reuse attack, which remains a common threat today. Meanwhile, security firms expanded their operations, antivirus software became a requirement for home computers, and organizations and individuals struggled with how to respond appropriately if they were attacked.

As the first decade of the 21st century closed, nation-states began to discover the power of cyberattacks. Candidly, governments had always viewed the Internet as a tool for intelligence gathering, but this period marked the beginning of large-scale, state-sponsored hacking campaigns. Advanced persistent threats gained mainstream notoriety. As described earlier, APTs refer to stealthy and methodical intrusions that remained embedded in networks for extended periods of time, known as dwell time.[5] Nation-states and their authorized affiliates leveraged this approach to silently siphon off intelligence data over long periods while avoiding detection.

While we typically don't think of a nation-state as a cybercrime syndicate, the definition truly depends on a country's perspective. For instance, what one nation considers state-sponsored cybercrime, another might view as a legitimate revenue stream for a foreign government. Consider, for example, the relationship between the United States and North Korea.[6] Based on geopolitical tensions and sanctions, organized cybercrime can serve the purpose of nation-state revenue and adversarial political agendas.

---

[5] https://www.connectwise.com/cybersecurity-center/glossary/dwell-time
[6] https://www.cnn.com/2019/03/01/politics/north-korea-cyberattacks-cash-bank-heists/index.html

CHAPTER 9   SYNDICATES

While nation-states were sometimes linked to espionage, these well-funded operations also helped shape the broader cybercriminal ecosystem, especially ones that are nation-state sanctioned. Some governments would willingly share sophisticated techniques with authorized cybercrime syndicates to aid their missions. Zero-day vulnerabilities, once the secret arsenal of intelligence communities, have been known to leak onto the dark web at astronomical prices, fracturing the trust between governments and sanctioned cybercriminal syndicates. In the end, this is only a footnote if the syndicate achieves their goal without being caught. And, make no mistake, nation-states target everything from critical infrastructure to government services. They are indifferent to individuals becoming collateral damage or being used as mules to achieve their goals.

Today, the cybercriminal playbook has evolved yet again. Ransomware, malicious software that encrypts victims' data until a ransom is paid, rose to prominence and wreaked havoc on businesses, hospitals, municipal governments, and individuals. At first, ransom demands were modest, but over time, criminal groups realized entire organizations could be crippled, losing millions of dollars every hour systems remained down. This high cost of downtime often incentivized organizations to pay the ransom.

However, once a cybercriminal group is identified, named, and a country is associated with the source of the attack, law enforcements gain the potential to catch up, and time may be ticking for the threat actors. Therefore, cybercrime syndicates strive to retain anonymity for the sheer purpose of operating in the dark. Figure 9-1 illustrates the process of a typical ransomware infection that may be used by a syndicate against an unsuspecting organization.

CHAPTER 9   SYNDICATES

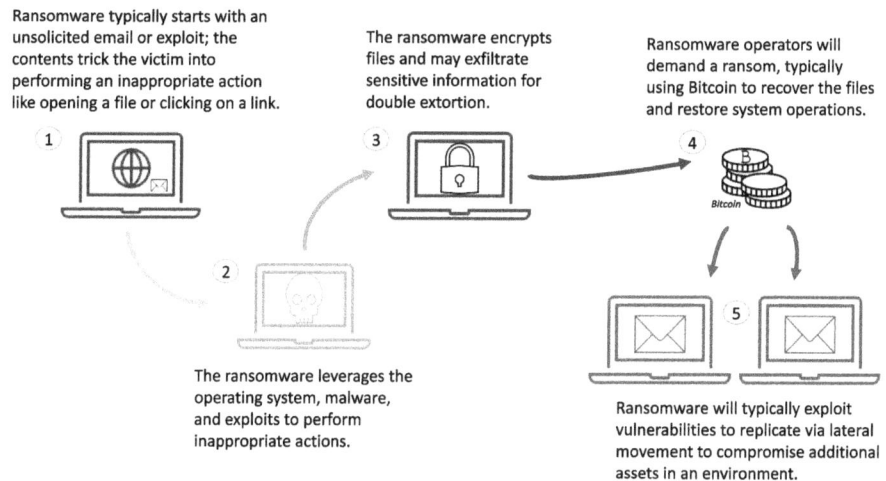

***Figure 9-1.***  *Process of a typical ransomware infection*

While money, greed, and deception are goals of these organizations, they can operate much like legitimate businesses, complete with regular correspondence, terms for payment, and even customer satisfaction surveys after you have been breached. As a business, they want to maximize their profits. This pursuit has led cybercrime syndicates to evolve ransomware into "double-extortion"[7] attacks.

In double-extortion attacks, attackers not only encrypt victims' data but also threaten to leak it publicly if payment isn't made. This tactic puts organizations in a difficult position, forcing them to choose between paying substantial ransoms and protecting their confidential information. For victim organizations, paying a ransom can be illegal (depending on regional laws) and the results could be damaging leaks, lawsuits, regulatory compliance fines, and reputational harm. These tactics have proven alarmingly effective, enriching cybercriminal groups and forcing cyber insurance companies to reevaluate their coverage terms and applicable exclusions.

---

[7]https://www.techtarget.com/searchsecurity/definition/double-extortion-ransomware

## CHAPTER 9  SYNDICATES

In recent years, cybercriminal syndicates have expanded their offerings with ransomware-as-a-service. This has provided novice cybercriminals with access to high-end tools for conducting ransomware campaigns. This commercialization of cybercrime has allowed the Internet's underworld to expand its reach, targeting small businesses and large corporations alike, from a growing multitude of attackers around the globe. Meanwhile, the anonymity of cryptocurrencies has made it possible for extortion money to vanish into digital wallets with nearly no legal methods for traceability or recovery.

In reflecting on the evolution of cybercrime syndicates over the last 25 years, it's evident that these groups are agile, relentless, and highly responsive to technological changes. In fairness, we're still playing the same cat and mouse game as we were two and a half decades ago. The lines between individual hackers, organized crime, and state-sponsored actors have blurred, but the chase is still on.

While the decentralized nature of the Internet and the borderless nature of these syndicates make them a tough takedown for traditional law enforcement, international cooperation and legislation fostered by the United Nations[8] have led to improvements. This includes enhanced intelligence sharing between countries and coordinated joint crackdowns on high-profile cybercriminal syndicates.

In the next few years, we'll likely see an increased use of artificial intelligence by criminals, automating attacks, mapping out vulnerabilities in real time, and even crafting highly convincing new deepfake campaigns to fool both individuals and institutions. Quantum computing, meanwhile, looms on the horizon, threatening to render classical encryption obsolete and open entirely new attack vectors against vulnerable encryption standards.

---

[8] https://www.un.org/counterterrorism/cybersecurity

## CHAPTER 9　SYNDICATES

We've witnessed cybercrime syndicates transform from scattered communities of curious hackers into vast, global enterprises that rival legitimate multinational corporations in both complexity and revenue. Through social engineering, malware distribution, ransomware extortion, and data breaches, cybercriminal syndicates have capitalized on society's reliance on technology, turning the Internet and human vulnerabilities into a multibillion-dollar revenue stream.

If history has shown us anything, it's that both cybercriminals and information security professionals will continue to escalate the stakes on both offensive and defensive strategies. And, to raise visibility on who these threat actors are, please refer to Appendix E, where I have compiled a list of the most prominent and known cybercrime syndicates and the attack vectors attributed to them.

# CHAPTER 10

# Social Engineering

For the past 25 years, social engineering has repeatedly proven that our most vulnerable cybersecurity asset is us—human beings. The fundamental premise of social engineering attacks is incredibly straightforward: why spend time reverse engineering code when, with a spoonful of charm and a sprinkle of deception, you can coax unsuspecting humans into divulging secrets to gain critical access and carry out attacks? After all, as is widely said today in the age of identity security, it's easier to log in than hack in.

And, humans, after all, are gloriously fallible, gullible, ignorant, arrogant, and blindly naive. If you appeal to their curiosity, kindness, or fear, you just might extract those secrets with minimal to no real effort. To be fair, modern digital social engineering started in mid-to-late 1990s, but charlatans have been duping gullible people for millennia. Over the last quarter century, we've seen social engineering evolve from simple phone-based scams to highly sophisticated, industrial-scale campaigns using deepfakes, SMS text messages, and even threats of incarcerating individuals for noncompliance. Now, let us revisit our time machine, jump a little more than 25 years, and see just how clever and brazen social engineers have become.

In the late 1990s, before the term "phishing" was even on the tip of everyone's tongue, social engineering typically involved direct phone calls, postal fraud, and improvised acts of human persuasion. Kevin Mitnick was a pioneer in the art of phishing, gaining notoriety for his actions. Mitnick famously exploited trust and confusion to coax system administrators into divulging passwords and other insider knowledge. He understood the immense pressure on IT professionals and would craft urgent, persuasive scenarios, often impersonating a colleague or executive in dire need. Even if an administrator initially pushed back, asking for proof of identity or more details, Mitnick would expertly leverage the target's sense of empathy and sympathy to gain trust. He'd then manipulate them into sharing credentials, resetting passwords, or granting inappropriate privileges, leading to system compromise. In the early days of personal computers, the average information technology worker wasn't necessarily tech- or security-savvy. Mitnick and his contemporaries found that a polite tone and credible jargon could unravel corporate security like deep-sea fishing (phishing) and a runaway line.

Now let's jump forward to the early 2000s. Email started gaining traction as the preferred method of communication within businesses and for correspondence at home. With it, we saw the emergence of the "Nigerian Prince"[1] or "419" scams. These emails often included a feigned air of desperation from a deposed royal figure who needed urgent assistance to move funds abroad, leading the phishing recipient to believe they would earn a lump sum payment for the simple favor of assisting with the transfer. While the stories presented in such attacks are often outlandish, those emails reached millions of inboxes, and if only a fraction of recipients responded, that fraction was enough to warrant continued attacks. According to cybersecurity researchers today, variations of this same scam today still produce millions of dollars in revenue for threat actors.[2]

We might laugh at these colorfully worded exhortations, heavy with capital letters, exclamation marks, and pleas for help, but they proved a masterclass in the power of targeting large volumes of people. Even a

---

[1] https://www.twingate.com/research/cybercrime-characters
[2] https://www.cnbc.com/2019/04/18/nigerian-prince-scams-still-rake-in-over-700000-dollars-a-year.html

## CHAPTER 10  SOCIAL ENGINEERING

very low conversion rate can still be highly profitable. Social engineering doesn't always rely on subtlety and targeted attacks; sometimes, it's a numbers game that rewards persistence, even when the response rate is low.

By the mid-2000s, "phishing" was a well-known term, despite its spelling still causing public awareness issues. Threat actors refined their approach, realizing that embedded URLS, bogus links, and official-looking websites were easy tactics to convince unsuspecting users to click, open a file, or execute a new program. Internet users were still catching up to the intricacies of digital threats, so an email cleverly spoofed to look like a PayPal, eBay, or bank notice had a higher percentage for success than a simple Nigerian Prince scam.

Remember the day you got that urgent "Your account has been compromised, click here to secure it" email? If you were having a busy day or were unaware of the risks, you might have clicked the link and entered your credentials. In doing so, you unwittingly handed your secrets to a spoofed website, giving threat actors immediate access to your bank accounts. Once again, psychological manipulation, fear of financial loss or urgent updates trumped any technology-based security measures or common sense to "trust but verify."

At this time, security tokens and multifactor authentication were still in their infancy, offering no additional security layers after falling victim such an attack. Threat actors walked right through the front door, courtesy of polite (or alarming) requests sent via email—and users, unfortunately, fell completely for their trap. Therefore, always think about Admiral Ackbar:[3] "It's a trap!"—before randomly interacting with any potential phishing attack (email, SMS texting, chat messages, direct messages, etc.).

Moving into the late 2000s and early 2010s, social media created new avenues for social engineering attack vectors. Platforms like Facebook, Twitter, and LinkedIn were no longer mere curiosities; they became integral to our daily lives and new methods for business communications.

---

[3] https://www.starwars.com/databank/admiral-ackbar

## CHAPTER 10   SOCIAL ENGINEERING

If you think an email that looks like it's from your bank is persuasive, imagine receiving a message from a close friend or an old business colleague via social media. Social engineers capitalized on the trust we place in familiar names and faces. Threat actors took to compromising social media accounts, then sent out messages to all or select contacts: "Help! I am trying to call mom, but she is not answering," "Do you remember our work at...," or, more cunningly, they used personal information gleaned from profiles—perhaps your mother's maiden name or your pet's name—to guess security questions after selecting "Forgot Password."

Even a humble "About Me" post can become a treasure trove of personal information, including maiden names, birthdays, children's names, etc. In an era where oversharing is a badge of honor, social engineers found an abundance of easy pickings. While the late 2000s saw an era of generic phishing, the early 2010s ushered in the dawn of spear phishing.[4] These were more targeted attacks on specific individuals that exploit gleaned knowledge to craft infinitely more believable messages with specific facts recognizable to the target.

Corporations, too, found themselves in the crosshairs of social engineering attacks. Elaborate phone-based schemes returned, this time disguised as official-sounding calls from "partners," "vendors," and "employees" potentially stranded overseas due to travel issues. Imagine a threat actor calling an employee from a number spoofed to look like an internal line. They introduce themselves as someone from the finance department with a pressing issue requiring immediate attention. The employee sees the number, hears the correct corporate lingo, and trusts the voice on the other end. In giant organizations, this type of ruse can result in a single misguided transaction worth hundreds of thousands of dollars, or the disclosure of additional information to perpetuate the attack. When these attacks occur via email, they are known as business

---

[4] https://www.dni.gov/files/NCSC/documents/campaign/Counterintelligence_Tips_Spearphishing.pdf

CHAPTER 10   SOCIAL ENGINEERING

email compromise (BEC)[5] scams. BEC attacks grew alarmingly common toward the end of the 2010s, and suddenly, it wasn't just individuals losing access to their bank accounts, but entire companies being targeted because of a few cunning words in an email or phone call delivered at just the right time.

Then there's the double whammy of big data and personalized scamming, a phenomenon that took off in the 2010s and continues to evolve today. We've already discussed how data breaches became disturbingly routine, making many individuals simply numb to the news of yet another compromise. Every year, we hear about a major corporation or government entity experiencing a breach. These incidents left a trove of personal records—names, emails, addresses, and phone numbers—floating around on the dark web. Armed with this data, social engineers could tailor their messages with eerie precision, merging datasets to build virtual profiles of their potential targets. Instead of "Dear Sir/Madam," a threat actor addresses you by your full name, references your city, or mentions a recent online purchase. With these simple facts, social engineering attacks become more believable, blurring the lines between a genuine email from a subscribed service and a clever fake.

We can see in near real time how threat actors borrow each other's methods, refine them, and adapt them each time to make the attacks more credible and, truthfully, scarier. In Figure 10-1, you can see an illustration of just how devious these emails have become. They play with multiple human emotions and, based on instilling fear alone, may compel you to engage with the threat actor.

---

[5] https://www.fbi.gov/how-we-can-help-you/scams-and-safety/common-frauds-and-scams/business-email-compromise

# CHAPTER 10  SOCIAL ENGINEERING

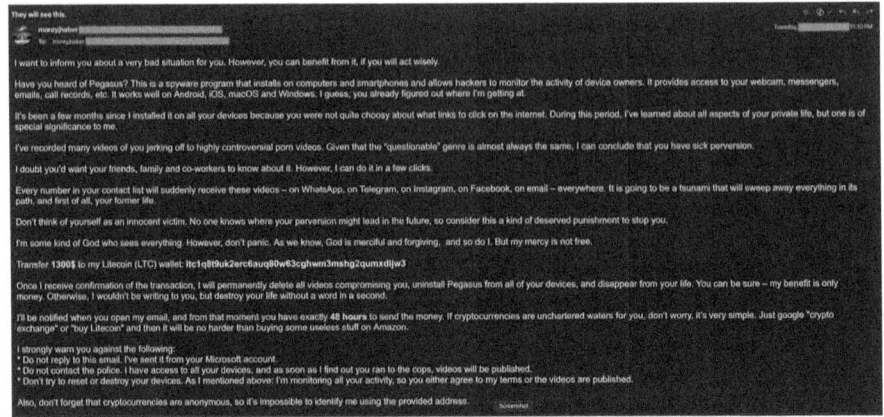

***Figure 10-1.*** *Sample of a malicious email extorting human emotion*

The last few years have witnessed an even deeper interplay between technology and psychology. With the rise of deepfakes and AI-based manipulation tools, the potential for deception using social engineering has skyrocketed. Imagine receiving a phone call that sounds exactly like your boss, complete with their accent and friendly laugh, instructing you to "buy some gift cards for clients at the conference." Or consider a Zoom call featuring a suspiciously lifelike impersonation of a colleague, with voice and face generated by AI. These scenarios were once considered science fiction, but they now are a reality, made possible with free tools on the Internet like ChatGPT or the Speechify[6] plugin.

Social engineers have always relied on illusions, but these illusions are becoming terrifyingly convincing. The mere knowledge that deepfake technology exists has introduced profound confusion and doubt. Am I speaking to a friend or a cunning simulation? Should I trust that video clip, or is it an elaborate hoax? When humans cannot even trust their own senses, you can bet social engineering will find a way to exploit that uncertainty.

---

[6] https://speechify.com

Throughout the decades, we've been continuously reinforced with lessons: no matter how advanced security technology becomes, no matter how many times we are reminded to install antivirus software, patch our systems, and avoid suspicious links, the "human factor" remains the Achilles' heel.[7] To that end, we even have a full chapter on human risks later in this book.

Despite the ongoing challenges, this isn't a message of doom and gloom. Instead, consider this a crucial reality check: cybersecurity awareness training demands greater seriousness from everyone. Modern defenses like phishing simulations, zero trust philosophies, and robust identity verification protocols are now standard for many companies to mitigate these risks. However, the responsibility isn't solely yours. Major Internet service providers like Google, Apple, and Microsoft have introduced new email protections, including advanced AI scanning that flags suspicious messages. Similarly, regulatory bodies worldwide have demanded stricter oversight on data handling, aiming to mitigate the effects of inevitable data breaches. Yet, the cat and mouse game persists, with social engineers continually finding innovative ways to challenge our defenses, particularly through email. To that end, even today, the best defense against social engineering attacks, especially email phishing, remains end-user awareness and training. Figure 10-2 provides the top ten email attributes to review in order to prevent these types of attacks.

---

[7] https://www.merriam-webster.com/dictionary/Achilles%27%20heel

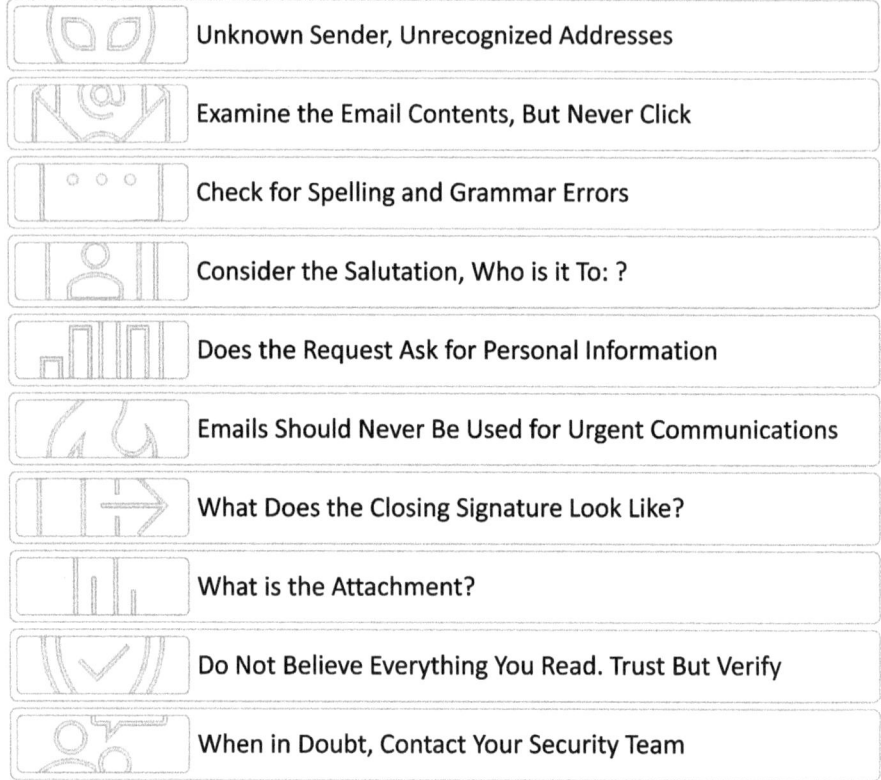

*Figure 10-2. The role of end-user awareness and training in recognizing email phishing attacks*

Over the past quarter century, technology has changed in leaps and bounds, but human nature adapts at a meandering pace. Our instincts for trust, empathy, and curiosity remain strong, making us prime targets for manipulative threat actors. Even as we deploy the latest firewalls, antimalware solutions, and encryption protocols, we must always maintain a healthy skepticism about the communications we receive. This means verifying unexpected requests, double-checking suspicious links, and pausing before responding to messages that attempt to instill fear or urgency. It means keeping up with (or at least being aware of) the evolving tactics of scammers, from phone-based "vishing" to elaborate AI-enabled spoofs.

If you are curious to learn more about how social engineering attacks have impacted businesses over the last 25 years, check out Appendix F. There, I have broken down the most important of these attacks and distilled simple lessons we can learn from each of them.

# CHAPTER 11

# Solutions

As we've stated in previous chapters, the escalation of cyber threats sparked the emergence of an entire market dedicated to addressing the diverse attack vectors that could compromise organizations, disrupt services, and extort money. Each solution, whether a product or a service, was developed in response to existing threats or anticipated emerging scenarios. In many cases, the very flaws within existing business solutions—initially developed to fulfill a business use case—spawned an entire new market of cybersecurity products because of their inherent flaws.

Threat actors quickly capitalized on these overlooked flaws. They learned unsigned executables allowed malware to run easily, that providing users full administrative privileges on their devices paved the way for lateral movement and unauthorized configuration changes, and that poor software coding created a myriad of easy-to-exploit vulnerabilities. Therefore, as we review each of these solutions in the market, we'll consider why it was developed, what threat it is designed to mitigate, and which previously discussed case studies could have been avoided with a mature deployment.

## Endpoint Security

Endpoint security has evolved nearly in lockstep with the growth of personal computing and the Internet. In the early days of personal computers, security measures focused on virus detection for individual

CHAPTER 11   SOLUTIONS

machines. During the late 1980s, as personal computers became more widespread, basic antivirus programs emerged to detect and remove malware. The 1990s saw the introduction of personal firewalls and more sophisticated virus protection, reflecting increased connectivity and more complex threats. As businesses embraced distributed networks in the early 2000s, traditional antivirus became insufficient, prompting the development of integrated endpoint protection platforms (EPPs) and suites of loosely coupled products. These solutions often combined antivirus, anti-spyware, intrusion detection, and disk encryption tools under a unified agent and management. At the same time, adjacent solutions were developed: endpoint privilege management (EPM) to enforce least privilege, and data loss prevention (DLP) to protect against data theft, leakage, and in appropriate data transfers. In the early 2010s, endpoint security further evolved to include advanced threat detection, heuristics, and behavioral analysis, responding to the evolving threat landscape. Today, zero trust models and continuous monitoring guide endpoint security, emphasizing proactive defense and real-time response across modern, distributed environments.

In the next few sections, we will cover the historical evolution of endpoint protection, from traditional antivirus through endpoint protection platforms to endpoint detection and response (EDR) solutions. This will help us understand how modern organizations address attack vectors against endpoints (both servers and workstations).

## Antivirus

The story of antivirus solutions began in the late 1980s. During this decade, the first computer viruses emerged, leading to the development of the earliest antivirus programs. As you may recall, one of the pioneering software in this regard was the "Reaper" program, designed to combat the "Creeper" virus, which was spreading among ARPANET users. Creeper, with its unexpected worm-style propagation, literally set the stage for the antivirus industry, demonstrating the necessity of such defensive software in a world that would become increasingly dependent on technology.

The 1990s also witnessed a significant evolution in both the complexity of computer viruses and the antivirus solutions designed to combat them. The rise of the Internet and personal computer email dramatically increased the potential for virus dissemination, leading to a surge in the development of more sophisticated antivirus software. These solutions emphasized the importance of proactive protection strategies, such as heuristic analysis and behavior-based detection, marking a significant shift from the traditional signature-based methods. The result was the commercialization of antivirus solutions, with companies like Symantec (Broadcom) and McAfee becoming household names.

If we fast forward to the current decade, the evolution of antivirus software is characterized by the integration of cloud-based technologies, artificial intelligence, identity security, and behavioral monitoring. While antivirus solutions still rely on signature-based technology for efficient identification and removal of older malware types, today's defensive strategies must mitigate evolved malware and the raw creativity of threat actors. By necessity, antivirus solutions themselves have evolved to become more adaptive, efficient, complex, and capable of rapidly responding to myriad attack vectors. AI-driven capabilities are a particularly strong force revolutionizing the AV sector, powering intelligent automation of complex tasks and predicting emerging threats based on behaviors occurring on a system.

The importance of antivirus solutions in our current digital landscape shouldn't be understated. With the exponential growth in the cloud and hybrid infrastructures, the proliferation of digital devices at home and at work, and the emergence of always-on connectivity, cyberattacks can occur at a faster pace than humans alone can respond. Modern antivirus solutions play a critical role in safeguarding personal and organizational data against these threats. It not only protects against known viruses but also offers defense mechanisms against new and evolving threats because history has a tendency to repeat itself.

CHAPTER 11   SOLUTIONS

And today, the role of antivirus solutions extends beyond mere malware detection and removal. Modern AV solutions are instrumental in maintaining system integrity, ensuring data privacy, preventing data leakage, and preventing human errors that would otherwise likely lead to a cybersecurity incident. This simply represents an evolution in technology to protect assets and users in every way possible.

Today, without an up-to-date AV solution, data breaches and cyberattacks can have devastating consequences, including the denial of disbursements from a cyber insurance company. AV capabilities are a required component of some regulatory compliance frameworks as well, to satisfy audited cybersecurity controls. In essence, AV is a cybersecurity best practice, has potential regulatory components to maintain and operate correctly, and is required by cyber insurance coverage in case of a breach.

The history of antivirus solutions is a testament to the relentless pursuit of digital security in an ever-evolving technological landscape. Understanding this history not only provides insights into the technological advancements in cybersecurity, but also highlights the indispensable role of antivirus solutions in maintaining a secure and trustworthy digital environment. As we navigate the complexities of the coming decades, the significance of these solutions remains more relevant than ever, underscoring their pivotal role in safeguarding assets and identities.

## Anti-spyware

The story of anti-spyware software is an intriguing one. It encapsulates a journey from being a standalone solution to becoming an integrated component in every modern antivirus security suite. Understanding this evolution is not just a foray into the history of cybersecurity, but also an insight into the changing nature of threats and the escalating sophistication employed by threat actors.

## CHAPTER 11   SOLUTIONS

In the late 1990s and early 2000s, the Internet's worldwide adoption brought along a wave of new security challenges. Among these was spyware, a subclass of malware designed to infiltrate and gather information from computers without user consent. These early spyware variants were often simple, designed to track online behavior, log keystrokes, or display unwanted advertisements. However, the privacy and security risks they posed were significant enough to prompt the development of specialized anti-spyware solutions.

Existing AV companies and startup cybersecurity vendors raced to create software that could detect and remove this new class of malware. These early anti-spyware solutions were standalone products, focused solely on combating spyware, not viruses or worms. The early to mid-2000s was the golden age of standalone anti-spyware software. Products like Ad-Aware, Spybot – Search & Destroy, and others gained popularity for their effectiveness in detecting and removing spyware. These tools offered a level of specialization that general antivirus programs lacked, and their user base grew rapidly as awareness of spyware threats increased.

As defenses matured, the nature of spyware also evolved to become more intrusive and destructive. Cybercriminals developed more sophisticated spyware capable of keylogging, screen capturing, and even remote control of infected machines. These new use cases escalated the risk, making the battle against spyware more complex and crucial.

Viruses, worms, spyware, and other malicious software began to overlap in functionality and sophistication. This convergence prompted companies to demand a single solution rather than licensing and deploying multiple agents, as the distinction between these early types of malware became increasingly blurred. In response, cybersecurity firms started to recognize the need for a more integrated approach, and the concept of endpoint security suites emerged. This recognition marked the beginning of the end for standalone anti-spyware products. Antivirus and broader security software suites began incorporating anti-spyware features, data loss prevention, and other features, acknowledging that

## CHAPTER 11   SOLUTIONS

effective digital defense required a multilayered approach. By the late 2000s, most leading antivirus programs had multiple capabilities in one bundle. Today, standalone anti-spyware software is a rarity, and when it does exist, it's targeted for a specific use case where a bundled solution is just not viable.

The transition from standalone anti-spyware software to integrated security solutions has taught us a few key lessons:

- **Technological Advancements:** Improvements in antivirus technology allowed for the effective inclusion of real-time anti-spyware and other malware defenses without compromising performance.

- **User Convenience:** Having a single, comprehensive security solution is more convenient and efficient for users than managing multiple standalone products from a licensing, deployment, and maintenance perspective.

- **Economic Factors:** For cybersecurity companies, developing and maintaining a standalone product for a single type of threat became economically unviable compared to offering an all-in-one solution.

The history of anti-spyware software is a testament to the adaptive nature of cybersecurity. It reflects how solutions must evolve in step with the changing nature of threats. While standalone anti-spyware software has largely become a thing of the past, its legacy lives on in the integrated defenses that continue to protect users from a multitude of cybersecurity threats in our increasingly hyper-connected world. This evolution underscores a fundamental truth in digital security: adaptation and integration are key to staying ahead in the never-ending race against cyberattacks.

# Endpoint Protection Platforms

Endpoint protection platforms (EPPs) represent a second stage in the evolution of antivirus solutions, adapting to the increasing complexity and sophistication of cyberattacks. Initially, antivirus software focused on detecting and removing computer viruses. Over time, as malware diversified, antivirus solutions expanded to combat Trojans, worms, and spyware. However, these traditional antivirus tools largely relied on signature-based detection, identifying threats based on known malware signatures. While effective against known threats, this approach struggled with new, unknown, modified, or obfuscated malware.

The limitation of traditional antivirus in dealing with novel threats led to the development of endpoint protection platforms. EPPs go beyond mere malware detection; they incorporate a range of security technologies to provide comprehensive protection against a broad spectrum of cyberattacks. This includes not only traditional malware, but also more sophisticated attacks, like zero-day exploits, advanced persistent threats, and ransomware.

A key aspect of EPPs is their use of advanced technologies, such as machine learning, behavioral analysis, and cloud-based intelligence. Machine learning enables EPPs to identify and respond to new threats by learning from patterns and anomalies in system and user behavior. Behavioral monitoring scrutinizes the behavior of applications and files, flagging any suspicious activity or deviations from normal operations. This approach is particularly effective against zero-day threats, which lack a known signature. Cloud-based intelligence is another crucial component, allowing EPPs to leverage vast datasets and threat intelligence from multiple sources to rapidly identify and respond to emerging threats. This collective, crowd-sourced approach ensures that even the most recent and sophisticated attacks can be identified and mitigated.

## CHAPTER 11  SOLUTIONS

EPPs also integrate various security functionalities that were once standalone products, in addition to previously discussed anti-spyware protection. This includes firewall management, intrusion prevention systems (IPS), device control, and data loss prevention (DLP). By consolidating these functions into a single platform, EPPs offered a unified and streamlined security posture, simplifying management and enhancing overall security.

Another significant advantage of EPPs was their adaptability to platform diversity. With the increase in Android, macOS, and other operating systems and the rise of personal devices used for business purposes (bring your own device–BYOD), the traditional network perimeter began to dissolve. EPPs began to cater to this change by securing endpoints irrespective of their location, ensuring devices are protected both inside and outside the corporate network, regardless of platform and connectivity.

The importance of EPPs as a period in cybersecurity history is a much longer story as we move into the next chapter. All EPPs still exist today; there is a preference for more modern solutions, which we will cover in a moment. To that end, cyberattacks are not only becoming more frequent, but also more sophisticated, with threat actors constantly devising new methods to bypass traditional security measures by blending attack vectors. The cost of these attacks, in terms of both financial and reputational losses, can be catastrophic for businesses.

With their advanced capabilities, EPPs offer a more robust defense against these evolving threats compared to standalone antivirus. However, the story doesn't stop there. The evolution from traditional antivirus solutions to endpoint protection platforms signifies a critical shift in the approach to cybersecurity. EPPs offer robust, integrated, and intelligent security measures that are crucial for protecting against the sophisticated and ever-changing landscape of cyber threats. This evolution reflects the necessity for proactive and advanced defense mechanisms, where cybersecurity is not just about protecting against known threats, but also being prepared for the unknown. This leads us into the next chapter of endpoint security defensive solutions.

# Endpoint Detection and Response

Endpoint detection and response (EDR) solutions represent the third generation of endpoint security solutions, following antivirus and endpoint protection platforms. As cyber threats have increased in sophistication, there's a growing need for more advanced security solutions that address the limitations of AV and EPP products. EDR fulfills this need by offering rich monitoring, detection, investigation, and response capabilities at the endpoint level. EDR solutions expanded on EPP by providing:

- **Continuous Monitoring and Data Collection:** EDR solutions continuously monitor and gather data from endpoints, creating a detailed activity log. This includes file executions, network communications, and changes in configurations, providing a more comprehensive view of potential security incidents.

- **Threat Detection:** Using advanced analytics, EDR tools detect suspicious activities that indicate a potential threat. This involves comparing behaviors against known threat patterns, anomaly detection, and utilizing machine learning to identify new, advanced threats.

- **Automated Response and Remediation:** Once a threat is detected, EDR solutions can automate responses, such as isolating affected endpoints, killing malicious processes, or rolling back changes made by malware. This quick response is crucial for containing and mitigating threats.

- **Forensics and Analysis Tools:** EDR solutions provide tools for in-depth analysis of security incidents. This helps in understanding the nature of attacks, identifying the source, and developing strategies to prevent future breaches.

- **Integration with Other Security Tools:** EDR often integrates with other security systems like Security Information and Event Management (SIEM) and threat intelligence platforms, enabling a coordinated and holistic security approach.

This evolution is why EDR is a cornerstone of modern endpoint cybersecurity for many organizations today. Based on the history of attacks, EDR effectively addresses the following use cases:

- **Malware:** Today's cyberattacks combine decades-old malware and new threats, including living-off-the-land (LotL) techniques that weaponize the operating system itself against assets. EDR solutions are designed to mitigate the risks from old attack vectors, malware-less attacks, and as-yet-unknown future threats.

- **Complex and Evolving Threats:** Modern cyber threats often bypass traditional security measures. EDR's advanced analytics and continuous monitoring are equipped to detect and respond to these complex threats, even if they have never been seen before.

- **Ransomware and Targeted Attacks:** With the rise in ransomware and targeted cyberattacks, organizations need more robust defenses that operate at multiple layers within an asset. EDR provides the necessary tools to quickly identify, mitigate, and quarantine these high-impact threats.

- **Insider Threat Detection:** EDR is not just effective against external threats, but also in identifying potentially harmful activities from within an organization, such as unauthorized data access, data exfiltration, or even a malicious insider operating within the confines of their role.

- **Faster Response and Remediation:** The speed of response is crucial in mitigating the impact of a cyberattack, especially since assets are always connected and online. EDR's automated response capabilities ensure threats are contained and addressed promptly, reducing the overall impact on the organization faster than typical human response times.

- **Compliance and Regulatory Requirements:** With increasing regulations around data protection and cybersecurity, EDR helps organizations comply with these requirements by providing detailed monitoring and reporting capabilities.

- **Remote and Distributed Workforce:** As workforces become more distributed, particularly in the era of remote work, securing endpoints outside the traditional network perimeter becomes critical. EDR's ability to monitor and protect endpoints regardless of their location effectively addresses this challenge.

Endpoint detection and response represents a significant advancement in endpoint cybersecurity. Its comprehensive approach to monitoring, detecting, and responding to threats—coupled with its capabilities for in-depth analysis and automated remediation—makes it an essential tool in combating the modern, ever-evolving cyberattacks organizations face.

As organizations continue to grapple with a challenging and dynamic threat landscape, EDR provides the necessary capabilities to ensure robust and resilient defenses. Looking closer at endpoint security, it's only a matter of time before we see a fourth generation of endpoint security tools emerge with new capabilities designed to address modern attack vectors.

CHAPTER 11   SOLUTIONS

# Networks

Network security has evolved significantly since the early days of interconnected systems. In the late 1980s, as the Internet emerged from academic and military projects, organizations recognized the need to protect their networks from intrusion. The concept of a firewall was introduced as the first line of defense, initially as packet filters, then advancing to stateful inspection and next-generation firewalls with deep packet and content inspection. Concurrently, the concept of virtual private networks (VPNs) arose, enabling secure communication over public networks through encryption and protocol tunneling.

As the Internet expanded, businesses and users faced new threats, prompting the development of firewalls at both the network and host levels that could perform actual content filtering based on a website's content (e.g., pornography, malware-infected websites, foreign geolocations). These tools scanned and filtered incoming data based on defined policies, blocking malicious or inappropriate material that would typically render on the end user's workstation or mobile device.

Together, firewalls, VPNs, and content filtering laid the foundation of modern network security, providing critical layers of protection against an ever-growing range of evolving cyber threats. In the next few sections, we will explore the history of these solutions.

# Firewalls

Firewalls quietly emerged in the late 1980s, initially as packet filters at the network perimeter. Early designs resembled digital fences with gates and knot holes, regulating data traffic between trusted and untrusted zones. As connectivity increased, next-generation firewalls integrated application-level inspection and intrusion prevention, to shield organizations from evolving threats. With each iteration, firewalls adapted to meet escalating

CHAPTER 11   SOLUTIONS

attack vectors, combining deep packet inspection with sophisticated analytics. Today, they are a cornerstone of cybersecurity architectures, essential for blocking unauthorized access, preventing malicious intrusions, and safeguarding sensitive data from exfiltration.

So, what is a firewall? At its core, a firewall is analogous to a wooden fence with holes, standing at the threshold of corporate networks, monitoring and regulating the flow of digital traffic inbound and outbound. By preventing malicious entities from trespassing and curbing unauthorized communications, firewalls uphold the integrity, confidentiality, and availability of business assets.

Firewalls, at their simplest incarnation, embody the principle of selective connectivity and visibility, much like the previous fence analogy. They operate based on predefined rules that determine what type of data packets (data) may enter or exit a network. These rules draw upon criteria such as source and destination Internet Protocol (IP) addresses, port numbers, encryption, and specific protocols.

In the real world, one can imagine a firewall as a fence with peep holes (wood knots), allowing various people and animals to see through and walk pass. A guard is ever-present, watching both inbound and outbound movement, preventing unauthorized passage. Only the known and trusted are granted entry through those holes in the fence, while others have no visibility or communication. Figure 11-1 illustrates the concept of a firewall.

# CHAPTER 11  SOLUTIONS

***Figure 11-1.*** *Illustration of a firewall using a fence analogy*

This seemingly straightforward role contradicts the required sophistication of modern firewall solutions, which have evolved in complexity alongside the evolution of cyber threats and technology.

As corporate networks expand, so does the complexity of threats—that's a given. Threat actors exploit system vulnerabilities, employee inattention, and outdated software to inject malware, gain unauthorized access, or steal precious data. Firewalls, therefore, have evolved beyond mere packet forwarding, now embracing intricate layers of threat analysis and prevention. Today's firewalls work in tandem with intrusion detection systems (IDS) and intrusion prevention systems (IPS), scrutinizing real-time traffic not only by IP addresses and ports but also by data content and behavioral patterns.

At the foundation of any firewall lies a form of access control that is based on policy, driven by electronic and corporate risk assessments. These policies can be as strict or as lenient as business needs dictate, to reflect an organization's risk tolerance. When establishing such a baseline policy, organizations must conduct a careful assessment: on one hand, maintaining stringent security; on the other, ensuring the smooth operation of legitimate business functions. An overly aggressive firewall policy can hinder daily operations by blocking essential communications, while a lax approach can open the paths to potential attacks. Striking that equilibrium requires thoughtful drafting, consistent review, and precise tuning as business needs and the threat landscape evolve.

Within a business context, firewalls also serve as the foundation for compliance initiatives and network segmentation. Various regulations, from industry-specific mandates (like PCI DSS for payment card processors) to general data protection laws (like GDPR in the European Union), impose rules on how organizations must secure sensitive data and manage their network boundaries. Firewalls form a crucial part of the compliance infrastructure, demonstrating that network barriers are in place to protect information from unwarranted exposure. Businesses typically maintain activity logs generated by firewalls, which track every connection attempt and flag every anomaly, as evidence of ongoing diligence during external audits and forensics.

In enterprises and multinational businesses, firewalls assume an even more complex role. Enterprises often host numerous subnetworks, cloud services, remote offices, as well as remote employees. To be successful, firewall technology must integrate seamlessly with other cybersecurity solutions, including encryption, virtual private networks (VPNs), multifactor authentication, etc., while managing secure connections for employees worldwide.

Network segmentation, which divides a network into smaller zones, prevents potential breaches from cascading throughout the organization via lateral movement. Simply put, a firewall is the orchestrator of segmentation policies, dictating who and what can communicate between network zones. This is often referred to as trusted or untrusted network segments or zones. If a malicious entity infiltrates one segment, additional firewalls placed at the boundaries of the next segment stand as a fence to prevent further attacks, lateral movement, and inappropriate access.

## CHAPTER 11  SOLUTIONS

Since the inception of firewalls, performance and the ability to enforce complex policies have become the features of choice. In the late 2000s, firewall technology evolved into next-generation firewalls (NGFWs) to address the evolution of attack vectors. Firewalls, once a tool of the network infrastructure team, morphed into the network security sphere. These advancements embraced old-school packet filtering and stateful inspection by delving into application awareness and, in some cases, employing machine learning techniques. By scrutinizing data at the application level, NGFWs can discern, for example, whether a user accessing port 80 (commonly used for unencrypted for web traffic) is engaging in legitimate website browsing or attempting to transport hidden malware. This application-aware approach allows organizations to control not just which ports can be used, but how applications within those ports behave. It's a crucial tactic for environments where employees rely on a multitude of cloud-based services and where unscrupulous threat actors try to hide nefarious activities behind common ports and protocols.

When viewed as a business enabling function, the value of firewalls for an organization is evident in the communications they foster. Should a cyberattack dismantle a company's infrastructure, losses can quickly accumulate from downtime, erosion of customer trust, legal ramifications, and sometimes irreversible harm to brand reputation. Firewalls contribute to business continuity by identifying suspicious behavior early, isolating infected networks and hosts, and preventing the spread of malware via lateral movement (e.g., worms, exploits, identity theft, etc.).

Today, a firewall's role extends beyond prevention to include intelligence. Activity and behavioral logs harvested from firewalls unveil patterns of attempted intrusions, malicious IP addresses, or emergent threats. Businesses able to interpret and learn from these logs can then implement advanced threat intelligence, real-time monitoring, and adaptive policies as a defensive response. Furthermore, firewalls maintain compliance and reinforce network segmentation to deliver valuable security intelligence. When businesses rely more than ever on data, remote workers, connectivity, and digital trust, the firewall's protective presence stands as both a fence and a guard against evolving threat actors.

## Intrusion Detection Systems

Intrusion detection systems (IDS) trace their origins back to the early 1980s, when computer security pioneers began seeking ways to detect unauthorized activities in increasingly interconnected networks.

In 1980, James P. Anderson authored a paper titled, "Computer Security Threat Monitoring and Surveillance," which laid the foundation for identifying and categorizing suspicious behavior. Building on Anderson's ideas, Dorothy E. Denning introduced her groundbreaking intrusion detection model in 1986. Her work established the concept of analyzing system audit trails using log data from operating systems and applications to identify anomalous behavior. During this period, research labs and universities explored host-based monitoring techniques, creating fundamental prototypes that would later evolve into more robust host-based detection mechanisms. These concepts would ultimately be merged into endpoint security solutions as the years progressed.

However, by the early 1990s, the IDS field gained momentum as network connectivity expanded, and new attack vectors emerged. Researchers shifted from purely host-based solutions to network-based IDS, analyzing packets traversing network infrastructures. (Note that, at this time, almost all network traffic was unencrypted.) This approach helped spot malicious activities, such as abnormal traffic patterns, port scans, and suspicious data payloads. Open source efforts, like Martin Roesch's Snort in 1998, propelled IDS into the mainstream by combining signature-based detection with real-time alerts. Snort's flexibility and community-driven rule sets empowered administrators to swiftly adapt to evolving threats, as commercial vendors introduced proprietary IDS solutions catering to diverse corporate needs.

CHAPTER 11   SOLUTIONS

Today, IDS plays a pivotal role in mitigating cyberattacks by providing early warning signals and facilitating rapid incident response. IDS solutions are still available as standalone technology, but they are often included as components or features within next-generation firewalls or EDR solutions.

IDS serves as an indispensable component of a layered defense strategy by continuously analyzing network traffic or host-based logs to detect deviations from normal behavior. This could be anything from an unusual spike in network bandwidth to an unexpected modification on a host itself. These alerts enable security teams to isolate compromised hosts, block malicious traffic, and update security policies to mitigate risks from the latest threats.

In addition, modern IDS solutions increasingly integrate machine learning to enhance detection accuracy, reduce false positives, and uncover advanced persistent threats. Ultimately, the history of IDS reflects a steadfast drive to protect assets. This underscores their importance in safeguarding systems and data by examining behavior on a host or network to detect malicious intent. By detecting intrusions early, IDS helps organizations respond decisively, preserving trust and continuity for business operations.

## Virtual Private Networks

The modern Internet was never designed to be accessed from a single location. Instead, its fundamental design allows access from anywhere, at any time, and by anyone. This translates to data exchange from one point to another, without a central switch, router, or firewall controlling all network traffic. Consequently, it has become more crucial than ever to ensure that communications remain both private and secure when specific, point-to-point communication is required. The virtual private network (VPN) addresses this need, becoming an absolute staple for businesses seeking to protect their communications across the open Internet.

## CHAPTER 11  SOLUTIONS

A virtual private network, in its simplest form, is a secure connection that extends a private network across a public one. For a straightforward analogy, imagine speaking into a voice changer[1] used by a musician. When the artist sings, the output could be completely unrecognizable, appearing as mere noise to the listener. However, the VPN recipient possesses a special decoder that returns the audible content to the singer's original voice. The result is that network traffic is obfuscated (encrypted) by the VPN solution and, even if "sniffed" (monitored) by a third party, the contents remain encrypted and indecipherable.

Of course, VPN solutions can transmit any type of data, and the musician analogy is simply one way to understand what happens to data in transit. As a real-world use case, imagine you are in a café with a laptop connected to public Wi-Fi, which is inherently unsafe. A VPN acts like a tunnel, enveloping your data in a protective shroud so that no prying eyes can intercept it while in transit. Indeed, VPN technology relies on encryption, and the results are decipherable only by the intended recipient.

The principle of this technology, it must be noted, is founded upon trust for network communications. When you connect to a VPN, you are effectively entrusting your data to a third-party solution that promises to protect and transmit it securely through the VPN tunnel, even though the communication is point-to-point. This typically occurs via VPN software loaded on the client device and a VPN appliance, software, or device that acts as the recipient. In a business context, this arrangement is particularly significant, as it allows employees to connect to company servers remotely without exposing sensitive information and internal assets directly to the open Internet. For example, a traveling employee in a foreign location can seamlessly access the same intranet resources they would from their office desk by using a VPN with strong encryption security protocols.

---

[1] https://www.yamaha.com/en/tech-design/research/reports/23_transvox/

CHAPTER 11   SOLUTIONS

But what does all this look like under the hood, so to speak? When a user connects to a VPN, a secure "tunnel" is established between the user's device and the VPN server. Any data that passes through this tunnel is encrypted, ensuring that even if a cybercriminal manages to "sniff" it, the content remains impenetrable. The VPN server, serving as a bridge, then sends this data out to its intended online destination. In this process, the user's IP address (an identifier akin to a digital home address) is masked, replaced by the VPN server's IP. From the vantage point of external websites or services, the traffic appears to originate from the VPN server rather than the user's actual device. This cloak of anonymity is often a key motivator for individuals and businesses alike when deciding to employ VPN solutions.

Now, from a business perspective, the benefits don't end with secure encrypted communications. For businesses operating across multiple regions, a VPN can unify different office networks under a singular, secure network. Think of it as building a wide area network with high-speed encrypted tunnels between disparate locations. For example, a European branch, American headquarters, or a newly established operation in Asia can all be connected over the Internet using a secure and encrypted tunnel. By seamlessly connecting these networks, employees can access shared resources, exchange files, and collaborate in real time without compromising the security of their communications. Figure 11-2 illustrates this connectivity.

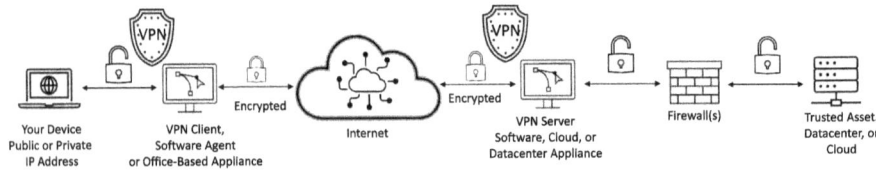

*Figure 11-2.* *Virtual private network architecture*

This is why VPN technology became so popular in the early 2000s and remains a popular technology today. However, that is slowly changing due to the reduction of on-premises technology, the shift to more software-as-a-service (SaaS) and cloud solutions, and the continued expansion of the borderless, work-from-anywhere world.

Security, collaboration, and anonymity aside, there's also the consideration of administration and cost. VPN license costs and overhead to manage and maintain them can be expensive, often requiring physical infrastructure and specialized appliances. Newer secure remote access technologies leverage existing Internet connectivity to provide a similar secure experience, but with less risk, lower administrative costs and expertise, and point-to-point communications at the application layer, versus at the network layer. With the right architecture, these can be a more flexible, scalable solution for employees, contractors, and vendors. This expands the initial "trust" principle to other entities that need access to your assets and data.

VPN technology, for all its greatness, has flaws. It's important to remember that a VPN, while robust, is not a cure-all. For instance, the security of a VPN connection is only as strong as the protocols it relies upon and the configurations implemented by the business. Outdated encryption standards, poorly configured servers, lateral movement within the network, unscrupulous VPN providers, stolen credentials, or compromised workstations can still leave vulnerabilities that cybercriminals may exploit. These reasons, along with a few more use cases, explain why VPN technology implementations are on a slow decline.

All in all, the virtual private network serves as a critical underpinning in the modern corporate environment. It unites distant offices and remote employees under a single secure umbrella, confers anonymity to sensitive operations, and ensures that data can flow securely across remote geolocations.

As threats continue to evolve, the role of VPNs will decrease in favor of remote application access, in lieu of remote network access. As we continue our cybersecurity history lesson, businesses should remain ever watchful, ever prepared, and ever committed to change technology when the risks and costs outweigh the benefits, and a better solution exists to solve the same use cases.

CHAPTER 11   SOLUTIONS

# Content Filters

While firewalls control the flow of data in and out of networks, and VPNs secure traffic from point to point, organizations of all sizes are still susceptible to content they may receive through the Internet via email, web pages, and file transfers. The solution to protect inappropriate or malicious content is content filters (email spam, web pages, images, etc.).

Content filters, at their most basic level, are solutions designed to control the information that flows in and out of an organization's network and what is appropriate to be received and rendered by an end user. A comprehensive look at content filters, especially through the lens of modern business operations, reveals a portfolio of distinctly separate solutions designed to manage threats, maintain compliance, and minimize risk.

The purpose of content filters is straightforward. Imagine a corporate environment where employees have unfettered access to the Internet. This freedom might seem like a breeding ground for creativity, but it can quickly spiral into a tangle of security risks, inappropriate content, and wasted productivity. Content filters set crucial guardrails for user behavior. The technology serves as a gatekeeper that monitors, scans, and controls online traffic to weed out malicious sites, spam or malicious emails, inappropriate images, or anything else that might compromise the network or productivity.

More than just a protective measure, these filters also support regulatory compliance. Certain industries, such as finance, healthcare, or education (Children's Internet Protection Act[2]) must abide by stringent data protection regulations. By scrutinizing outbound and inbound content, filters help ensure sensitive data doesn't leave company servers

---

[2] https://www.fcc.gov/consumers/guides/childrens-internet-protection-act

in violation of legal and ethical standards. This is crucial not only to shield a business from substantial fines, but also to protect its reputation with clients, partners, and regulators.

Content filters are not a one-size-fits-all solution. Instead, think of them as a segment of a multipronged defensive strategy. They often work in tandem with firewalls, antivirus solutions, and intrusion detection systems. Their function is to isolate and classify the nature of online content, whether it is textual, visual, or embedded in attachments. By scanning websites in real time, filters can detect harmful code or potentially objectionable materials, blocking them before they reach the end user.

While security and compliance remain top of mind, productivity is another key reason businesses deploy content filters. It's no secret that social media and streaming services can take a toll on workplace efficiency. By instituting rules that block or restrict recreational websites during work hours, organizations can preserve focus and encourage employees to stay on task.

No two businesses have the exact needs, which means deploying content filters can be a complex endeavor. An organization must consider factors such as employee privacy, organizational structure, and the nature of its industry. In some cases, too rigid a filter can hinder legitimate research or creative tasks. For example, a software developer might need to visit coding forums, even if they contain certain flagged keywords or links. Striking the right balance between security and freedom of innovation is crucial.

In addition, employee pushback can also be significant. Content filters may be seen as intrusive or overbearing, especially if they block personal activities during breaks. Therefore, transparent communication is essential. Companies should outline why filters are in place and ensure employees understand the risks they mitigate. By clarifying that the objective is not to micromanage but to protect the organization as a whole, leadership teams can secure greater adoption and compliance.

CHAPTER 11   SOLUTIONS

Today, with the progression of social engineering and malicious online content, content filters of all types form a critical line of defense. They do more than shield a business from threats; they support employee productivity, minimize risk, and facilitate smoother compliance with legal standards. By embracing clear and acceptable online policies, employing the right blend of technologies, and engaging employees with open communication, organizations can seamlessly integrate content filtering into their broader strategic framework to mitigate cyber risks.

## Secure Remote Access

Secure remote access (SRA) stands as one of the newer pillars in modern business infrastructure, especially in an era where the workforce is increasingly dispersed and secure application access is a primary concern. Today, SRA is emerging as a replacement to VPN technology for end-user access, primarily due to its application tunneling benefits compared to network tunneling. In essence, secure remote access technologies allow authorized users to connect to a company's network, systems, and resources from anywhere in the world based on applications or remote sessions—without routing all network traffic to a destination's IP range. By enabling employees, contractors, vendors, etc., to work securely and efficiently from remote locations, SRA has evolved into an extension of locally installed applications.

At the heart of modern secure remote access lies the principle of trust for anyone that an organization deems worthy of application access. This access allows only trusted, authenticated, and approved users access to critical business data and services. The process typically involves robust identity and access management (IAM) mechanisms, ensuring that each user's credentials, like passwords, tokens, biometric inputs, or multifactor authentication (MFA) codes, are verified with a high level of confidence. Every aspect of SRA ties into the broader conversation around a zero trust architecture (ZTA), where no user or device is inherently trusted, and every interaction with an application is scrutinized since access could ultimately involve third-party entities. The collaboration between SRA solutions and IAM ensures that only the right people can access the right resources, regardless of their location.

One of the most significant benefits of modern SRA technology is operational flexibility. In a world where employees are no longer confined to traditional office spaces, companies can recruit top talent from across the globe, support flexible working arrangements, and ensure business continuity during crises, such as natural disasters or public health emergencies. With the right SRA strategy in place, organizations can switch to remote operations for specific applications without the risk of a VPN that potentially opens wide swaths of networks and network traffic to exposure.

From a strategic perspective, SRA plays a crucial role in shaping a company's security posture, managing data exposure, and facilitating regulatory compliance reporting. Clients, partners, and regulatory bodies increasingly scrutinize businesses' data protection measures, and a strong SRA strategy signals that a company takes these responsibilities seriously.

Many industries, particularly those handling sensitive data, like healthcare, finance, manufacturing, and government sectors, face stringent compliance requirements for any and all application and data access. SRA solutions can help align with regulations like HIPAA, PCI DSS, and GDPR, ensuring sensitive data is managed in accordance with legal mandates, since information is rendered at the application layer or per session versus unrestricted network access as provided by other common remote access technologies.

The concept of secure connectivity is no longer a luxury, but rather an imperative that touches every facet of business, from customer trust to operational efficiency. With an increasingly global workforce and rising cyber threats, companies that fail to invest in strong secure remote access strategies put themselves at a competitive disadvantage.

CHAPTER 11   SOLUTIONS

By safeguarding remote connections through encryption, authentication, continuous monitoring, and user education, organizations ensure that the promise of modern work can be realized without sacrificing security. In short, secure remote access shapes the future of business by drawing lessons from past system hacks, enabling growth and resilience, and above all, lowering risk.

# Security Information Event Management

Logs, logs, and more logs. Nearly every piece of technology produces activity and diagnostic security logs based on interaction, activity, and operations. When a security event occurs, reviewing these logs is paramount to determining the root cause. Consolidating these logs and events before an incident is detected can streamline the forensics process. Cohesively streamlining this process is essential for determining whether a security incident is in process or about to occur, based on rules, policies, pattern matching, or AI-based analysis. This consolidation and analysis of all the security logs within an organization is the responsibility of a Security Information Event Management (SIEM) solution.

SIEMs have become the ombudsman in the modern organization's security framework serving as the focal point for all logged activity and providing comprehensive answers to any security query through a unified view of events and logs. As contemporary business operations rely on more and more technology, the risk surface increases with the addition of each new device, service, asset, database, and data. SIEM solutions are designed to collect and analyze security events and logs in real time and serve as the source of truth for any and all activity from every connected resource within an implementation.

From a broad perspective, SIEMs represent the fusion of two complementary disciplines that are no longer separate products in the industry:

- **Security Information Management (SIM):** Focuses on collecting data from various sources and storing it for long-term analysis.

- **Security Event Management (SEM):** Zeroes in on real-time monitoring, correlation, and prompt notification of potential threats through a wide variety of analysis techniques.

When the two disciplines are merged, the results enable organizations to see a more complete picture of their security and behavioral landscape. The outcome is akin to having both a historian and a police officer perform functions on the same dataset:

- The historian catalogs events from the past, making them available for extended analysis and compliance audits.

- The police officer stands alert to detect and raise alarms at the first sign of unusual activity.

In a typical deployment, a SIEM solution integrates with numerous endpoints—from servers, applications, and firewalls to routers and other devices—capturing logs and events generated across an entire network and the cloud. These logs, at first glance, can seem dauntingly voluminous. However, herein lies the true strength of SIEM. Its design is to aggregate, normalize, and contextualize massive amounts of raw data into meaningful, human-readable results. Think of it as an expert puzzle-solver who can assemble a thousand scattered pieces of log data faster than you can read this sentence. By standardizing event formats from various platforms and devices, SIEMs can more readily compare apples to oranges, identifying anomalies and suspicious patterns that a security analyst might otherwise overlook if forced to review logs manually.

CHAPTER 11   SOLUTIONS

This ability to identify anomalies and suspicious patterns by standardizing and aggregating diverse log data based on a correlation engine is the brains of most SIEM solutions. By applying rules, heuristics, and, for newer solutions, artificial intelligence, SIEM solutions can identify connections between individual events and build context around them. For instance, if a single user logs into the corporate network from two geographically distant locations within minutes of each other, the correlation engine might flag this as a probable case of compromised identity and associated credentials. In addition, advanced rule sets and machine learning algorithms can detect multistage attacks, whereas a sequence of small anomalies that seem insignificant on their own together form a clear signal of malicious intent. This primary use case is what sets SIEM platforms apart from simpler log management tools.

The function of SIEM in a business context extends well beyond mere detection. Regulatory compliance remains a major reason for adopting this technology. Whether it's GDPR in Europe, HIPAA in healthcare, or PCI-DSS in credit card processing, organizations confront a tangle of regulations requiring meticulous log tracking, alerting, and incident reporting. SIEMs streamline these tasks by automating report generation and providing a concise, centralized dashboard from which auditors can review historical and real-time data. In essence, a SIEM not only hardens defenses, but also keeps the compliance burden in check, saving both time and resources.

Another use case for SIEM lies in incident response. When an anomaly is detected, it's not enough to merely know that something unusual has taken place. Security automation in a modern enterprise is essential. Most modern SIEM platforms integrate with incident response workflows, orchestrating everything from ticket creation to automated remediation steps.

Consider a scenario where the system detects malicious traffic from a known bad actor based on content filtering or a firewall. The SIEM might automatically trigger a block at the firewall, notify the security operations center (SOC) team, and quarantine affected endpoints for further investigation. By consolidating these responses in one central console, SIEM helps reduce reaction time, minimize damage, and enhance an organization's ability to learn from each incident.

Today, Security Information Event Management represents both a philosophy and a practice. It reflects an understanding that, in an always-connected world, harnessing data for real-time threat detection and historical forensics is not merely an option but a fundamental requirement. By gathering, correlating, and analyzing events from across an environment, SIEM implementations help organizations visualize activity across their networks and applications. When combined with a well-rehearsed incident response plan and ongoing policy refinement, SIEM offers a powerful safeguard against present and emerging threats. And, as history has shown, being aware that an attack is coming, or occurring, is critical to formulating and mitigating a response.

# Vulnerability Management

By definition, vulnerability management (as outlined in *Asset Attack Vectors*[3] by Morey Haber and Brad Hibbert, 2019) is a disciplined approach to discovering and remedying software flaws in a company's technology stack. Consider it akin to regularly scheduled building inspections, where each inspection reveals a list of water leaks, wiring violations, or cracks in the foundation and supporting structure. While some issues might be cosmetic, others, if left unaddressed, can lead to the entire building crashing down. In this sense, a robust vulnerability management program helps an enterprise maintain a watchful eye on everything from aging servers and legacy applications to freshly deployed cloud-based services and the myriad endpoints employees use daily. This oversight includes identifying published vulnerabilities across these assets. What sets

---
[3] https://a.co/d/gjrzxHq

## CHAPTER 11   SOLUTIONS

vulnerability management apart from a one-time assessment is its cyclical nature. Vulnerability assessments should be performed periodically, preferably in near real time, to identify potential risks and document them as a part of a formal management process.

Much as with any continuous improvement cycle, vulnerability assessments typically begin the process by identifying risks. Specialized tools and security scanners assess the network for known vulnerabilities, including many of the threats and breaches we've seen in our history lessons: software misconfigurations, missing patches, and outdated operating systems. The findings are then analyzed, categorized, and assigned a level of severity or risk. Next, the skill of information security practitioners lies in deciphering which vulnerabilities genuinely pose a risk to the business and how quickly they should be remediated. After all, any given network could have thousands of identified vulnerabilities. An organization must choose where to focus its time and resources as a part of risk management and governance. Attempting to resolve all issues simultaneously could devote manpower to vulnerabilities that aren't truly exploitable.

This vulnerability management workflow leads naturally to prioritization. Not all vulnerabilities are created equal, and the stakes vary widely. The presence of a remotely exploitable flaw on a critical server, for instance, will typically demand immediate action. Meanwhile, an easily exploitable weakness in a noncritical system might rank below a more complex but business-essential risk. This is where cross-functional collaboration discussions and established policies for prioritization become important. Effective vulnerability management teams do not operate in a vacuum; instead, they coordinate with IT, development, and leadership. Each stakeholder brings invaluable insight into the operational requirements and strategic objectives of the business. By cross-referencing threat intelligence, compliance obligations, and organizational priorities, teams can better assess which vulnerabilities pose the greatest risk and should be remediated first.

CHAPTER 11  SOLUTIONS

The workflow of vulnerability assessments doesn't stop at risk identification and the passing of information to patch management teams (an approach that largely ended in the early 2010s). Today, organizations rarely pause operations simply because a patch needs to be applied or a configuration needs to be revised. Many industries function on 24/7 cycles, with only the slimmest maintenance windows available. Rolling out a series of patches for operating systems or company-wide applications can be as delicate as brain surgery. Any operation changes and patch deployment must be tested in controlled environments, adhere to change control procedures, and be accompanied by comprehensive communication to all potentially affected personnel. For certain high-risk vulnerabilities, emergency measures may even be required during business hours.

Finally, the cycle doesn't end with a newly patched server or a fresh firewall configuration—verification is essential. Postremediation scans and tests confirm that vulnerabilities have been adequately addressed. Just as doctors might schedule a follow-up appointment to ensure their patient is healing well, a vulnerability assessment and potential penetration test checks whether the fix has completely remediated the risk without creating new findings. Subsequently, the lessons learned from each assessment feed into future policy and procedure refinements. This iterative cycle cultivates a culture of constant improvement, ensuring the business remains proactive, rather than reactive, in the face of new attack vectors.

For many organizations, vulnerability management also serves as a bridge to broader governance, risk, and compliance (GRC) frameworks. As regulatory compliance continues to evolve, organizations are, too, becoming more security conscious. It's imperative that they can demonstrate a mature vulnerability management program including patch management. Indeed, their security maturity in this regard can either give them the edge to win a lucrative contract or cause them to lose out to a competitor based on their own auditable processes. It's not only about internal security, but also the business's ability to satisfy auditor requirements and potentially demonstrate a secure computing environment necessary to secure future business.

CHAPTER 11   SOLUTIONS

Vulnerability management remains an indispensable process for business continuity. It ensures an enterprise's deployed and future technology is robust enough to support day-to-day operations, while gracefully evolving alongside new innovations and software development. Vulnerability management is a cyclical process, and a disciplined methodology—from identification to verification—helps organizations methodically stay ahead of threat actors, regulatory changes, and the breaches that can ensue from unmitigated vulnerabilities. After all, as history has shown, vulnerable assets that are easily exploitable are prime targets for threat actors. Why an organization wouldn't invest in remediating them in a timely manner, given all the lessons learned to date, still baffles most cybersecurity professionals.

## Penetration Testing

Penetration testing, often referred to as "pentesting," is a proactive method of assessing an organization's cybersecurity posture by simulating real-world attacks on its infrastructure, applications, and networks via vulnerabilities and their associated exploits. Penetration testers, referred to as "pentesters," act as ethical hackers, seeking out system vulnerabilities before threat actors do. This practice not only reveals which vulnerabilities are truly exploitable but also provides evidence to vulnerability management teams for prioritizing remediation. In today's threat landscape, it's no exaggeration to say that hacking your own systems does have risk. With that aside, wouldn't you want your own trusted team to prove something is a risk versus a threat actor proving so by infiltrating your environment?

From the moment a business stands up its first Internet-facing service or web application, it announces to the world that countless attack vectors are possible from known vulnerabilities that are not patched, or from potential vulnerabilities that will be identified over time. These threats can manifest as opportunistic attacks by unsophisticated hackers or as deliberate, highly orchestrated campaigns by nation-state threat actors.

Penetration testing serves as an empirical line of defense by continuously challenging digital services, just as a potential threat actor would. In essence, penetration testing aligns with the principle of "trust but verify." Even if an organization has implemented sophisticated security controls, adopted a modern security policy, and trained its employees extensively, it's still wise to assume that something might have been missed or be vulnerable through shadow IT. Penetration testing provides the reality check that businesses need. Just as with vulnerability management, pentesting should be a cyclical process to continuously test against all the layers of technology deployed within an organization. This is true for every asset and every solution, including other security solutions themselves. After all, every piece of technology deployed has a risk surface, including the tools used to defend the organization.

Penetration testing also has a direct impact on regulatory compliance and client confidence. Many industries, such as finance, healthcare, and retail, must abide by stringent data protection standards based on regional regulatory laws. Failing to demonstrate due diligence in securing systems can result in costly fines or regulatory action. On the flip side, regularly scheduled tests and the consequent improvements not only help ensure alignment with compliance initiatives but also become a powerful testimonial of the company's commitment to security and the mitigation of identified risks. This supports some of the incident response planning and rehearsals (tabletop exercises) we have touched upon earlier in this book. By understanding how threat actors might breach their environment, organizations can refine their incident response plans.

Controlled testing uncovers not only potential entry points, but also reveals how quickly internal teams can detect, contain, and remediate threats. Many times, the difference between a minor security incident and a major data breach boils down to the speed and efficiency of the response. This is commonly referred to as dwell time. A well-prepared incident response plan, shaped by the insights gleaned from managed penetration testing, can minimize damage and downtime.

CHAPTER 11   SOLUTIONS

Ultimately, penetration testing is not a standalone exercise, but rather a pivotal aspect of a multipronged security strategy. It aligns with robust policies, continuous monitoring, employee training, threat intelligence, and incident response plans. By adopting a holistic vulnerability management and penetration testing approach, businesses can fully prioritize risk identification and remediation.

As networks become more complex and threat actors grow more sophisticated, it's this ongoing, iterative commitment to testing and improvement that helps companies safeguard their data, fulfill regulatory obligations, and maintain trust. And, as history has yet again shown us, identification and remediation of risks is the first step in secure computing and preventing the latest attack vectors.

# Data Loss Prevention

Regardless of a threat actor's intent, the data contained within information technology systems can be compromised in only two different ways:

- **Denial of Service (DOS):** Data becomes inaccessible due to an outage, ransomware, deletion, corruption, or service interruption.

- **Stolen:** Data—regardless of its sensitivity—is copied, stolen, or leaked to an unauthorized entity outside of the organization.

As a discipline, data loss prevention (DLP) is designed to ensure that data, regardless of its type, stays only within authorized systems and that only approved users can access, copy, or alter information. No matter the industry—be it finance, healthcare, retail, or technology—data forms the intellectual property by which operations are measured, analyzed, and propelled forward.

At the same time, data is a prize for threat actors who seek to exploit vulnerabilities. As cyberattacks have progressed over the years with tactics such as ransomware, phishing, and advanced persistent threats, organizations of every size stand to lose if their data is compromised. That's where DLP steps in, acting as a security discipline with a wide variety of solutions to guard proprietary information, customer details, and intellectual property from inappropriate behaviors. DLP is not just one security tool; it's a business function that leverages many cybersecurity tools to achieve its goals. DLP can encompass endpoint security solutions (previously discussed), dedicated technology, and configuration options to stop file transfers, block removable media, inspect visibly seen onscreen content, and so on.

To better grasp the scope of DLP, consider its formal definition and the following use cases:

1. **Defining Data Loss Prevention:** DLP is both a strategy and a set of solutions designed to detect and prevent the unauthorized transmission, disclosure, or deletion of sensitive information. In other words, it ensures that confidential data—ranging from trade secrets to personal identifiable information—stays where it should be and is used in compliance with internal policies and external regulations. The overarching goal is to maintain the confidentiality, integrity, and availability of data, so organizations can better protect their competitive advantages and meet stringent legal obligations.

2. **The Importance of Data Loss Prevention:** The significance of DLP in the modern business environment can't be overstated. The legal and financial repercussions of a data breach can be astronomical, encompassing fines, lawsuits, and

compensation payouts. Beyond the monetary toll lies something more intangible to the health of a business: its reputation. When headlines announce a major breach, public trust erodes. Customers become wary, partners grow cautious, and future deals can be compromised. DLP solutions reinforce confidence among stakeholders, signaling that the organization is serious about safeguarding data, and, by extension, the trust vested in them. In addition, regulatory agencies worldwide, from the European Union's GDPR to the US state-level privacy laws, all require the protection of data. Noncompliance not only leads to hefty penalties but also endangers the long-term viability of the organization's operations.

3. **Functional Data Loss Prevention Requirements:** DLP programs often revolve around three core functional areas and use cases:

    - **Visibility:** Enables organizations to identify where their data resides—whether on local machines, in the cloud, or in transit between endpoints— and categorize it according to risk profiles. Understanding the nature and location of data is crucial; you can't protect what you can't see.

    - **Monitoring:** Ensures that any transfer or usage of data is tracked in real time. Advanced DLP solutions can monitor everything from email attachments to cloud-based file sharing, instantly flagging anomalies or policy breaches. If, for instance, an employee attempts to email a customer database to a personal address, DLP systems raise immediate alerts or block the transfer altogether.

- **Enforcement:** Refers to the mechanism through which DLP takes corrective action, either by restricting access, encrypting files, or quarantining suspicious activity. These enforcement measures mitigate human error and malicious intent alike, ensuring sensitive data remains behind carefully guarded virtual walls.

And again, it can take multiple solutions and tools to achieve these use cases across a modern enterprise.

4. **Integrations:** DLP rarely operates in isolation. For it to be effective, it must integrate seamlessly with other security layers. Firewalls, intrusion detection systems, and endpoint security measures all play supporting roles. DLP solutions may work alongside threat intelligence platforms to stay updated on emerging risks, or tie into identity and access management (IAM) systems so that user permissions are enforced in a granular manner. When integrated properly, DLP becomes part of a holistic cybersecurity strategy that adapts to evolving threats and ensures protective efforts remain both consistent and comprehensive.

5. **The Human Element:** A robust DLP initiative recognizes that data breaches often occur due to human factors, whether accidental or malicious. Corporate culture plays a key part in DLP's success. It's not enough to install sophisticated monitoring software and then wait for alerts. Employees must be educated about cybersecurity best practices, data handling guidelines, and the consequences

of noncompliance. Regular training sessions, workshops, and clear policies help cultivate a sense of shared responsibility. When everyone understands the value of data and the risks of mishandling it, the organization as a whole becomes a shield against data leakage.

6. **Business Functions:** DLP is more than a technological safeguard; it's a business function that touches multiple layers of an organization. From the legal department worried about compliance to the marketing team entrusted with large volumes of customer data, every department has a stake in the effective prevention of data loss.

7. **Implementation:** Rolling out a successful DLP solution demands thoughtful planning and cross-functional collaboration. An organization must first conduct a comprehensive risk assessment to identify and locate all sensitive data, potential vulnerabilities, and the stakeholders involved. This evaluation informs the choice of DLP solutions, ranging from endpoint-based tools to network and cloud-based systems. Next comes the pilot phase, where the chosen technology is tested in a trusted beta group, measuring its accuracy in flagging risks without overloading teams with false positives. Once the pilot is successful, the DLP solution is rolled out in stages, accompanied by training sessions for staff and ongoing monitoring to ensure the system adapts to real-world conditions and allows for approved exceptions.

8. **The Future:** As businesses increasingly move data to the cloud and adopt remote work models, DLP continues to evolve. Today's solutions employ machine learning and AI-driven analytics to detect even subtle anomalies. Additionally, the scope of what constitutes "sensitive data" is broadening, as regulations tighten around biometric data, genetic information, and geolocation data. The future promises more intelligent, context-aware solutions capable of dynamic adaptation, further extending the protection of all data types.

Data loss prevention stands as a cornerstone of modern enterprise security. It reinforces organizational resilience, safeguards brand reputation, and aligns with ever-evolving regulatory mandates. By offering visibility, monitoring, and enforcement mechanisms, DLP addresses both external and internal threats, whether malicious or accidental in nature. Most importantly, it doesn't merely lock data behind barriers; it instills a culture of security, ensuring that every employee, from the mailroom to the boardroom, understands the intrinsic value of information and what can happen if it's compromised.

# Identity and Access Management

Identity and access management (IAM) may, at first glance, appear to be a purely technological construct to address user access and permissions. In reality, IAM encompasses a sophisticated conglomeration of protocols, permissions, and cryptic passkeys that address access on a need-to-know basis, least privilege, and regulatory compliance initiatives.

At its core, IAM is a business enabler that orchestrates enterprise access. It unites digital and human elements covering processes, technologies, and policies around a central premise: the right people

CHAPTER 11   SOLUTIONS

should have the right access at the right time. The simplicity of that statement contradicts its depth, for IAM is about more than just letting an employee log into a workstation. It provides the structure and oversight organizations need to protect their data, maintain compliance, and streamline operations. That complexity is represented in all the primary security disciplines that currently make up IAM, illustrated in 11-3.

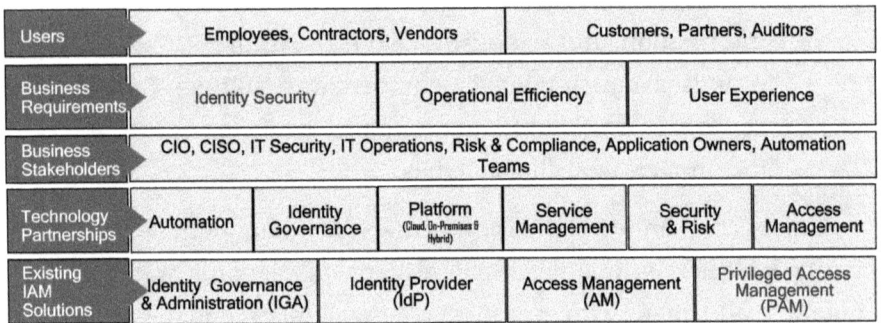

*Figure 11-3. A complete IAM architecture illustrated as a block diagram*

One of the remarkable things about IAM is how it touches every part of a modern organization, though many employees seldom realize it. When you open a new SaaS application, it's IAM that authenticates you. When HR onboards a fresh hire and grants them access to relevant systems, it's IAM that ensures they are assigned the correct permissions. When an external partner accesses a shared portal, IAM polices that gateway. In each instance, the invisible orchestration of IAM arranges who gets in, what they can see, and how their actions are monitored.

At its most foundational, IAM begins with the creation and management of identities and their associated accounts. In a business context, identities encompass more than just the human usernames and passwords a trusted individual uses to log in; they also include nonhuman identities (NHI) or machine identities. These identifies include all the distinguishing attributes (name, department, role, security clearances, owner for NHI, etc.) that define someone (or something) within the organization's network. Software components, application-to-application communications, integrations, and automated workflows also have some form of identities and accounts, enabling electronic services to communicate securely with one another. Managing these identities means ensuring they are accurate, consistent, and up to date.

Once identities are established, IAM addresses the question of access: what should each identity be able to do? This is where policies, roles, privileges, entitlements, and permissions converge to shape the degree of access. Role-based access control (RBAC) remains a hallmark of IAM, assigning users to roles (e.g., "Finance Analyst," "IT Administrator") that will predefine the level of access they require. More modern approaches, like policy-based access control (PBAC), further refine this principle by examining dynamic attributes such as location, device type, or time of day before granting entry. Taken together, these measures allow organizations to uphold the principle of least privilege, a security best practice that dictates users receive only the privileges necessary to perform their duties. After all, if a threat actor gains excessive privileges, as we have seen from history, they can essentially "own" an organization.

Governance, oversight, and compliance reporting are crucial to demonstrating IAM success. IAM is, after all, the bridge to regulatory compliance. Whether an organization is bound by GDPR, HIPAA, SOX, or any other alphabet soup of regulations, there are common denominators: data security, privacy, and auditability. IAM solutions ensure only authorized personnel can access sensitive data, which is crucial for maintaining compliance. In addition, audit trails and records of who accessed what and when prove essential for demonstrating adherence to governing bodies.

By seamlessly integrating compliance controls with operational processes, IAM not only reduces the burden on internal teams, but also instills confidence in stakeholders that the business handles data responsibly. Governance stands as the framework that ensures processes are followed, audits are conducted, and user access remains aligned with regulatory mandates and internal policies. From a practical viewpoint, governance is what compels businesses to routinely review user access (especially for employees in sensitive positions) and to perform account revocation for unnecessary privileges or changes as part of the joiner, mover, and leaver cycle. (If this topic interests you, please review *Identity Attack Vectors*,[4] Haber and Rolls 2024.)

Another oft-overlooked dimension is the positive impact of IAM on user experience and productivity. Effective IAM embraces single sign-on (SSO), privileged access management (PAM), and multifactor authentication (MFA) for employees juggling a multitude of applications with different privileges. This implies streamlined provisioning processes that eliminate the lag time between a new hire's first day and their access to the tools they need. It means automated workflows that reduce manual errors and free up the IT department to work on strategic projects rather than resetting passwords or tinkering with isolated user directories. Ultimately, the pursuit of a seamless user experience supports the goal of enhancing user efficiency, while maintaining strong security standards that address the threats of the past and future.

Today, IAM is the foundation against identity-based attacks. Through the years, IAM vulnerabilities have provided a critical path for threat actors to compromise an organization. IAM is a multifaceted discipline that straddles technology, governance, user experience, and corporate culture. Moving into the future, IAM must be viewed as a foundational element and an enabler that grants the right people the right privileges at precisely the right moments. When threat actors can insert themselves into this process, or compromise an identity, their actions can mimic trusted identities and infiltrate organizations. Strong IAM practices help to ensure that this attack vector is unlikely, and if it does occur, the detection methods—from endpoint security through SIEM, and identity security—can promptly identify the attack.

---

[4] https://a.co/d/57CPKTb

CHAPTER 11   SOLUTIONS

# Identity Security

As we've discussed the history of cyberattacks, it should now be apparent that a single compromised account can jeopardize an entire enterprise. To that end, the security of identity and access management (IAM) itself and its implementation within an organization demands a dedicated cybersecurity strategy. Identity security has emerged as an indispensable safeguard for everything identity-related in response to modern threats. This includes subdisciplines like PAM, CIEM, ITDR, SSO, MFA, etc., all of which manage identities, authentication, and access, but can be compromised like any other solution and become the initial attack vector in a breach.

Identity security is not merely about controlling who uses IAM solutions, but rather a complete discipline to log, audit, and ensure that all identities, regardless of type, are behaving within expected parameters based on the solutions used to manage them. By examining what identity security entails, and why it functions as a guard in modern enterprises, we can better grasp how IAM is functioning and any risks that may emerge from its implementation.

Identity security, at its core, focuses on verifying a user's identity and monitoring what the user can do once authenticated, a process often invoked by IAM's automation or adjacent IAM solutions. Consider a new employee walking into the company on their first day: behind the scenes, identity security processes monitor their onboarding in tandem with human resources and IT. The employee receives credentials, often linked directly to the company's identity provider or directory services, and gains access to the single sign-on (SSO) portal. Those credentials grant them the specific privileges needed for their role. If this person later moves into a different department, identity security tools automatically monitor their permissions, ensuring they retain only the privileges they need for their new position. When the employee eventually departs the organization, the same identity security solutions verify their access across all systems has been revoked, sealing any potential backdoors.

This lifecycle approach is critical in upholding the principle of "least privilege," wherein users get exactly the level of access needed—no more, no less. Too often, businesses discover hidden pitfalls in outdated or poorly maintained identity systems. A user might accumulate permissions over multiple years and roles, granting them unintentional access to databases and critical tools they no longer need. From a security perspective, every extra privilege opens another possible avenue for malicious actors. Identity security ensures each account remains tightly controlled and monitored, thereby reducing risk and promoting both compliance and operational efficiency, regardless of which IAM tools are used to create these processes.

Beyond user provisioning and de-provisioning, identity security also monitors behavior. A robust identity security solution can detect unusual activity, such as an insider threat actor downloading vast amounts of data late into the night, or an employee logging in from two countries within a short time frame. Such anomalies can be flagged and promptly investigated, minimizing potential data breaches.

Organizations that adopt identity security as an integral function stand on firm legal and ethical ground. For many regulated industries, like finance, healthcare, and government, strict guidelines demand that businesses know exactly who has access to what systems and precisely when that access is granted or revoked. Failing to maintain identity security controls could lead to noncompliance with critical regulations such as the General Data Protection Regulation (GDPR) or the Health Insurance Portability and Accountability Act (HIPAA). Noncompliance can prove costly from both a financial and reputational perspective. Identity security, in this sense, serves not only to protect against external threats, but also to maintain a company's standing with regulators, clients, and the public.

CHAPTER 11  SOLUTIONS

As enterprises increasingly migrate to the cloud, adopt software-as-a-service (SaaS) platforms, and rely on remote work, the importance of strong identity security becomes even more critical to combat new attack vectors. Today, identity security is the guard on which modern business stands, enabling flexibility, collaboration, and trust through extensive monitoring of everything related to IAM processes. Identity security ensures every digital identity is properly accounted for and its usage is appropriate.

## Identity Governance

In any large enterprise, it's been my experience that no single individual understands all the complexity around their IAM implement. The identity governance (IG) security discipline focuses on creating a clear picture of all identities through processes, systems, and attestation reporting. IG and, by extension, identity governance and administration (IGA) ensure that the right individuals have appropriate access to technology resources at the right times and help certify that identity-based exposure is not unchecked.

By design, identity governance orchestrates how employees, contractors, partners, and even customers interact with a business's digital assets, balancing security, compliance, and efficiency. Identity governance is a subset of IAM and differs from identity security in one distinct way. IG automates and instruments the management of identities from creation to deletion, while identity security focuses on monitoring everything related to that identity during its normal runtime and interactions within an environment. With that said, it's important to note that this distinction is blurry. Just as anti-spyware has merged with antivirus solutions, identity security is slowly becoming a component of other IAM solutions, like privileged access management (PAM) and IGA.

# CHAPTER 11  SOLUTIONS

Identity governance, at its core, is about policy-driven identity management. On the surface, granting someone access to a system might seem straightforward: a new employee joins, you provide them with login credentials, and they are ready to work. However, beneath this simplicity lies a myriad of tasks to be performed and a mountain of potential risks, especially as organizations expand, roles shift, and regulations change. This is why identity governance goes beyond mere "identity and access control." It establishes the policies, processes, and controls that ensure each user only has the permissions they need for their given business role. The objective is not to hamper business by defining what is appropriate for every employee, but rather to cultivate a secure environment where stakeholders can confidently operate, share information, and collaborate without exposing the organization to unnecessary attack vectors.

In practice, identity governance comprises several key use cases. Access requests, as an example, require approvals from managers to grant access to a resource. Rather than employees hunting down system administrators to grant or revoke permissions, well-structured identity governance solutions offer self-service portals with clear workflows and approval mechanisms to streamline the process. This function goes hand-in-hand with certification reviews or attestation reporting. Periodically, managers or designated reviewers confirm that users still require the privileges they've been assigned. This ongoing governance deters "permission creep" and helps organizations remain compliant with regulatory compliance initiatives. Additionally, sophisticated analytics and reporting capabilities allow auditors to trace when, where, and why access was granted or revoked, boosting accountability throughout the organization.

Today, identity governance is far more than a set of technical controls and solutions. It has become a living philosophy of mindful stewardship over application access and data governance. By ensuring each identity and account relationship is accurately created, modified, or destroyed based on their legitimate needs, organizations lessen threat exposure, reduce compliance headaches, and cultivate trust among their employees, contractors, and vendors.

Properly implemented, identity governance is akin to a well-oiled lock-and-key mechanism, opening doors that should be opened and securing those that should remain shut, in the form of identity and account management. As businesses look to the future, where data, machine learning, and interconnected services continue to fuel innovation, identity governance will only grow in importance to ensure threat actors don't compromise, create, or even delete the identities and accounts needed to operate a business. After all, if a threat actor can create their own administrator or root account with no one noticing, they've essentially jeopardized the entire organization.

## Identity Provider

Today, it's become a forgone conclusion that it's easier for a threat actor to log in as opposed to hacking in. This rings true because, in this era of dissolved perimeters, edge computing, identity proliferation (especially machine/nonhuman identities), and work-from-anywhere, "identity" is the most fertile attack surface for threat actors.

Identities can be loosely assembled across an organization (local accounts) and managed by identity governance solutions or centrally orchestrated via an identity provider (IdP) solution (preferred). Through this crucial piece of infrastructure, enterprises can orchestrate secure user authentication, centralized identity management (cradle to grave), and manage access to a wide variety of resources, on-premises or in the cloud. The goal of a centralized identity provider is not only to reduce the risk of data breaches due to inconsistencies in identity and account management, but also to foster efficiencies by streamlining the login experience for employees, partners, contractors, vendors, and customers alike.

CHAPTER 11   SOLUTIONS

At its core, an identity provider is often a cloud-based service that creates, stores, and manages digital identities and associated accounts. Rather than juggling multiple sets of login credentials, a user interacts with an IdP once, typically during a single sign-on (SSO) process. The IdP then authenticates the user's identity and delivers secure tokens or assertions to multiple software applications on the user's behalf. This reduces the friction often associated with repetitive logins and password resets and enables end users to switch between systems without reauthenticating on every single one.

From a practical standpoint, consider an employee who needs to access customer relationship management (CRM) software, an internal project management platform, and a billing system. Without an IdP, this might require three separate sets of login credentials, three unique passwords, and a complex workflow for managing three separate systems. With a centralized identity infrastructure, including IdP and IGA, the user logs in once, and the infrastructure handles the rest, providing authentication tokens to all relevant applications. In turn, identity security solutions like Identity Threat Detection and Response (ITDR) monitor for inappropriate behavior or errant changes in privileges. This allows an identity provider to play a profound role in bolstering enterprise security.

When an organization embraces a complete identity management system, it enforces consistent security policies and automation. Whether the enterprise has a few hundred employees or spans a global workforce of thousands, the IdP oversees everything from enforcing password complexity all the way through multifactor authentication (MFA) enforcement. This enforcement of best practices helps prevent common vulnerabilities we've seen in the past, like weak, shared, and reused passwords. Best practices should also include oversight and alerting of administrators whenever there are suspicious account activities, such as logins from unrecognized devices or unexpected geolocations.

CHAPTER 11 SOLUTIONS

One of the primary functions of an identity provider is extensive integrations with other IAM solutions and other vendors across the entire landscape of digital solutions. The IdP performs this function using various protocols and standards within the identity and access management (IAM) ecosystem. Commonly used protocols include Security Assertion Markup Language (SAML), OAuth 2.0, and OpenID Connect. By leveraging these open standards, the IdP can grant or deny access to external systems, such as cloud-based applications or partner networks, without forcing each separate platform to store credentials locally. In effect, the IdP functions like a gatekeeper, bridging communication between different services, each with its own architectural nuances. This interoperability ensures businesses that rely on external partners or software-as-a-service (SaaS) applications can confidently implement concepts like least privilege and just-in-time access without building unique workflows for each and every application.

Today, an identity provider is much more than just an identity database and authentication mechanism. It's an integrated solution within IAM that ties together an organization's digital footprint, enabling secure, efficient, and user-friendly access to a wide variety of applications and services. By standardizing authentication processes, integrating proven security protocols, and automating the administration of user accounts, the IdP significantly reduces risk while maximizing productivity. By consolidating the management of identities and use cases for authenticated access, IdPs solve modern challenges present in current identity attack vectors.

## Single Sign-On

Single sign-on (SSO) is the underrated hero of modern corporate access and security. It's a vehicle that lets a single credential (like a username, password, and MFA) unlock access to an entire estate of enterprise applications and systems that have been assigned to a role. If you've ever

CHAPTER 11   SOLUTIONS

found yourself breathing a sigh of relief when that one authenticated login got you into your email, your project management platform, your data analytics tool, and even that fancy new HR portal, you've experienced the power and authentication consolidation of SSO. Today, where employees juggle an ever-expanding assortment of applications, SSO quietly coordinates an authentication balancing act by making everyone's job easier. SSO means only having to remember one complex password to get access to multiple systems/applications, requiring authentication once per session, all while fortifying cybersecurity.

So how does SSO work? Think of it as a trusted doorman in a building filled with multiple rooms (applications). Without SSO, you'd have to knock on each door, present your ID, maybe answer a few annoying questions (multifactor verifications), and only then would you be permitted restricted entry. With SSO, you present your credentials once to the doorman; they verify your identity and then vouch for you to enter all the other rooms within the building. That doorman is typically an identity provider (IdP), a system specifically designed to verify your credentials and pass authentication tokens around the building. As you move from room to room (application to application), that one token works like all an-access day pass to your favorite theme park, telling each new attraction (application), "They have been verified with confidence; let them in."

From a cybersecurity standpoint, this arrangement is incredibly beneficial. SSO isn't just a convenience feature for employees who are tired of memorizing hundreds of passwords (or worse, storing them in sticky notes under their keyboards or in a notepad on their mobile device). Rather, it's a strategic measure to prevent security authentication vulnerabilities. When employees are asked to manage multiple passwords across numerous platforms, people often settle for easily guessable credentials or rely on the same password for everything, creating two major cybersecurity risks. SSO consolidates password management and lessens the chance of insecure workarounds. Additionally, because the entire authentication process is automated and centralized, businesses can also enforce additional security policies like MFA or biometric checks for all human identities. Instead of applying these layers of security to every piece of software, administrators can enforce them once, ensuring a consistent and higher standard for best practices everywhere.

In addition, SSO helps reduce the overhead costs of IT and service desk support. If you've ever worked the helpdesk lines, you know the number of calls related to lost or locked-out passwords can be downright staggering. By giving everyone a single set of credentials to remember, the total volume of password resets naturally drops. SSO's role in modern businesses goes beyond employee convenience for individual departments. It's also critical for compliance and regulatory requirements. Whether an organization must adhere to HIPAA, GDPR, FINRA, or other industry-specific regulations, demonstrating sound identity management practices is often mandatory. Centralizing authentication data with SSO means that documenting and auditing user access becomes markedly simpler and easier to evaluate, especially when connected to Identity Security solutions.

Today, SSO's rise underscores a broader truth about technology in the workplace: that behind every streamlined workflow, every reduced error margin, and every cut in administrative overhead, there is a well-designed system that remains mostly invisible to end users. Single sign-on is precisely that: a gateway to a better, more efficient business environment. It's the doorman, the box office, the theme park ticket taker, all wrapped into one. If you're looking to usher your organization into a more secure, user-friendly future, SSO is one of the first and best steps to address future cybersecurity concerns and mitigate many of the risks of the past.

## Multifactor Authentication

Based on an analysis of past cybersecurity breaches, stealing a username and password is a highly common and successful tactic attackers use to gain unauthorized access to an organization and its resources. Truth be

CHAPTER 11  SOLUTIONS

told, credentials are simple secrets that make it too easy for threat actors to compromise an environment when poor password management practices are the norm. When poor identity hygiene is involved, it's only a matter of when, not if, an identity compromise will occur.

Widely adopted across diverse industries today, multifactor authentication (MFA) provides a high confidence in authentication by verifying that the credentials used are from the individual who owns them. When properly deployed, MFA provides additional safeguards against unauthorized access and thus stands as a basis of modern cybersecurity best practices.

At its core, multifactor authentication is a layered security system that requires individuals to verify their identities through two or more independent mechanisms before gaining access to a resource, application, or system. MFA mechanisms generally require satisfaction in these three categories to provide confidence in an identity:

1. **"Something you know":** Most often takes the form of a password or a passphrase as part of your credentials.

2. **"Something you have":** Could be a mobile device, security token, or smart card that contains a unique verification code.

3. **"Something you are":** Might be a biometric identifier such as a fingerprint, facial recognition data, or an iris scan that is unique to your identity.

The inclusion of multiple factors ensures that, if one layer is compromised—like an employee's password—access can still be denied, unless the threat actor possesses the other two required factors.

Multifactor authentication isn't a new concept, though its modern incarnation is shaped by ever-increasing cyberattacks against digital identities. Consider, for example, the physical equivalent for building access. In the past, the usage of both a physical key and a photo ID card might have been required to authorize access at high-security facilities. Even before the digital age, such methods exemplified two distinct factors of authentication: possessing the key (something you have) and matching an identification photo (something you are). Today, however, with cyberattacks occurring any place a device is connected to the Internet, the attack vectors have changed, and a physical presence for authentication is no longer a trusted method to gain access. Thus, MFA transitioned from a convenience or optional feature to a mainstream necessity.

MFA supports regulatory compliance regulations to ensure only the appropriate individuals have access to the applications and data governed by their business roles. Many data protection standards, such as the GDPR, HIPAA, and PCI DSS, either explicitly or implicitly require multifactor authentication as part of their stringent security frameworks. Demonstrating proactive compliance helps businesses avoid punitive fines, legal liabilities, and damaging publicity due to inadequate security practices.

Today, organizations can select from an array of MFA methods, each tailored to different levels of security requirements and user convenience. A common example combines a traditional password with a one-time code generated in a dedicated authenticator application. This approach works well for large, distributed teams that rely on mobile devices as a primary means of communication. SMS texting however is considered insecure and should not be used for business MFA. Unfortunately, this is a common approach for business to consumer grade security.

Another MFA method involves hardware tokens that generate time-based codes; though arguably more secure than text message codes, they can be more cumbersome to manage at scale because they are frequently lost, damaged, or stolen. In addition, biometric verification, such as fingerprint or facial recognition, is increasingly popular in environments requiring high levels of confidence in a user's identity. Their advantage is that these factors are nearly impossible to replicate, although concerns

CHAPTER 11   SOLUTIONS

about privacy and data protection must be carefully addressed. When these techniques are merged with some advanced implementations, like geolocation or device health and hygiene monitoring, the level of assurance helps businesses strike an effective balance between rigorous security measures and user convenience.

Today, multifactor authentication, when viewed in isolation, may appear as one item in a long list of security controls. Yet, in today's interconnected and attack vector-riddled world, MFA stands out as an essential security control against malicious intrusions. By requiring multiple forms of proof, MFA reduces the risk of compromised credentials, ensures compliance with regulatory mandates, and instills greater confidence among all stakeholders that access is appropriately delegated with confidence, to mitigate modern identity attack vectors.

## Privileged Access Management

Privileged access management (PAM) is one of the most critical protective mechanisms an organization can implement. To paint a thorough picture, consider the modern workplace with intricate complexities that no one person in the organization knows everything about. It's a city of applications, access, privileges, and residents that navigate streets, alleys, tunnels, and public transportation on a daily basis. To that end, its systems, networks, and databases bridge the distance between departments, and the streets crisscross city districts. In such a world (city), employees and various automated processes step in and out to perform the construction of new buildings and maintain existing infrastructure. Each time this occurs, privileges are required to perform these tasks and should be protected from everyday citizens to prevent a mistake or compromise a mission-critical service. These elevated tasks demand the right privileges to fulfill their responsibilities, like servicing a traffic light or pouring the foundation for a new building. In this metaphor, PAM emerges as the

CHAPTER 11  SOLUTIONS

system that ensures the right individuals have the right keys to the city's ongoing maintenance functions and new construction. After all, you wouldn't want a street food vendor having the ability to decide when the subway schedule operates and how close the trains can operate on the same track.

Privilege is not always about grand authority figures wielding absolute control (root or administrator) within an organization's technology landscape. The term "privileged access" covers any form of elevated permission that grants a user or system greater command over business processes than ordinary (standard user) accounts. This might be a senior systems administrator who can alter critical server configurations, or a database administrator with the power to access and extract confidential data. In some businesses, privileged access lies in the hands of third-party contractors brought in to optimize certain components as a part of managed services. The broader reality is this: any entity holding privileged rights automatically becomes a potential vulnerability if access is abused.

To understand PAM, you must picture it as a robust suite of policies, processes, and tools designed to oversee and control these powerful accounts. It imposes the principle of "least privilege," ensuring that individuals have only the precise level of access they need, precisely when they need it. But while the principle of least privilege might read as a straightforward statement, its real power comes from how it's implemented, and that is where PAM solutions support a wide variety of use cases to accomplish their goals. The principle of least privilege stipulates that a user should possess only the minimum permissions required to fulfill their responsibilities. Whether it's a network engineer accessing infrastructure or a marketing specialist managing social media channels, limiting privileges helps reduce the attack surface. In the event of a malicious actor or an insider threat, the damage in a least privilege environment is contained because the compromised privileged account lacks the rights to extend its reach through the organization.

## CHAPTER 11  SOLUTIONS

At the heart of any effective PAM implementation is the discovery, inventory, and management of privileged accounts themselves (both human and nonhuman). Often, organizations lose track of how many privileged accounts actually exist, or which departments rely on them. Over time, especially as workplaces expand or transition to the cloud, unmonitored privileged accounts can pile up like forgotten skeleton keys in old, dusty drawers.

In a typical PAM environment, discovering privileged accounts is only the first step. This process will typically include auto-onboarding and categorizing accounts by risk level. During this process, dormant privileged accounts—those not being actively used—should also be identified and removed if they are no longer needed. PAM solutions help businesses rotate, store, and protect privileged credentials within secure vaults, safes, or encrypted repositories. Every time a privileged user needs to enter a particular system, they check out the required credentials from the vault using an approved workflow designed and designated for their role. Once the user finishes their task, the password is typically changed automatically, closing the door behind them and preventing credential theft. This practice prevents multiple individuals from quietly reusing static credentials and drastically reduces the window of opportunity for a malicious actor to capitalize on a stolen or hacked password. It also provides accountability, as each password checkout can be tied back to a specific event and user, creating an audit trail of activity and session monitoring for behavioral analysis.

For modern enterprises, the PAM function extends far beyond just protective measures for privileged accounts and implementing least privilege. In many respects, it also carries significant compliance implications. Regulations like HIPAA, PCI DSS, SOX, and GDPR mandate diligent handling of sensitive data and controls around the users who can access it. Having an effective PAM strategy in place signals to stakeholders, auditors, and regulators that you have taken the appropriate steps to protect the organization's most valuable data and assets.

Today, privileged access management is much like a fortified castle gate in the kingdom of corporate infrastructure. It has become an indispensable, many-faceted cybersecurity solution to keep watch over who passes in and out of restricted and sensitive areas. Without PAM, businesses risk exposing their most sensitive data to both internal errors and external threats. With PAM, organizations embrace best practices around controlled privileged credential usage (from privileged account passwords to SSH keys, DevOps secrets, and more), gain the ability to identify and quarantine suspicious activity, and enforce compliance standards with confidence when users access privileged functions and features. When privileged accounts and activity are monitored, managed, and governed correctly with PAM, a threat actor now can be detected when trying to elevate privileges or compromise an asset or data within an organization. That is, all privileged activity, regardless of the attack vector or sanctioned usage, is being tracked and monitored for inappropriate access and behavior.

## Quantum Computing

While we have explored existing solutions in detail, the future really does lie in what technology is emerging and how it will change life forever as we know it. Today, quantum computing is inching closer to practical reality whether through room temperature super conductors or quantum on silicon. The foundation for today's encryption technology is under an existential threat. Most encryption methods used across the Internet including RSA, ECC, and Diffie-Hellman[5] rely on mathematical problems that are easy to verify but hard to solve without massive computational

---

[5] https://www.keyfactor.com/education-center/types-of-encryption-algorithms/

CHAPTER 11   SOLUTIONS

power. Quantum computers, however, can solve these equations with relative ease using algorithms like Shor's[6] and just brute force computing power.

This looming risk is not hypothetical. Threat actors today could be harvesting encrypted data and storing it until they have the means to decrypt it. This tactic is known as "harvest now, decrypt later."[7] Financial records, health data, and classified government files transmitted now could be compromised in the near future if not protected with quantum-resistant cryptography.

That's why the urgency to adopt quantum-resistant encryption, also called postquantum cryptography (PQC), cannot be overstated. These new algorithms are designed to resist attacks from both classical cracking techniques and quantum computers, ensuring long-term confidentiality and data integrity. The US National Institute of Standards and Technology (NIST)[8] is leading initiatives for standardizing PQC algorithms, with updates appearing on a periodic basis.

Organizations should begin their quantum readiness, planning, and budgeting now. This includes identifying where vulnerable cryptography is used, evaluating PQC candidates, and planning for a hybrid cryptographic transition that combines classical and quantum-safe protections until all resources can be mitigated.

The shift to quantum-resistant encryption is more than just a technical upgrade. It is a generational transformation of cybersecurity just like deploying personal computers for the first time. Acting now means ensuring that the information we protect today remains secure tomorrow.

---

[6] https://www.classiq.io/insights/shors-algorithm-explained
[7] https://www.keyfactor.com/blog/harvest-now-decrypt-later-a-new-form-of-attack/
[8] https://www.nist.gov/news-events/news/2022/07/nist-announces-first-four-quantum-resistant-cryptographic-algorithms

Organizations who delay embarking on this strategy may find themselves unprepared for a future where today's encryption is no longer enough and all your data could potentially be decrypted and exposed.

# Artificial Intelligence

The promise of artificial intelligence (AI) is seductive. We all know humans can be impatient and having faster decisions, smarter automation, and the potential to solve problems that have stumped humans for decades are all attractive lores. Beneath the innovation lies an undeniable truth: AI, like all innovative human solutions, can be weaponized, manipulated, or skewed against someone's best interests or undeniable truth. In order for us not to become a victim of our own creations, we need start building technical, legal, procedural, and operational guardrails now as a part of secure by design initiatives. Otherwise, the risks will outpace the benefits.

The most imminent concern today for AI is model manipulation.[9] Threat actors are already testing AI models with adversarial inputs to confuse and mislead output that servers their nefarious mission. For example, there are techniques to corrupt a chatbot into providing harmful instructions, disclosing privileged information, and even executing code that could have devastating consequences. AI has no common sense like humans and can be "dupped" simply by asking it leading questions or training it with wrong information. When the output is believable, then human frailties come into play. This is a blurry line between social engineering and trusted content.

---

[9] https://www.nist.gov/news-events/news/2024/01/nist-identifies-types-cyberattacks-manipulate-behavior-ai-systems

## CHAPTER 11   SOLUTIONS

Next, we need to consider the risks of AI hallucinations.[10] AI models, especially large language models, can fabricate convincing but false information. In regulated industries like healthcare, finance, legal, government, or cybersecurity, this could have devastating consequences. A mistyped diagnosis, a fabricated threat alert, a fake legal claim,[11] all delivered with confident syntax and fabricated reference information could dup unsuspecting users and cause a myriad of risks from bad instructions to faux legal cases. We must confront the risk of autonomy without accountability as a part of the solution and a potential problem. When AI systems make decisions or produce content without human oversight, or operate in black-box architectures, it becomes nearly impossible to trace the logic or rationale behind their results. This is not just a technical problem. It is a governance failure waiting to happen, and as we have established, humans are incredibly gullible when information is presented that looks authentic, yet is fictitious. AI has no morals about creating content that exacerbates this risk.

So how do we mitigate these risks with AI and future AI-embedded solutions?

- We need explainability by design. AI systems must be built with transparency and interpretability as core principles, not optional features. If you can't audit an algorithm, you shouldn't deploy it. This implies all output can have credited sources and explanations built in to determine how AI came to its conclusions.

---

[10] https://www.ibm.com/think/topics/ai-hallucinations
[11] https://www.reuters.com/technology/artificial-intelligence/ai-hallucinations-court-papers-spell-trouble-lawyers-2025-02-18/

- Enforce human-in-the-loop (HitL)[12] and secure by design architectures. Critical decisions generated by AI for safety, security, compliance, etc., should always involve human validation. Autonomous decision-making without oversight is not innovation; it is potentially negligence. If you are an avid science fiction fan, consider the premise of rogue AI in *Star Trek: Discovery*.[13] In the future, autonomous AI is illegal specifically due to the potential threats of not having human supervision.

- We need adversarial quality assurance testing and red team penetration testing for AI from day one. Just as we perform penetration test networks and simulate phishing campaigns, we must stress-test AI models against malicious prompts, poisoning attacks,[14] and bias exploitation.

- Compliance and regulations must be developed in lock step with AI adoption. It is truly time for standards on AI data integrity, model transparency, and acceptable use within verticals and for consumers. In my personal opinion, letting the market self-regulate AI is a recipe for exploitation and jokingly may warrant a second edition of this book based on all the potential exploits that could occur.

The future for AI is truly incomprehensible at this time for any one individual to articulate. We have so many types of AI from narrow, to generative, to general AI that are emerging with specialty functionality

---

[12] https://cloud.google.com/discover/human-in-the-loop
[13] https://www.imdb.com/title/tt5171438/
[14] https://www.cloudflare.com/learning/ai/data-poisoning/

for tailored workflows and use cases. Security, transparency, and accountability must be embedded at every stage of the AI lifecycle from design through development, deployment, and maintenance. Otherwise, today's innovation will become tomorrow's existential threat.

## End-of-Life Solutions

Attack vectors never die. Old malware, exploits, and social engineering attacks may not be as relevant as patches become available, but rest assured, they're still present. End-of-life systems and shadow IT will always have some form of presence on the Internet. Using end-of-life (no longer supported by the developing vendor) cybersecurity solutions presents a unique risk surface in organizations. While attacks never fade away, the products to defend against them certainly do. Using end-of-life (EOL) cybersecurity software introduces significant security, compliance, operational, and financial risks to an organization. Below are key considerations before continuing operations within an EOL environment longer than absolutely necessary:

**Security and Operational Risks**

- **No Security Patches:** Once a product reaches EOL, a vendor will cease the release of security updates and vulnerability notifications. This leaves the software with undocumented and unpatched vulnerabilities in embedded open source libraries and proprietary code vulnerable to attacks.

- **Increased Attack Surface:** Threat actors will target outdated software because vulnerabilities can't be remediated, increasing the risk of zero-day exploits.

- **Lack of Compatibility:** Many EOL solutions don't support modern encryption, authentication, or endpoint security solutions, making them susceptible to attacks based on their dependencies and compatibility.

- **Vendor Support:** With no official vendor support, organizations are left without technical assistance, increasing the difficulty of troubleshooting security and performance issues.

- **Reputation and Trust:** If a breach involving EOL software, customers and stockholders may lose confidence in the organization's ability to protect data, and organizations using outdated software may face media scrutiny, damaging brand reputation and stock value.

**Compliance and Regulatory Risks**

- **Violations of Industry Regulations:** EOL software fails to meet security standards in regulations such as HIPAA, PCI DSS, SOX, FISMA, and CMMC, leading to potential audits, fines, and loss of certifications. The following are specific regulatory compliance initiatives that specify EOL systems are a violation:

  - **PCI DSS (Payment Card Industry Data Security Standard):** PCI DSS Requirement 6.2[15] states that organizations must "ensure that all system components and software are protected from known vulnerabilities by installing applicable vendor-supplied security patches." Using EOL security solutions without patches violates this standard, increasing the risk of cardholder data breaches.

---

[15] https://pcidssguide.com/pci-dss-requirement-6/

- **SOX (Sarbanes-Oxley Act):** SOX requires companies to protect financial data and IT systems from security threats. Using EOL security solutions can lead to noncompliance with SOX Section 404,[16] which mandates internal controls over financial reporting, including IT security controls.

- **SEC Cybersecurity Rules:** The SEC requires companies to disclose cybersecurity risks and controls. Running EOL security solutions increases the risk of breaches, and failure to disclose reliance on unsupported software could violate Regulation S-K Item 106.[17]

- **FISMA (Federal Information Security Management Act):** FISMA mandates federal agencies to maintain risk-based security controls under NIST SP 800-53[18] guidelines. Using EOL software violates NIST controls such as SI-2 (Flaw Remediation) and SA-22 (Unsupported System Components), leading to noncompliance.

- **CMMC (Cybersecurity Maturity Model Certification):** CMMC requires companies to follow NIST 800-171[19] controls, including 3.14.1 (identify, report, and correct system flaws). If a security solution is outdated and unpatched, it cannot meet these requirements, leading to compliance failure.

---

[16] https://www.sarbanes-oxley-101.com/SOX-404.htm
[17] https://www.ecfr.gov/current/title-17/chapter-II/part-229/subpart-229.100/section-229.106
[18] https://csrc.nist.gov/pubs/sp/800/53/r5/upd1/final
[19] https://csrc.nist.gov/pubs/sp/800/171/r3/final

- **Legal Liabilities:** A data breach caused by outdated software can result in lawsuits, class actions, and regulatory investigations.

- **Loss of Cyber Insurance Coverage:** Many cyber insurance policies require up-to-date security controls, and running EOL software may void coverage in the event of a breach.

Using EOL cybersecurity software is a major security liability that exposes organizations to breaches, compliance violations, operational failures, and financial losses. The best practice is to upgrade to supported solutions as soon as strategically possible, implement proactive patch management, and identify any and all systems before they become obsolete in order to avoid this risk.

# CHAPTER 12

# The Human Threat

As we look back on all the attacks and breaches throughout the past few decades, we come to a startling revelation: "What if I didn't…?" Human beings, with all of our emotional flaws, are prime attack vectors for social engineering. Simply put, we are prone to gullibility, ignorance, arrogance, and, often, carelessness. With this in mind, how do we "patch" people? How do we improve the "HumanOS," so we don't make these mistakes? This chapter focuses on the human vulnerability across the history of cyberattacks.

Today's world is technology-dependent. Almost everyone has multiple devices—from televisions and computers to mobile devices—that require security updates on a regular basis to stave off the latest vulnerabilities and exploits. Yet, amidst the rapid pace of software delivery using Agile processes, one constant vulnerability remains: humans.

Like any operating system, the HumanOS (the human identity interacting with any resource) can be manipulated, exploited, and corrupted, if left unmanaged. Addressing this vulnerability is no longer a business option; it's a critical requirement for any organization to prioritize identity security. While security teams continue to deploy, upgrade, and replace traditional security technologies like firewalls and endpoint protection, the real challenge lies in "patching" the human element and shielding them from modern cyber threats.

At its core, cybersecurity is about people and data. Firewalls, intrusion detection systems, and antimalware solutions play their parts, but humans still remain the most frequent entry point for threat actors. From phishing attacks to advanced social engineering using deepfake artificial intelligence schemes, cybercriminals rely on exploiting human behavior far more than exploiting a software vulnerability or misconfiguration.

It's been well known for decades that if threat actors gain access to a privileged account (typically root or domain administrator), it can be a "game over" event for an organization. This is why privileged access management (PAM) is a foundational element to prevent inappropriate human exposure to critical accounts. In securing modern organizations, reducing risks associated with both threat actors and inadvertent insider threats necessitates ensuring the concept of least privilege and appropriate access for any and all sessions. However, technology alone cannot fix a poorly educated or gullible workforce. It's not enough to secure systems if the individuals interacting with those systems are mentally vulnerable. In many ways, patching the HumanOS is as important as deploying any cybersecurity solution.

Like software, the HumanOS contains weaknesses, but fixing these flaws is not as simple as deploying a software patch—not by a longshot. Some of these vulnerabilities are well-known to threat actors and have been demonstrated as repeatable risks. People are inherently trusting and often fail to recognize sophisticated social engineering tactics, especially if the source is spoofed from a known trusted individual or entity. Phishing emails continue to be one of the most successful methods for gaining unauthorized access to systems because they prey on human instincts of urgency, trust, and curiosity.

Social engineering attacks alone aren't the only vulnerabilities in the HumanOS. Human errors due to lack of knowledge or failures in process play a significant role in many security incidents. Whether due to a misconfiguration, a failure to update systems in a timely manner, shadow IT, or the accidental exposure of sensitive data, even well-planned workflows can lead to the exploitation of assets and data. This reality makes the case for ongoing education, training, and the right tools to reduce HumanOS risks.

Patching the HumanOS starts with understanding that education, training, and role playing are insufficient. In many organizations, cybersecurity training is seen as a one-off yearly event, designed to satisfy compliance requirements. However, threats don't develop once a year; they evolve daily, and this approach to training is dangerously outdated. A more comprehensive strategy involves continuous learning, continuous reinforcement, and embedding cybersecurity best practices into the organization's technology infrastructure and, most importantly, culture!

1. **Cybersecurity Cultural Trait:** At its most effective, cybersecurity awareness isn't a campaign, burden, requirement, compliance initiative, or an annual training module—it's a cultural imperative; just like accountability, reliability, or passion. Organizations must embed a security mindset into the daily routines of all employees, contractors, and vendors. This can be done by encouraging a culture of vigilance where employees feel empowered to report suspicious activities without fear of repercussion, even if they make a mistake. By aligning cybersecurity with business operations, companies can create a workforce that instinctively approaches situations with security in mind and incorporate security checkpoints throughout any appropriate workflow to ensure security requirements are being met.

2. **Adaptive Learning Techniques:** The HumanOS isn't static, and neither are the threats we face. Just as software patches need to be regularly applied, so too must employee training and role playing exercises be performed on a periodic basis. In addition, adaptive learning techniques, such as

scenario-based simulations, can be highly effective when merged with daily workflows. As an example, phishing simulations offer employees real-time learning opportunities that reflect current threat tactics that could appear in their email inbox or via phone calls. By experiencing simulated attacks in a controlled environment, employees are better prepared to recognize them in the wild and know how to report them to the appropriate internal team. The goal is to reinforce the concept of muscle memory in cybersecurity and enable quick recognition of potential threats and reflexive action.

3. **Privileged Access Management:** One of the most powerful ways to reduce human-related vulnerabilities is through least privilege and protection of access to privileged accounts, for both HumanOS-based and NHI (nonhuman identities). In many organizations, employees are granted more access than they need to do their jobs. They are essentially overprivileged with permissions, rights, and entitlements, introducing excessive human risk. These excessive privileges increase the risk of both intentional and unintentional misuse. PAM ensures users only have access to the information and systems necessary for their roles, significantly reducing the attack surface and also mitigating the risk from threat actors performing lateral movement due to excessive privileges that can be obtained during a successful attack. In addition, modern PAM applies the concept of just-in-time (JIT) access, which eliminates the risk of standing

privileges by ensuring credentials are granted only when approved and needed, and immediately revoked after use. This minimizes the window of opportunity for misuse and significantly reduces the risks associated with credential theft and privilege escalation attacks. By intelligently automating access control, organizations not only protect themselves against external threats, but also address the internal risks posed by human error or malicious insiders.

4. **Gamification/Incentivization:** The key to any effective training is engagement. Traditional cybersecurity training often lacks the interactive elements necessary to hold employees' attention. For example, "watch this video, attend this session, and answer these test questions" are the most common approaches. Gamification, the process of applying game-style elements to other modes of learning, can change the success of engagement and effectiveness of training. Organizations are finding success by using point-based systems, tangible rewards, and leaderboards to make security learning more engaging for humans. As an example, employees compete to spot phishing attempts, report suspicious behavior, identify flaws in workflows, etc., all designed to solidify best practices through additional gamified engagement. These techniques foster a sense of personal responsibility in cybersecurity, a measure of success and pride, and allow alignment for individual goals within the organization's security framework.

5. **Supplementing Human Defenses with Automation and AI:** Two of the most powerful tools available to organizations today are automation and artificial intelligence (AI). By automating routine tasks, such as patch management, access reviews, and incident response, organizations reduce the likelihood of human errors that can pose risks to workflows. When AI is applied to cybersecurity, anomalies in human behavior can be identified in a timely manner and elevated for automation or additional intervention by security teams. These technologies act as an additional line of defense, ensuring that threats are identified and neutralized before extensive exploitation from a human-related incident occurs. This concept of containment based on a timely initial detection is one of the foundational components for zero trust (ZT). As an example, advanced AI-driven analytics can automatically flag unusual behavior or unauthorized access attempts, prompting immediate investigations or automation to block access by source or for an account. It's important to note that automation does not fully replace human intervention, but rather acts as a necessary supplement, reducing the manual intervention for repetitive workflows or investigations, allowing people to focus on other tasks that require applicable attention.

As identity-based cyberattacks continue to rise, the human element (the HumanOS) will always remain a critical point of vulnerability. However, by implementing a layered technology and human resource approach that includes continuous education, identity security, adaptive training, and strategic use of automation and AI, organizations can effectively "patch" the HumanOS. This shift isn't just about deploying the right cybersecurity tools; it's about fostering a security-first mindset throughout the organization. By addressing the human side of cybersecurity with the same rigor as technical defenses, companies can transform their greatest vulnerability into their most powerful defensive weapon.

# CHAPTER 13

# Lateral Movement

Lateral movement is a postexploitation activity during which a threat actor tries to compromise adjacent IT systems. After gaining initial access to an asset or network, the attacker begins to authenticate or exploit vulnerabilities in digitally connected assets to execute commands or gain visibility into additional resources. The goal is typically to escalate privileges, access sensitive data, or deploy additional malware to further the threat actor's nefarious mission.

Representing one of the first phases of a cyberattack, lateral movement is only able to occur after a threat actor has gained an initial foothold within a network or assets. The most common techniques used for the initial breach include identity attack vectors, entitlement misconfigurations, and software vulnerability exploitation. Then, based on an account's True Privilege™, exploitation can occur to other accounts and assets that represent a higher risk. The entire flow in Figure 13-1 represents a path to privileged access.

# CHAPTER 13   LATERAL MOVEMENT

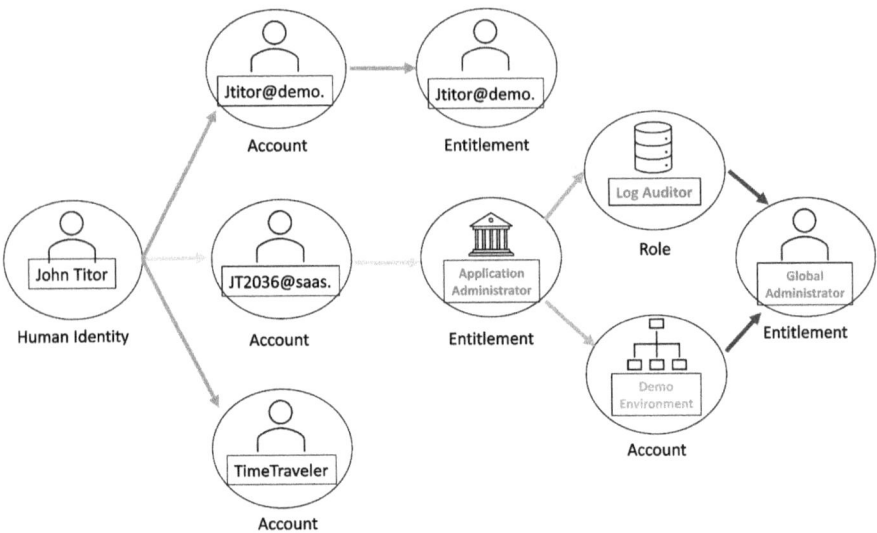

*Figure 13-1. True Privileges providing a path to privileged access*

Unlike the initial breach, which may involve less subtle penetration tactics (like brute force attacks and password sprays), lateral movement is often conducted with great care. To remain undetected, the threat actor will use techniques to blend in with legitimate network traffic and host authentication, authorization, and remote access. The challenge for cybersecurity professionals is to detect and block unwanted lateral movement before the threat actor navigates to the next asset, ultimately creating a path to privileged access.

Typically, a threat actor probes for weak spots, looking for an initial entry point. However, rarely is that initial entry point the end goal of the attacker. Once a beachhead is established, a threat actor can try to use that foothold to launch a further attack by compromising adjacent systems.

Lateral movement can entail compromising other assets on the network, applications sharing resources, and even escalating privileges to gain access to far more valuable identities and accounts. Ideally, each phase of the attack chain evades detection to maximize the penetration

CHAPTER 13   LATERAL MOVEMENT

and monetization of the compromised systems. Figure 13-2 illustrates lateral movement and key attributes, defenses, and models for detection, containment, and remediation.

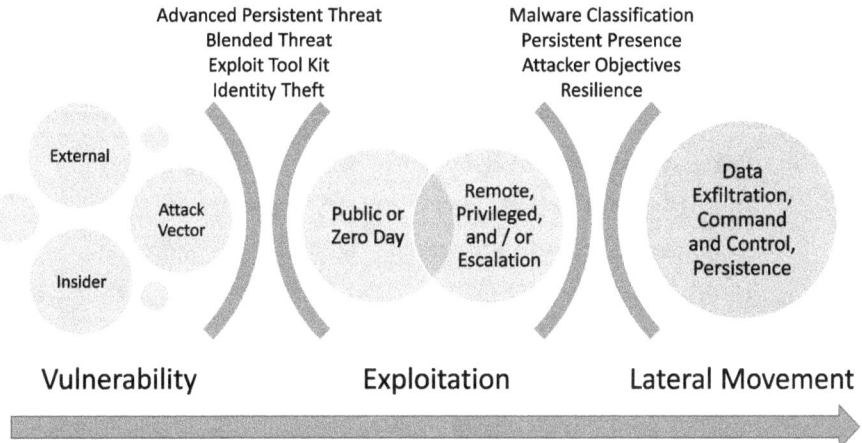

*Figure 13-2. How a vulnerability and exploitation lead to lateral movement*

To a cyber threat actor, lateral movement means all the difference between compromising a single asset and potentially navigating through an enterprise to establish a persistent presence. While a threat actor might initially succeed in infiltrating an environment via a number of methods—such as an opportunistic phishing attack or a targeted spray attack based on stolen credentials—lateral movement is the primary vehicle to compromise an entire environment.

Once an environment is breached, threat actors will employ a myriad of strategies to accomplish lateral movement. The most common lateral movement techniques include:

- **Credential Dumping**: Extracting and reusing credentials from compromised systems to access other systems within the network

- **Pass-the-Hash (PtH)**: Utilizing hashed passwords to authenticate without knowing the actual plaintext password

219

- **Exploitation of Trust Relationships**: Leveraging identity-based trust via account relationships to move across network segments without raising alarms

- **Remote Services**: Using legitimate remote desktop services or other remote access tools to move between systems

- **WMI and PowerShell**: Utilizing Windows Management Instrumentation (WMI) and PowerShell scripts to execute commands and transfer files across systems as remote commands

- **Vulnerability Exploitation**: The exploitation of known or zero-day vulnerabilities within software is used to execute code remotely or provide information for maintaining a persistent presence

- **Misconfiguration**: Simple misconfigurations, or the lack of system hardening, which allow for lateral movement based on applications and services using default credentials, exposed resources, and poor cybersecurity hygiene

Lateral movement poses detection challenges because it often appears as legitimate network activity. After all, the goal of a threat actor is to remain undetected. However, several indicators of compromise (IoC) can suggest inappropriate lateral movement, including:

1. **Unusual Authentication Patterns**

   - Unexplained logons to systems outside of normal business hours or from unexpected locations

   - Multiple failed login attempts followed by a successful login, potentially indicating a brute force attack

- Logon attempts to systems not typically accessed by the identity
- Authorization for a command or configuration change without a prior authentication event
- Privileged authentication attempts without MFA
- Authentication requests for applications and commands not approved for privileged or standard user access, including those used in living-off-the-land attacks

2. **Anomalous Network Traffic**

- A sudden spike in network traffic between systems that do not usually communicate or using unusual ports
- Unexpected use of remote access protocols, such as RDP or SSH especially in unusual patterns or between unexpected systems

3. **Anomalous Applications**

- PowerShell scripts or WMI activity on systems, where such activity is uncommon or not authorized
- Use of system tools in an unusual manner, potentially indicating a living-off-the-land attack
- Installation of malware using unsigned applications or digital signatures not authorized by the organization

4. **Privilege Escalation Requests**
   - Attempts to access privileged accounts or use of privileged commands from nonadministrative accounts
   - Sudden changes in user privileges, or the appearance of new administrative accounts
   - Privileged access without the use of MFA
   - Access to sensitive data and sensitive assets from privileged accounts that should normally not have any interaction with a system

In fairness, this is not an exhaustive list of potential lateral movement detections, but rather the most common examples every organization should be able to detect within their environment.

Given the sophistication of modern attacks, traditional detection methods are increasingly insufficient. Organizations must consider implementing advanced techniques that leverage artificial intelligence, behavior analysis, and real-time monitoring to detect lateral movement.

1. **Identity-Based Behavioral Analytics:** This entails establishing baselines of normal behavior for human and nonhuman identities and then detecting deviations that might indicate lateral movement. Examples of suspicious behaviors may include an identity that suddenly begins accessing multiple systems in succession, or a machine identity requesting adjacent system access. These types of threats are normally detected via inappropriate authentication requests in a SIEM or an identity threat detection and response (ITDR) solution.

2. **Endpoint Detection and Response (EDR):**
   Deploying EDR solutions that monitor and record endpoint activity in real time is crucial for detecting and containing any lateral movement. These tools can detect anomalies, such as unusual process executions, unexpected file modifications, or new network connections, which often indicate lateral movement.

3. **Network Traffic Analysis:** Using network traffic analysis tools to monitor traffic on the same VLAN or subnet can help identify lateral movement, especially when assets are not in the same physical location but rather logically connected. By analyzing the flow of data between systems, these tools can detect abnormal traffic patterns and alert on unexpected connections or unusual port usage.

4. **Deception Technology:** Deception technologies, such as honeypots, decoy systems, or other Trojan horse-style tools can lure threat actors into revealing their presence. These technologies are designed to collect as much information as possible from a threat actor during an interaction. Defensive deception technologies can also trigger alerts and allow security teams to respond or stealthily perform monitoring as the attack progresses further.

While detection is crucial, preventing lateral movement is the ultimate goal. This requires a combination of proactive security measures, including network segmentation, least privilege access, and continuous monitoring.

CHAPTER 13    LATERAL MOVEMENT

1. **Mature Zero Trust Security Controls**

   Advancing zero trust principles and implementing a zero trust architecture (ZTA) are high-level strategies that, by design, aim to reduce the attack surface and restrict unwanted lateral movement. Zero trust principles also espouse putting controls in place for continuous monitoring and accelerating detection and response.

   Most of the best practices that follow play a key and necessary role for advancing zero trust security.

2. **Implement Network Segmentation**

   Segment your network into distinct zones with strict access controls between them. This limits the attacker's ability to move laterally by isolating the breach within a single network logical segment, or even individual asset.

   For example, sensitive data should reside in an isolated network segment accessible only through secure remote access via proprietary technology. Avoid using RDP, SSH, and HTTPS directly between network zones. When these protocols are required, proxy them through an appropriate gateway technology.

3. **Apply Least Privilege**

   Ensure identities, accounts, users, and machines operate with the minimum privileges necessary to perform their functions. This reduces the blast radius if an account is compromised by limiting the potential for authentication and lateral movement into adjacent systems. Regularly review and right-size privileges and permissions, particularly for administrative accounts, using entitlement and privileged access management (PAM) solutions. As much as is feasible, your least privilege model should strive toward a zero-standing privilege (ZSP) state by implementing just-in-time (JIT) access.

In addition, organizations should enforce privilege separation and separation of duties. When applied to users, this involves segmenting user privileges across separate users and accounts and ensuring certain duties can only be performed with specific accounts. Thus, if one account is compromised, the range of privileges it affords the attacker is restricted in scope.

4. **Implement Privileged Account and Session Management (PASM)**

   Secure passwords, keys, and DevOps secrets in a centralized safe, and actively manage them according to security best practices. PASM, also called privileged password management, prevents numerous identity-based attacks and account hijacking threats outright, while reducing the effectiveness of others. For instance, implementing one-time passwords (OTPs) for highly privileged accounts will prevent password reuse attacks. Frequent rotation of credentials, or dynamic generation of secrets, also means the threat window during which an account can be compromised via stolen credentials is time limited. PASM solutions should also pair active credential management with real-time privileged session monitoring and management, overlaying threat detection and response capabilities to stop attacks in their tracks.

5. **Address the Privileged Pathways**

   A primary goal of threat actors is to elevate low-level accounts (standard users) to privileged accounts (superuser, local administrator, domain administrator, application owner, or root). If the threat actor can elevate privileges, then lateral movement and a complete compromise of the entire environment are possible. The linkage of a low-level account to a privileged account can be mapped as a Path to Privilege. Some environments have unidentified Paths to Privilege™ due to nested groups, domain trusts, and misconfigurations. Unfortunately, many paths to privilege are not obvious and require advanced detection capabilities to link accounts based on common identities. By proactively discovering Paths to Privilege, organizations can harden identity security posture to reduce risks and attack pathways.

6. **Implement Multifactor Authentication (MFA)**

   Enforce MFA for all users—period. If that isn't possible, at minimum, enforce MFA on all remote access, privileged accounts, and critical systems. By requiring an additional verification step to provide confidence in an identity, MFA significantly reduces the risk of credential theft leading to lateral movement.

7. **Perform Regular Audits and Monitoring**

   Conduct regular audits of identities, accounts, permissions, and network configurations to identify and mitigate potential software misconfigurations outside of planned vulnerability assessment scans. Continuous monitoring of network activity, combined with real-time alerting, helps detect suspicious activity early. In addition, ensure policies, alerts, and audits follow a Shared Responsibility Model. This type of security framework helps define the division of responsibilities between an organization, vendors, employees, and entities like cloud service providers. As an example for this model, the provider is responsible for securing the cloud infrastructure (such as hardware, networking, and virtualization), while the customer is responsible for securing their data, applications, user access, and configurations within the cloud. Audits, escalations, and findings should therefore be routed to the appropriate teams for investigation and remediation based on ownership. It is not enough just to audit and monitor, knowing who is responsible is equally as important.

8. **Vulnerability, Configuration, and Patch Management**

   Keep systems and software up to date with the latest security patches in as timely a manner as physically possible. Various lateral movement techniques commonly exploit known vulnerabilities. Timely patching and configuration management can close these vulnerability gaps. Monthly vulnerability assessments are a common practice, but what happens in between these scans? Consider staggering assessments, ad hoc statistical assessments, and real-time scanning to eliminate gaps in monitoring that could otherwise be exploited for lateral movement.

9. **Identity Security**

    Identity security encompasses a broad range of controls for protecting digital identities. Poor identity hygiene and gaps in protection give threat actors the footholds they need to land an attack as well as many pathways to conduct lateral movement. The hygiene and runtime of an organization's identity governance program, deployment of identity directory services, and PAM solution (which includes PASM) coverage are crucial for protecting against lateral movement attacks. In addition, all nonhuman identities, application integrations, and privileged accounts should be managed and monitored for potential abuse that can occur during lateral movement. In addition, identity threat detection and response (ITDR) capabilities are becoming essential for modern environments to provide unified identity security visibility across heterogeneous domains. This requires strong and broad integrations with PAM and other solutions.

10. **Operationalize Effective Incident Response**

    Develop and role play your incident response playbook to ensure a swift and effective response to detected lateral movement. This includes having predefined playbooks for isolating affected systems, conducting forensic analysis, recommending updates, and restoring normal operations.

Detecting and preventing unauthorized lateral movement is pivotal for any modern cybersecurity strategy. As threat actors become more proficient at evading traditional defenses, organizations must adopt advanced detection techniques to ensure lateral movement after exploitation is rapidly detected and mitigated. Minimizing the dwell time for threat activities is crucial to preventing an all-out breach.

By understanding the symptoms of unauthorized lateral movement, deploying intelligent monitoring solutions, addressing paths to privilege, and adhering to identity security and vulnerability management best practices, organizations can significantly reduce the likelihood of successful lateral movement by a threat actor.

# CHAPTER 14

# Return on Investment

There is an unspoken truth for executives in the cybersecurity industry. When selecting a solution for a business use case to mitigate risk, how do you justify its cost? Do you first measure risk and offset the cost of a potential incident to justify the solution? Or do you budget based on the need to satisfy a compliance initiative or audit finding? Truthfully, a CISO can apply many other approaches to justify the cost of a product that a board may accept or reject. However, in this CISO's opinion, one calculation is emerging that can readily meet the scrutiny of even the most stringent economic buyer: the minimization of dwell time or outage costs.

For every CISO, the fundamental goal is to minimize and prevent the time an attacker spends inside a system. This is called dwell time for an incident or breach. The longer a breach goes undetected, the higher the potential financial and reputational damage, which is directly related to the cost associated with the dwell time.

According to the IBM Cost of a Data Breach Report,[1] the average cost of a data breach in 2024 is $4.88 million, with a significant portion attributed to the time taken to detect and respond to incidents and breaches. The report explores how organizations can calculate the return on investment (ROI) from licensing solutions that can directly reduce dwell time by detecting, preventing, and mitigating a threat before excessive dwell time occurs. Based on this concept, a simple financial model can demonstrate

---

[1] https://www.ibm.com/reports/data-breach

CHAPTER 14   RETURN ON INVESTMENT

the cost per minute of an event. If an incident or breach is managed at its earliest possible point of detection, the financial savings can justify the cost of a solution to mitigate the risk.

By definition, dwell time is the period between when a breach or incident occurs (an event) and when it is detected and contained. Each minute a threat actor remains undetected within a system amplifies financial, operational, and reputational risks for the organization. For example, a distributed denial-of-service (DDoS) attack in 2024 cost an average of $6,000 per minute. In addition, other forms of cyberattacks are estimated at $5,600 per minute, according to a recent report.[2] Similarly, breaches involving ransomware, where threat actors exfiltrate sensitive data before encrypting systems, result in financial loss not just from ransom payments, but also from business disruptions, legal liabilities, and recovery efforts. Minimizing the dwell time for these types of attacks not only minimizes the associated scope of the attack, but also the service disruption costs incurred during the event.

To justify licensing cybersecurity tools that shorten dwell time, organizations need to model a dwell time reduction as a measurable ROI factor. This cost justification model revolves around two key variables:

1. **Baseline Dwell Time Versus Reduced Dwell Time:** Solutions like endpoint detection and response (EDR), endpoint privilege management (EPM), and identity threat detection and response (ITDR) help organizations detect intrusions faster based on malware, exploits, and identity-based attack vectors. To understand this better, the baseline dwell time is calculated when these solutions are not present, and detection and containment occur only after

---

[2] https://www.helpnetsecurity.com/2024/08/21/ddos-attacks-duration-surge/#:~:text=DDoS%20attack%20duration%20increases,rate%20of%20$6%2C000%20per%20minute.

a noticeable environmental impact. The reduced dwell time is calculated when information about the threat is provided in a timely manner, even when, operationally, everything appears normal.

2. **Cost Reduction from Faster Detection:** Every minute of dwell time increases the financial loss for the business. Therefore, every minute of reduced dwell time translates into lower costs, reduced resource losses (such as prevention of additional ransomware encryption), blocked lateral movement, and faster mitigation from the threat.

When dwell time is reduced by days or even hours, the potential savings can be modeled directly as avoided event costs. Below are several use cases that illustrate how reduced dwell time translates into substantial financial benefits and ROI for solution justifications.

# Example 1: Ransomware Incident Containment with an EPM Solution

**Scenario:**

A mid-sized healthcare provider licenses an EPM solution to remove local administrative privileges. Without the EPM solution, their baseline dwell time for ransomware incidents was one day, costing approximately $300,000 per hour based on previous breaches and in line with estimations provided by Gartner.[3] The new tool reduces dwell time to one hour.

---

[3] https://www.gartner.com/en/publications/ransomware-in-midsize-enterprises

**Financial Impact:**

- **Baseline Cost:** $7.2m per incident (one-day baseline dwell time)
- **Post-tool Cost:** $300,000 per incident (one-hour reduced dwell time)

The healthcare provider justifies the annual licensing fee of the EPM solution by showing net savings of $6.9m per incident and demonstrating clear ROI for the technology by minimizing dwell time and reducing costs. Of course, the financial costs for your organization will vary, but the 1-hour mitigation cost of a single host being compromised is clearly much better than an infection of an entire environment over 24 hours.

# Example 2: Preventing Paths to Privileged Escalation with an ITDR Solution

**Scenario:**
A financial services firm faces constant phishing attempts that target employee credentials. Without an Identity Threat Detection and Response (ITDR) toolset, threat actors often linger for 30 days before being discovered, leading to data breaches costing approximately $5 million each. Implementing an ITDR system with real-time monitoring reduces dwell time to less than one day.

**Financial Impact:**

- **Baseline Cost:** $5 million per breach (30 days dwell time)
- **Post-tool Cost:** $166,000 per breach (one-day dwell time)

The firm spends $1 million annually on the ITDR solution, generating net savings of over $4 million in a single budget lifecycle.

# Example 3: Malicious Command Execution Due to Remote System Access

**Scenario:**

A mid-sized manufacturing organization licenses a secure remote access solution to mitigate the risks of privileged remote connectivity into an OT (operational technology) environment. Without this solution, their baseline dwell time could be impacted by:

- Living-off-the-land attacks and malicious commands
- Exploitable remote access protocols (RDP, SSH, Telnet, HTTP, etc.)
- Inadequate behavioral monitoring

If you consider it can take up to 30 days to identify a problem, and it costs approximately $300,000 per hour based on previous breaches, the new solution can reduce dwell time to 8 hours based on a daily review process.

**Financial Impact:**

- **Baseline Cost:** $7.2m per incident (1-day baseline dwell time, 24 hours × $300,000)
- **Post-tool Cost:** $300,000 per incident (eight-hour reduce dwell time)

The product manufacturer justifies the annual licensing fee of the secure remote access solution by showing a net savings of $6.9m per incident and demonstrating clear ROI for the technology by minimizing unexposed assets crucial for employee or contractor connectivity into an OT environment. Of course, the financial costs for your organization will vary, but an eight-hour mitigation window for a single host accessed inappropriately with secure remote access technology installed is a significant improvement. This allows for rapid escalation of any deviations

## CHAPTER 14  RETURN ON INVESTMENT

compared to traditional log reviews and threat hunting through a SIEM based on session anomalies. In addition, without a secure remote access solution, actual session recording and command blocking don't occur, making forensics much more difficult due to the lack of activity details.

To further formalize the ROI calculation for cybersecurity investments, organizations can apply the following formula:

$$ROI = (DT_b - DT_r) * \$E * f_r$$

Legend:

- ROI: Return on investment expressed in annual cost
- $DT_b$: Baseline dwell time without a solution
- $DT_r$: Reduced dwell time with a solution
- $\$E$: Financial cost per event in standard unit of time (minutes, hours, days, etc.)
- $F_r$: Frequency of event occurrence per year

This formula emphasizes how an organization can save costs from faster event detection, lower dwell time, and quicker response compared to licensing a solution, on an annual subscription basis.

Some common numbers used for calculations include the following:

- Corero indicates a DDoS attack cost an organization $9,000 per minute[4] in 2024.

- IBM estimates the average cost of a data breach is $4.8 million from their 2024 Cost of a Data Breach Report.

---

[4] https://www.corero.com/true-cost-of-a-ddos-attack/#:~:text= Distributed%20denial%2Dof%2Dservice%20(,now%20averages%20$6%2C000%20 per%20minute.

## CHAPTER 14   RETURN ON INVESTMENT

- The average ransom in 2024 is $2.73 million, almost an increase of $1 million from 2023, as reported by Sophos.[5]

- The average downtime a company experiences after a ransomware attack is 24 days, as reported by JumpCloud.[6]

While the monetary impact of minimizing dwell time can be significant, there are other business benefits that cybersecurity solutions can bring to the organization:

- **Improved Customer Trust:** Faster detection of an incident limits customer data exposure, helps uphold brand reputation, and limits customer trust issues that might require third-party engagements, such as for credit monitoring or legal exposure.

- **Regulatory Compliance:** Reducing dwell time ensures faster breach reporting, keeping the organization in line with regulations like GDPR or CCPA.

- **Operational Continuity:** Solutions that reduce dwell time help maintain business operations, especially for verticals that drive income from web services or ecommerce.

Dwell time is a critical metric in evaluating cybersecurity effectiveness. Reducing dwell time provides measurable financial and operational benefits. By modeling dwell time reduction as a ROI financial metric, organizations can align their cybersecurity budgets with real business

---

[5] https://www.sophos.com/en-us/press/press-releases/2024/04/ransomware-payments-increase-500-last-year-finds-sophos-state
[6] https://jumpcloud.com/blog/2024-ransomware-attack-statistics-trends-to-know

## CHAPTER 14  RETURN ON INVESTMENT

outcomes based on cyber mitigation risks. The sample use cases presented for ransomware containment and identity threat prevention illustrate how investing in tools like EPM and IDTR can yield substantial savings. If your organization or vertical has financial models to calculate downtime, DDoS, or outages, they can be easily applied to dwell time calculations to yield similar results.

The cost of breaches continues to rise due to long dwell times and the cost of mitigation. Leveraging dwell time as a metric within a financial model not only helps ensure better protection but also provides a clear business case for licensing cybersecurity solutions. Organizations that adopt this ROI-focused approach will be better positioned to safeguard their assets and users, while avoiding unexpected financial instabilities stemming from a negative cyber event.

# CHAPTER 15

# It's Not If, But When

At any given time, any organization could become the victim of a cybersecurity breach. It's a matter of when—not if—it will happen. The Internet has revolutionized businesses, innovation, and commerce, but it has also evolved into a battlefield where cyberattacks are not merely probable; they are inevitable. For organizations, a mentality change is required from "we will never be breached" to "when a breach happens, how should we respond and to whom?" The emphasis on an honest discussion about disclosure subsequent to a security incident is vital, not just for regulatory compliance, but also for maintaining trust with stakeholders. This chapter will delve into best practices that organizations should adopt for transparent communication postincident. It will also explore common mistakes organizations make out of fear, ignorance, lack of expertise, or unfortunately, arrogance.

Our dependency on technology has created a risk surface unlike any technological advancement in the last 100 years for businesses. Data breaches are no longer just information technology anomalies; they are a real business risk and, potentially, a game over business event. Transparency in the wake of a cyber incident demonstrates accountability, mitigates reputational damage, and fosters trust, despite the incident. Customers, partners, and regulatory bodies expect organizations to handle breaches with honesty, integrity, and in a timely manner. Failure to clearly and truthfully disclose a breach can lead to compounded losses, legal repercussions, and irreparable harm to brand equity and customer trust. With that stated, here are a few recommendations for honest public disclosure:

1. **Punctually Acknowledge the Breach**: The moment an incident is confirmed, time is of the essence. Any delays in disclosure often aggravate the situation by allowing rumors and misinformation to spread. A swift acknowledgment of the incident or breach (and there is a difference) demonstrates a proactive posture and a commitment to honesty regarding the situation and remediation activities.

2. **Institute a Crisis Response Team**: A multidisciplinary team comprising cybersecurity experts, legal counsel, public relations professionals, and executive leadership should manage the entire communication process end-to-end. This ensures disclosures are accurate, timely, and align with both legal obligations and the organization's ethical standards. All employees should be informed of the situation on a regular basis. External responses should be coordinated through a central path of communications (email, website, phone number, etc.) to ensure consistency in messaging.

3. **Provide Clear, Transparent, and Actionable Guidance**: Clearly outline what happened, the overall impact, and the procedures taken to mitigate the situation. For affected parties, provide specific actions they can take, such as changing passwords or requesting credit monitoring reports, to instill confidence that they can safeguard themselves

from further compromise. Underestimating or downplaying the criticality of a breach can backfire when the full scope is eventually revealed. It's better to overcommunicate than to appear ambiguous. If certain details aren't yet known, acknowledge that investigations are ongoing and commit to providing regular updates.

4. **Legal and Regulatory Compliance**: Different geolocations and business verticals have varying requirements for breach notification. It's legally imperative that these are met in a timely fashion. This can be done by consulting with legal experts familiar with data protection laws, such as GDPR, CCPA, HIPAA, etc.

5. **Periodic Updates**: A single, broad company announcement is typically never sufficient. All affected parties need ongoing assurance that the organization is actively addressing the breach and that the organization has remediation plans in place to prevent future incidents. Consistent updates reinforce the message that the situation is being managed correctly and thoughtfully.

6. **Display Empathy and Accountability**: A human response is often overlooked in these situations, but it's a key trait for a successful recovery. Humanizing the response by acknowledging the inconvenience and impact its causing others goes a long way in maintaining trust. Accountability also means avoiding shifting the blame, making excuses, or deflecting the situation to a third party. An empathetic tone will go a long way in laying the foundation for the organization's ultimate recovery.

## CHAPTER 15   IT'S NOT IF, BUT WHEN

While most organizations have the best of intentions, there are some common mistakes and pitfalls that occur with the disclosure or management of a breach:

1. **Delaying Disclosure**: Attempting to "fix" the issue or waiting for the right time (like after quarterly financial statements, as an example) before making it public can lead to legal and compliance penalties and erode customer trust. Those impacted by a breach are more forgiving of organizations that act promptly and responsibly with timely disclosure and honesty.

2. **Withholding Information**: Omitting critical information about the breach can create an impression of dishonesty. Transparency is crucial, even when the details are uncomfortable or unprecedented.

3. **Shifting Blame**: Blaming third-party vendors, employees, or other entities deflects accountability and damages the organization's credibility. Focus on the incident and resolution rather than pointing fingers and trying to hold someone else accountable.

4. **Using Technical Jargon**: While technical information may be necessary for some audiences, most affected parties need clear, plain language explanations that are decisive and actionable. Avoid overwhelming them with complex terminology and technical jargon that is unreadable by the affected community.

5. **Setting Unrealistic Expectations**: For any organization in this situation, avoid making sweeping assurances about security measures unless they are genuine and actionable. Empty promises about the current or future state of the situation will only delay the erosion of trust.

For all organizations, it's time to prepare for "when" a breach occurs, not "if." The key to effective incident and breach disclosure lies in preparation. Organizations should always:

- Develop and regularly update an incident response plan with all key stakeholders. This plan should include external legal counsel and cyber insurance brokers, as appropriate, to ensure all necessary communications and workflows are known and documented.

- Conduct tabletop exercises to simulate breach scenarios and refine communication strategies for a wide variety of incidents and breaches—from ransomware to physical asset theft and data leakage. Each event will require a slightly different response, so knowing how to base them on common scenarios will help when and incident occurs.

- Build relationships with legal, public relations, and cybersecurity experts who can provide guidance during a crisis. This includes having an incident response retainer with an independent third-party organization and media agency that can help manage inbound and outbound communications.

Organizations must embrace honest disclosure as a cornerstone of their incident response strategy. By prioritizing honesty, truthfulness, promptness, transparency, empathy, and accountability, they can mitigate

CHAPTER 15   IT'S NOT IF, BUT WHEN

the fallout of an incident and, hopefully, safeguard their reputation. Remember, the vast majority of people value integrity. When the inevitable occurs, let your business actions demonstrate that you are not only prepared, but also committed to doing the right thing when something inevitably goes awry.

# CHAPTER 16

# Supply Chain Attacks

Part of my daily routine is to read the news, particularly articles and websites covering cybersecurity. In the last few years, there has been a disturbing trend of vendor breaches that impact very high-profile customers. Despite the severity, you can't help but become numb from the unceasing litany of these incidents.

As our businesses have become more dependent on interconnected technology, your business's security is only as strong as one any one individual link—and it might not even be the weakest in the chain, just the one that's stressed the most. In addition, that link may not even be within your organization, but within your supply chain. When a trusted vendor experiences a security breach, the ripple effects need to be taken seriously to avoid a cascading event. The compromised data or access may provide threat actors with a direct line to your systems. How you respond to such a supply chain threat can mean the difference between mitigating the fallout and becoming collateral damage.

Here are some actions your organization can take to better withstand supply chain attacks.

CHAPTER 16   SUPPLY CHAIN ATTACKS

# Step 1: Confirm the Breach and Understand the Scope

The first step is to avoid panic. Just because a vendor has suffered a breach doesn't mean your business has been directly impacted. Take swift action to determine your current status.

- Communicate immediately with the supplier (vendor) to confirm the breach and ask the following questions (at a minimum):
    - What was the nature of the breach? (e.g., ransomware, data exfiltration, credential compromise)
    - What systems or data were affected?
    - How did the breach occur, and has it been contained?
    - Is there any additional risk of exposure?
    - Has remediation (a patch) been developed and implemented?
    - Are there any recommended steps we should take? (e.g., log reviews, password resets, taking an application offline, looking at IoCs, etc.)
- Assess your complete exposure and how your organization interacts with the vendor.
- Assess whether the vendor has access to sensitive data, privileged accounts, or key infrastructure. This will determine the level of risk to your business and how you proceed with next steps. (e.g., How are you impacted?)

CHAPTER 16 SUPPLY CHAIN ATTACKS

# Step 2: Activate Your Incident Response Plan

Your organization should already have an incident response (IR) plan for cybersecurity incidents. If not, now is the time to establish the necessary policy owners, protocols, and procedures. These steps should only be initiated if it has been determined that you've been impacted. Otherwise, diligent monitoring of the situation is highly recommended.

- Activate your IR plan and bring together stakeholders from IT, legal, compliance, and PR to coordinate efforts. Ensure clear roles and responsibilities.

- Temporarily suspend connections with the vendor's system or applications if they pose an immediate risk or the breach is ongoing. This may involve disabling API access, changing credentials, or rerouting workflows.

- Monitor for indicators of compromise (IoCs) and work with your security team to identify unusual activity, such as unauthorized logins, changes in data flow, or access attempts tied to the breach timeline. All of this information will be needed and should be securely documented.

# Step 3: Informing Stakeholders

Transparency is critical during a vendor breach, but communication must be strategic and precise. Conflicting, unstructured, or inaccurate information can lead to legal issues and stakeholder frustration. All external information should be reviewed by legal counsel.

- Inform your leadership team and relevant departments about the breach, its potential implications, and the steps being taken to address it. This information is confidential and should be treated as such.

- External communications should always be readily available (even a public email address will suffice). If customer data is at risk, you may need to notify affected parties to maintain trust and comply with regulatory compliance regulations. Again, work with legal counsel to craft clear, concise messaging that avoids speculation.

## Step 4: Defense-in-Depth Review

After stabilizing the immediate risk, focus on bolstering your organization's security posture. No one wants to find themselves in the same situation again or be impacted multiple times by the same security breach. Once the immediate crisis has passed, conduct a postmortem with the vendor to identify lessons learned.

- As a general precaution, immediately update passwords and API keys associated with the vendor in all instances, just in case some form of lateral movement was missed.

- Audit the level of access your vendor had to your systems and data. Limit access in adherence to the principle of least privilege.

- Provide additional focus on monitoring tools to flag suspicious behavior and identify potential vulnerabilities that may be related to the breach.

- The offending vendors should provide transparency into what happened, how it was mitigated, and the steps they're taking to prevent future breaches via an incident report. Ensure your organization has received and thoroughly reviewed it.

- Review your vendor agreements to include clear security requirements and incident response obligations for any potential future events.

# Step 5: Third-Party Risk Management Program

A vendor breach highlights the need for a robust third-party risk management (TPRM) framework. Use this incident as a catalyst for improvement and to ensure any regulatory scrutiny will be satisfactorily met. This is especially important if sensitive data was exposed, as your organization may need to comply with regulatory reporting requirements. Regulations such as GDPR, CCPA, or industry-specific standards like HIPAA often mandate timely disclosure of data breaches and should be connected to your third-party risk management program.

- Regularly evaluate vendors for their security maturity, ensuring they meet your compliance standards. This evaluation should occur before onboarding, during contract reviews, and after a breach.

- Implement the foundational principles of zero trust to third-party vendors. This means no implicit trust outside of the organization for any vendor.

- Ensure all notifications are handled correctly, and all timelines are reflected in all communications. These documents (internal and external) could be used against the vendor if a legal situation arises, so ensuring their accuracy is critical.

- Maintain detailed records of your response actions, vendor communications, and remediation efforts. These can be critical in demonstrating compliance and mitigating liability if additional situations arise.

A vendor security breach is a stark reminder that security exposures and risks can occur anytime, anywhere. Every team member is tasked with protecting the organization; and you are a part of a broader ecosystem where every link in the chain matters. By acting decisively, communicating transparently, and continuously strengthening your defenses, your business can weather these events and emerge more resilient to future attacks.

# CHAPTER 17

# Been Hacked?

In order for resources to interact using different technologies, vendors, and platforms, organizations use secrets (credentials, API keys, tokens, etc.) to authenticate and automate workflows. This basic process ensures communication between machines, applications, and AI agents is authorized and appropriate. If secrets are stolen or lost, a cybersecurity breach is a potential result. When secrets carry administrative privileges, these small strings of code wield enormous power and are often referred to as "keys to the kingdom." These administrative secrets and the privileges they grant can unlock doors to sensitive systems, proprietary data, and critical operations, making them an irresistible target for threat actors. If such a secret falls into the wrong hands, what can happen? For this chapter, we will answer that question and also explore how to detect when secrets have been compromised and strategies for swift remediation.

When a secret or key is stolen, the repercussions can ripple throughout an organization, affecting internal operations, client environments, and potentially leading to legal issues. The severity and scope of the impact depend on the compromised data and services. Secrets are designed to authenticate applications and services for machine-to-machine interactions, bypassing traditional user credentials. Here are some implications of stolen secrets:

1. **Unauthorized Access**: Threat actors can exploit stolen keys to gain direct access to cloud services, databases, and APIs. This bypasses additional authentication methods, like MFA, that are typically required for human-based accounts.

2. **Data Exfiltration**: Sensitive information—such as customer data, proprietary algorithms, or financial records—can be siphoned off at line speed (the speed of the Internet connection) with little time for someone to react or acknowledge the compromise.

3. **Supply Chain Attacks**: Secrets often link multiple services, partners, vendors, integrations, and advanced automation. A compromised key can trigger a ripple effect, impacting third-party systems and escalating the breach into client environments and other vendors.

4. **Financial Impact**: Cloud resources can be hijacked to mine cryptocurrency or launch other malicious attacks, resulting in substantial service bills due to increased network utilization and/or CPU/GPU costs.

5. **Reputation**: Trust is hard-won and easily lost, especially in the technology sector. A breach involving secrets can tarnish an organization's credibility, resulting in customer churn, regulatory scrutiny, and lost future opportunities.

The clandestine nature of secrets makes their early detection challenging for any organization. However, focused monitoring and robust detection mechanisms can uncover anomalies before they escalate if a secret key is compromised:

1. **Traffic Patterns**: Unusually high volume of API calls, requests from unfamiliar IP addresses, or access outside of normal business hours may indicate unauthorized secret authentication attempts.

2. **Behavioral Analytics**: Modern cybersecurity solutions embed machine learning (or artificial intelligence) to establish baselines for normal secret usage. These solutions can flag deviations that warrant investigation, forming a key part of a mature and vigorous approach to secrets management.

3. **Access Logs**: Regularly audit logs for signs of unauthorized access or activity from deprecated keys. These outdated keys should be removed as part of a comprehensive lifecycle management process for machine identities and secrets management.

4. **Rate Limiting**: Excessive requests or exceeding predefined thresholds can indicate misuse, not only for the secret itself but also for any databases, applications, or services accessed via API keys.

5. **Error Logs**: An increase in log error events, such as failed authentication requests, could indicate malicious attempts to exploit stolen keys and initiate lateral movement within the network.

Time is of the essence when a secret compromise is discovered. A prompt, structured response is crucial to minimize damage and prevent future recurrence:

1. **Key Revocation**: Immediately disable the compromised secret to prevent further unauthorized access. Many platforms offer dynamic key revocation and creation. If this isn't available, place the secret under management using a privileged access management (PAM) solution.

2. **Communications**: Promptly inform all affected teams, customers, and partners. Transparency fosters trust and enables collaborative mitigation, which is especially important if the event is subject to regulatory compliance.

3. **Least Privilege Access**: Limit all secret permissions to the minimum necessary for its function. This curtails the potential damage should a key be stolen.

4. **Review Secrets Security**:

    - **Privileged Pathways**: Ensure that secrets do not have a path to privileged access for administrator or root accounts. If compromised, such secrets offer a straightforward path for threat actors to gain the most important "keys to the kingdom."

    - **Use IP Allowlisting**: Restrict secrets access to known, trusted IP ranges. Consider incorporating geolocations, business hours, and other trusted attributes for API key access.

    - **Adopt Token-Based Authentication**: Replace static secrets with ephemeral tokens to reduce exposure risk. This should be a requirement for all new system implementations.

CHAPTER 17   BEEN HACKED?

5. **Postmortem Analysis**: Analyze the breach to identify root causes, improve defenses, and build in additional controls for future monitoring.

While remediation is crucial, prevention is always better. Protecting secrets requires a multilayered approach:

- **Secrets Storage**: Never hard-code secrets into applications. Instead, use a secure secret safe, such as a PAM solution. These tools provide best practices for storage, inventory, and management.

- **Rotation**: Periodically rotate secrets to limit the window of exploitation if one is ever compromised. The frequency of these rotations and testing of "break glass" access procedures should be an integral part of this process.

- **Monitor Access**: Where feasible, implement real-time monitoring and anomaly detection of all secret usage to avoid a breach.

- **Developer Education**: Educate development teams and require them to follow secure coding practices. They need to understand the potential risks to the business if secrets are compromised.

- **Vulnerability Assessments**: Conduct regular vulnerability assessments, penetration testing, and secrets inventory reviews. These practices help uncover vulnerabilities in secret implementation—from faults in depreciated APIs to stale instantiations.

The consequences can be dire when secrets are compromised. By acknowledging these risks, prioritizing detection, and acting swiftly to remediate breaches, organizations can regain control and minimize

CHAPTER 17    BEEN HACKED?

the impact, both internally and for their clients. All organizations must treat secrets with the same vigilance as user passwords and any sessions that allow privileged access. After all, if the "keys to the kingdom" are stolen, the cost of complacency far outweighs the price of appropriate preparation.

# CHAPTER 18

# History Lesson

Over the past three decades, the Internet has undergone a profound transformation—from a fledgling curiosity to the beating heart of global commerce and social interaction. Parallel to this growth, a sophisticated wave of cybersecurity threats has emerged, initiating a cat and mouse game between threat actors and defenders.

Cybersecurity incidents from the last 30 years—from early worms like Slammer and Blaster to notorious campaigns like WannaCry and NotPetya—reveal not only the technological evolution of digital threats, but also the persistent human patterns behind these breaches. Even the most advanced exploits often hinge on a handful of familiar mistakes: unpatched systems, weak authentication methods, social engineering, and a lack of routine oversight.

What follows are ten recommendations drawn from these past lessons, meticulously reconfirmed by the countless breaches that have shaped modern cyber defense strategies. Each of these guidelines echoes an underlying principle: proactive, consistent, and well-communicated measures are critical for safeguarding against modern attack vectors. While each recommendation stands on its own, in practice, they intertwine into a holistic strategy that demands constant updating, monitoring, and refinement in response to new threats. Moreover, these recommendations can be adapted to almost any organization, aligning with the straightforward approach of improving your security posture 1% at a time, as discussed in the introduction.

1. **Embrace a Culture of Security Awareness:** One of the most critical lessons from the past quarter century is that technology alone cannot solve the cybersecurity equation. Humans remain both the weakest link and the strongest shield. Threat actors commonly exploit human error through spear phishing, social engineering, or simple oversight. While the Morris Worm (1988) was an early harbinger, modern attacks like the 2020 Twitter breach show how one unsuspecting user can open the door to a catastrophic compromise. Therefore, every business should invest in regular, engaging security training sessions. Encourage employees to report suspicious emails or activities, even if they prove benign. Develop a "security-first" mindset at all levels of the organization so that due diligence and caution become second nature, rather than an afterthought.

2. **Apply the Principle of Least Privilege:** Traces of high-profile attacks often show that once threat actors gain a foothold—whether through stolen credentials or a system vulnerability—they can pivot laterally with relative ease if internal privileges are not tightly regulated. Implementing the principle of least privilege means ensuring every user—from the newest intern to the CEO—has precisely the minimum level of access required to perform their job duties. Administrative privileges, in particular, should be carefully monitored and granted on a strict need-to-use basis. This approach significantly limits the "blast radius" of any single compromised

account. Pairing a least privilege model with continuous reviews of user permissions ensures that access rights remain accurate and up to date, further reducing the risk of exploitation.

3. **Patch Early and Patch Often:** A stark revelation from the last two decades is how many successful breaches could have been prevented with diligent patch management. The infamous WannaCry ransomware, for instance, spread rapidly in 2017 by largely exploiting a known vulnerability in Microsoft Windows for which a patch was already available. Yet, countless organizations failed to apply the update in time and paid a steep price in data loss and downtime. A robust patch management program involves regularly scanning systems for missing updates and streamlining deployment so that critical patches reach endpoints as swiftly as possible. While automated solutions help, even the best tools require consistent oversight and immediate response when new vulnerabilities surface.

4. **Encrypt Everything, Especially Sensitive Data:** With data breaches happening with alarming regularity, encrypting sensitive data—both in transit and at rest—is no longer optional. High-profile incidents, from early credit card data theft to major social media platform breaches, underscore encryption's critical role. Even if cybercriminals steal your data, encryption can turn that haul into useless gibberish. Beyond customer data, businesses should encrypt internal communications, backups, and removable storage

devices to ensure unauthorized access doesn't lead to a catastrophic leak. Remember to keep encryption keys secure and rotate them periodically, just as you would privileged passwords.

5. **Invest in Real-Time Monitoring and Incident Detection:** The damage inflicted by threat actors often multiplies when a compromise goes undetected for weeks or even months. In the early 2010s, numerous state-sponsored attacks relied on "low and slow" infiltration techniques, stealthily exfiltrating intellectual property from large corporations over extended periods. Real-time security monitoring, powered by well-configured intrusion detection systems, Security Information and Event Management (SIEM) tools, and advanced threat intelligence feeds, can help your team identify anomalous behavior before it escalates. Proactive detection isn't an extravagance; it's a necessity to curb breaches in their early stages and efficiently manage damage control. Invest in the right tools, but also ensure staff have clear processes, training, and funding to respond to alerts and escalate critical events.

6. **Segment Your Network:** Network segmentation is another core lesson learned from major breaches. When a single infected laptop can freely traverse the entire corporate environment, threat actors can hop from an innocuous user endpoint to mission-critical databases in minutes. Proper segmentation compartmentalizes systems, isolating development, production, and guest environments. Moreover,

sensitive data repositories should be stored in separated networks with stricter access controls. If threat actors compromise one part of the network, segmentation contains the breach, giving security teams time to detect, isolate, and remediate before intruders spread further.

7. **Adopt Strong Authentication Measures:** A lesson consistently reinforced over two decades is that passwords—especially weak, reused passwords—pose a looming threat. The phenomenon of credential stuffing, where threat actors try troves of stolen credentials across multiple platforms, is more rampant than ever. Multifactor authentication (MFA) can significantly mitigate this risk by mandating an additional layer of verification, whether through a hardware token, mobile app, or biometric factor. The shift away from purely password-based security measures is not just advisable; it's essential. Furthermore, businesses should consider moving toward passwordless solutions, or at least robust policy frameworks that enforce complexity requirements and regular rotation.

8. **Maintain Comprehensive Backups and a Tested Recovery Plan:** Ransomware attacks vividly demonstrate the importance of backups as an integral part of any security strategy. If your data is properly backed up and can be restored swiftly, the ransomware threat loses much of its leverage. However, simply having backups isn't enough; they need regular testing to ensure functionality and

clearly documented restoration processes. Keeping offline, air-gapped backups prevents malware from encrypting both live systems and the backups themselves. A well-tested recovery plan, practiced via periodic drills, gives your team the confidence to handle emergencies swiftly and minimize disruption.

9. **Foster Transparency and Collaborate with the Wider Community:** If the past 25 years have proven anything, it's that no single organization can handle cyber threats alone. When an attack wave begins, sharing timely intelligence—like indicators of compromise (IoCs) and malicious IP addresses—can thwart threat actors from rapidly scaling their campaigns. Similarly, organizations that openly disclose breaches, detail their remediation steps, and share lessons learned not only uphold integrity but also strengthen the collective response to cyber threats. Industry alliances, threat information sharing forums, and close partnerships with law enforcement agencies can mean the difference between being blindsided by an emerging tactic and having the foresight to thwart it.

10. **Commit to Periodic Audits and Continual Improvement:** One consistent theme that resonates across all major breaches is the dynamic nature of cybersecurity. A static security policy, no matter how robust at inception, erodes in effectiveness as new threats emerge and business operations shift. Regular external and internal audits illuminate overlooked vulnerabilities or misconfigurations and

verify that security policies align with real-world practices. Consider engaging in penetration testing to simulate an attacker's techniques, thereby revealing the most immediate threats. Commit to iterative improvements, merging each new finding into your security posture. Just as technologies change, so do attack vectors. What worked five years ago may not stand firm tomorrow.

These ten recommendations reflect lessons learned through countless incidents, remedial steps, and slow transformations in corporate culture. But even as we adopt them, we must remember that cybersecurity remains a living, breathing discipline. A well-patched network from last month can quickly become vulnerable if IT staff neglect newly announced patches. An organization that once enforced rigorous multifactor authentication can find itself exposed if new employees are onboarded without proper training. A data encryption scheme can prove fruitless if the encryption keys remain unsecured on a publicly accessible server.

Equally important is the acknowledgment that robust security isn't the exclusive domain of large enterprises. Small- and medium-sized businesses can benefit just as much, if not more, from disciplined security practices, especially since they often lack the resources to easily rebound from a major breach. Tools and processes that seemed expensive or reserved for tech giants a decade ago have become more affordable and user-friendly, thanks to advances in automation and cloud technologies. Yet, effectively adopting these resources demands strategic planning and a willingness to learn past missteps.

Above all, the last few decades have demonstrated that complacency is the ultimate enabler of threat actors. They rely on overlooked updates, ill-prepared workforces, and neglected security protocols, operating with the certainty that some businesses will inevitably let their guard down. Defending against this mindset requires an enduring commitment to

## CHAPTER 18  HISTORY LESSON

vigilance. By creating and sustaining a culture where security awareness is an integral part of daily operations, businesses can make it infinitely harder for malicious actors to succeed.

Reflecting on the timeline of past attacks and adopting the ten recommendations presented here ensures that organizations treat each high-profile breach not merely as a cautionary tale, but as a catalyst for growth. Cybersecurity, after all, is a journey rather than a destination—a cyclical process of learning, adapting, and strengthening. The most enduring defenses often begin by consistently embracing the simplest, smartest steps over time.

# CHAPTER 19

# Conclusion

As we reach the closing pages of this history lesson, it's helpful to pause and reflect on how far we've come and how much further we still need to go. Think back to the earliest documented computer worms that crept onto unsuspecting networks through what were then revolutionary new communication channels. While they seem rudimentary by today's standards, these early incursions offered a glimpse of the chaos that would follow.

Over decades, we've watched attacks grow in sophistication, from mischievous pranks to meticulously planned strikes by organized cybercriminals and nation-state actors. In parallel, organizations have grappled with the rising costs of these breaches, along with reputational fallout that can be even more devastating than direct financial loss. Yet, threaded through all these episodes is a recurring insight: relatively simple improvements in cyber hygiene could drastically reduce the success rate of these threats and the scope of any damage.

It's easy to think of the modern cyber landscape as a battlefield rife with elaborate tactics, zero-day exploits, ransomware, social engineering, and deepfakes. However, many of the most damaging breaches still exploit the same fundamental deficiencies: weak passwords, unpatched systems, and human error. From a corporate vantage point, the core lesson might seem painfully obvious: the tighter your security standards, the harder it is for malicious actors to gain a foothold. But "obvious" doesn't always translate to "easy," or "user-friendly." With a constantly shifting workforce, a never-ending parade of third-party vendors, and overlapping networked

## CHAPTER 19 CONCLUSION

systems, ensuring consistent safeguards is far from trivial. Yet "far from trivial" is not synonymous with impossible. If there's one message that resonates through our journey in these pages, it's that victory lies in methodical, incremental fortifications—steps that might look small in isolation but collectively form a robust cybersecurity strategy.

One prevailing reason simple cyber protection measures fail to take root is the perception that cybersecurity demands advanced, expensive technology accessible only to large, well-funded companies. Certainly, a broad market offers state-of-the-art solutions boasting complex detection algorithms and real-time threat analytics, and these solutions have their place. However, most successful intrusions can be traced back to, for instance, an unpatched server running outdated software or an unsuspecting employee unwittingly clicking a malicious link. These are threat surfaces that are addressable with well-documented, affordable best practices. Implementing multifactor authentication (MFA), for example, can block a large proportion of unauthorized access attempts. Training staff to recognize social engineering attacks is another low-cost, high-impact measure. For many organizations, the much-needed fix isn't necessarily more technology, but rather the consistent application of processes already within their reach.

The costs tied to these breaches, both financial and reputational, often serve as a stark reminder that ignoring the fundamentals isn't a viable option. By now, we've seen high-profile data leaks leading to class-action lawsuits, regulatory fines, and widespread public outcry. These consequences can chip away at a company's standing in the market, eroding customer trust built over years, if not decades. Consider the potential reputational damage alone: the moment news of a breach hits the headlines, social media discussion flares, outraged customers demand explanations, and competitors seize the moment to reiterate their commitment to data protection. In today's digital landscape, the speed at which such news travels is alarming; a single misstep can quickly spiral into an ongoing crisis. From there, the financial toll might surface in the form of lost contracts, plummeting share prices, or expensive remediation efforts. What intensifies the frustration for many executives is the realization that many of these breaches could have been prevented with disciplined, routine actions.

Still, there is a silver lining. While charting cyberattacks from clumsy sabotage efforts to the refined infiltration techniques of the present day, we also encounter the resilient spirit of defenders—security teams, IT experts, ethical hackers, and forward-thinking executives—who, through their diligence and collaboration, have spurred an entire industry focused on safeguarding our digital ecosystem. Training programs now abound, aimed at instilling a security-first mindset from the factory floor to the corner office. Awareness campaigns have evolved from sporadic, mandatory compliance videos to more dynamic engagements, including simulated phishing exercises that push employees to recognize real-world threats. Community-driven endeavors, too, have emerged, offering open source tools for scanning and patching vulnerabilities, ensuring that organizations of all shapes and sizes can find accessible avenues to fortify their defenses.

In the broader scope, policy and regulatory forces are now shaping expectations for cyber hygiene and breach communications. Various data protection laws, like the General Data Protection Regulation (GDPR) in the European Union or the California Consumer Privacy Act (CCPA) in the United States, have extended legal accountability far beyond voluntary corporate promises. While initially perceived as a compliance burden, this has also standardized foundational security measures and spurred more strategic conversations in boardrooms worldwide. For many organizations, regulatory deadlines catalyzed action that had long been postponed. And while compliance itself should never be the sole driver of security investments, these legal frameworks lay out guidelines that significantly overlap with proven best practices, effectively guiding even reluctant organizations toward a better security posture.

# CHAPTER 19  CONCLUSION

Perhaps the most empowering realization through all of this is the knowledge that, even when threats escalate or seem insurmountable, one of the most effective defenses lies in nurturing a culture of awareness. When employees understand that opening an unusual attachment could lead to ransomware, or that plugging in an unknown USB stick might trigger a data breach, they become the first line of defense. When executives view cybersecurity spending not as a mere sunk cost, but as a strategic investment protecting everything from brand reputation to intellectual property, they shift organizational mindsets.

Simple steps like segmenting the internal network, ensuring a breach in one department doesn't cascade through the entire organization, or regularly reviewing user privileges so staff have only the access needed for their roles, can be transformative. Clustering together these "small wins" eventually fosters an environment where lapses in security become less likely, and anomalies are identified and contained faster.

In concluding this book, it's worth underscoring that cybersecurity is less a finish line and more an ongoing journey, one that requires constant learning and adaptation. While we've traced how attacks have morphed from novel pranks into strategic assaults on individuals, businesses, and governments, the underlying moral still stands: neglecting basic defenses underestimates the craftiness of malicious actors. Their techniques may evolve, but so can the simplest countermeasures. Patching, password discipline, system monitoring, employee education, and multifactor authentication remain some of the most potent forms of deterrence.

Ultimately, the history of cyberattacks is not just a timeline of increasingly sophisticated exploits; it is also a chronicle of business leaders, security professionals, and everyday individuals who have learned, time and again, that vigilance is vital. The costs of breaches and poorly handled security incidents to businesses, measured in dollars, jobs, and reputations, serve as cautionary tales. Yet they also highlight a silver thread running through every breach: the reminder that prevention is possible and often starts with the fundamentals. By weaving these basic protections into an organization's everyday rituals and championing a culture that values security as part of collective responsibility, we can write the next chapter of cybersecurity with more confidence.

While no security posture is ever foolproof, each well-placed safeguard, each educated user, and each timely patch substantially narrows the window of opportunity for threat actors. And in that spirit, our concluding insight is clear: to protect our digital future, we must remain nimble, transparent, and steadfast in the knowledge that every small effort counts.

# APPENDIX A

# Malware

Below is a curated list spotlighting 50 of the most notorious computer viruses (and broader malware, including ransomware) of roughly the last quarter century, arranged in chronological order. Each entry includes its approximate year of emergence, a brief description of its history/origins (where known), its behavior, and estimated financial or economic impact. Although exact figures for damages can vary by source, these estimates provide a sense of the widespread fallout each malware strain inflicted. These history lessons are key in helping form our best practice recommendations from this book.

## APPENDIX A    MALWARE

| Year | Designation | History | Behavior | Impact (USD) | Reference |
|---|---|---|---|---|---|
| 1998 | CIH (Chernobyl) | Allegedly created by a Taiwanese student. This virus targeted Windows 95/98/ME systems. | Overwrote a computer's BIOS chip, rendering machines unbootable. | Over $80 million globally, affecting both home users and corporate networks. | https://www.f-secure.com/v-descs/cih.shtml |
| 1999 | Melissa | Crafted by David L. Smith. Spread via Microsoft Word documents attached to emails. | Exploited Outlook to automatically send itself to the first 50 contacts in the victim's address list, causing widespread email server slowdowns. | About $80 million (mostly from lost productivity and IT cleanup costs). | https://www.fbi.gov/news/stories/melissa-virus-20th-anniversary-032519 |
| 1999 | ExploreZip | Believed to have originated in Israel. Masqueraded as a genuine message from known contacts, prompting victims to unzip a malicious file. | Once activated, it destroyed or corrupted files on a company's network by overwriting data. | Estimates range from tens of millions of dollars (primarily from damage to corporate systems). | https://money.cnn.com/1999/06/10/technology/virus/ |

## APPENDIX A  MALWARE

| | | | | |
|---|---|---|---|---|
| 2000 | ILOVEYOU (Love Bug) | Traced back to creators in the Philippines. This worm enticed users to open an infected attachment based on early social engineering. | Overwrote critical files (e.g., images) and used Microsoft Outlook to replicate all contacts in the user's address book. | Believed to exceed ~$10 billion worldwide, once considered one of the most destructive worms. | https://www.computermuseumofamerica.org/2023/02/07/i-love-you-virus/ |
| 2001 | Code Red | Exploited a vulnerability in Microsoft's Internet Information Services (IIS). First identified by eEye Digital Security in the early years of vulnerability assessment technology. | Defaced affected websites with messages like "Hacked by Chinese," launched DDoS attacks against the White House, and spread quickly with no user intervention. | Between ~$2.0 and ~$2.6 billion. | https://www.giac.org/paper/gsec/1162/code-red-worm/102232 |

(*continued*)

APPENDIX A   MALWARE

| Year | Designation | History | Behavior | Impact (USD) | Reference |
|---|---|---|---|---|---|
| 2001 | Nimda | Named "admin" spelled backward, spread via multiple vectors: email, compromised websites, and network shares. | Rapidly elevated privileges, modifying web documents and existing files to facilitate further infection. | Roughly ~$530 million (mainly in cleanup and lost productivity). | https://www.f-secure.com/v-descs/nimda.shtml |
| 2001 | Klez | Origin remains uncertain, but it proliferated via mass-mailing techniques similar to Melissa and ILOVEYOU. | Used "spoofed" sender addresses to trick recipients into opening content, often included multiple variants that disabled antivirus software. | Hundreds of millions (due to widespread email network infection and antivirus service recovery). | https://www.f-secure.com/v-descs/klez.shtml |

APPENDIX A  MALWARE

| Year | Name | Description | Impact | Reference |
|---|---|---|---|---|
| 2003 | SQL Slammer | Exploited a buffer overflow vulnerability in Microsoft SQL Server. Believed to have originated among underground malware groups. | Caused massive Internet slowdowns, crashed bank ATMs and airline systems due to exposed database network services. Over ~$1 billion (due to lost productivity and emergency network rebuilds). | https://learn.microsoft.com/en-us/security-updates/securitybulletins/2002/ms02-039 |
| 2003 | Blaster (Lovsan) | Capitalized on a Windows DCOM RPC vulnerability. Based on subsequent analysis, professionals believe it emerged in the United States or China. | Crashed systems by forcefully rebooting them and threatened an attack on Microsoft's windowsupdate.com service. Up to ~$525 million (total damages from lost business continuity and system repair costs). | https://learn.microsoft.com/en-us/troubleshoot/windows-server/security-and-malware/blaster-worm-virus-alert |

(*continued*)

275

# APPENDIX A   MALWARE

| Year | Designation | History | Behavior | Impact (USD) | Reference |
|---|---|---|---|---|---|
| 2003 | Sobig | Written by an unknown author, spread via spam emails, forging sender addresses to entice recipients to open infected attachments. | Included multiple versions (Sobig.A through Sobig.F). Sobig.F was especially virulent and set records for the fastest-spreading email worm at the time. | ~$500 million or more, primarily from overwhelming email servers worldwide. | https://www.cnn.com/2003/TECH/internet/08/21/sobig.virus/index.html |
| 2004 | MyDoom | Believed to have origins in Russia. Arrived as an email attachment disguised as an error message. | Opened a backdoor on infected PCs allowing remote control; launched DDoS attacks against websites like SCO Group. | Over ~$38 billion (often cited as the fastest-spreading email worm ever). | https://www.okta.com/identity-101/mydoom/ |

| | | | | |
|---|---|---|---|---|
| 2004 | Sasser | Authored by a German teenager. Exploited the LSASS (Local Security Authority Subsystem Service) vulnerability in Windows. | Forced computers to crash and reboot repeatedly, spreading automatically without user intervention. | ~$18 billion (damages and productivity losses). | https://www.f-secure.com/v-descs/sasser.shtml |
| 2004 | Bagle | Detected in various forms across Europe. Circulated as an email attachment that unleashed a backdoor Trojan. | Targeted a wide range of Windows versions, formed "botnets," and attempted to disable security programs. | Hundreds of millions of dollars in global cleanup operations. | https://www.microsoft.com/en-us/wdsi/threats/malware-encyclopedia-description?Name=Win32%2FBagle |

(*continued*)

APPENDIX A  MALWARE

| Year | Designation | History | Behavior | Impact (USD) | Reference |
|---|---|---|---|---|---|
| 2004 | Netsky | Written by the same author who coded the Bagle (eventually unmasked as Sven Jaschan). Spread via email attachments and peer-to-peer networks. | Famously engaged in "trash-talking" with Bagle's creators within the virus code, spurring a so-called "virus war." | Over ~$100 million (not including countless hours devoted to removing the worm from corporate and home PCs). | https://www.f-secure.com/v-descs/netsky-v.shtml |
| 2004 | Santy | Exploited a vulnerability in the phpBB forum software. Precise origin is unknown. | Defaced websites running vulnerable phpBB installations by replacing pages with "This site is defaced!!!" messages. | Tens of millions of dollars (website restoration and software patching costs). | https://www.f-secure.com/v-descs/santy-a.shtml |

APPENDIX A  MALWARE

| | | | | |
|---|---|---|---|---|
| 2004 | Witty | Struck computers running Internet Security Systems (ISS) firewall products, presumably authored by a highly skilled group or individual. | Notable as the first Internet worm to effectively destroy data, writing random bits over the hard drive. | Millions (limited volume, but high damage to specifically targeted security software and systems). | https://www.caida.org/archive/witty/ |
| 2007 | Storm Worm | Origin unknown; named for initial email subject referencing "230 dead as storm batters Europe." | Transformed infected machines into a colossal botnet, used for spam and DDoS attacks. | High hundreds of millions (mostly in global spam-related costs and system outages). | https://www.secureworks.com/research/storm-worm |

*(continued)*

APPENDIX A    MALWARE

| Year | Designation | History | Behavior | Impact (USD) | Reference |
|---|---|---|---|---|---|
| 2007 | Zeus (Zbot) | Believed to have originated in Eastern Europe/Russia. Often distributed via phishing emails or malicious downloads. | Specialized in stealing online banking credentials; formed large botnets to siphon sensitive data from victims. | Over ~$100 million (direct theft from bank accounts, plus remediation costs). | https://www.crowdstrike.com/en-us/cybersecurity-101/malware/zeus-malware/ |
| 2008 | Conficker (Downup, Downadup) | Exploited vulnerabilities in Windows RPC services. Believed to be from a sophisticated cybercrime operation. | Created massive botnets by locking users out of administrative controls, disabling security systems, and patching certain vulnerabilities to block rival malware. | Up to ~$9 billion (total global damage and containment efforts). | https://www.cisa.gov/news-events/alerts/2009/03/29/conficker-worm-targets-microsoft-windows-systems |

# APPENDIX A MALWARE

| 2008 | Koobface | Specifically targeted social networks like Facebook and MySpace, luring victims with bogus links and videos. | Transformed infected systems into botnet nodes, harvesting login credentials for social platforms. | Over ~$100 million (largely due to mass identity theft and fraudulent campaigns). | https://www.f-secure.com/v-descs/net-worm-w32-koobface.shtml |
|---|---|---|---|---|---|
| 2010 | Stuxnet | Believed to be jointly developed by US and Israeli intelligence agencies to sabotage Iranian nuclear facilities. | Targeted industrial control systems (Siemens PLCs), marking one of the earliest examples of cyberwarfare. | Tough to quantify, but Iran's nuclear program faced significant setbacks; costs likely in the hundreds of millions. | https://www.csoonline.com/article/562691/stuxnet-explained-the-first-known-cyberweapon.html |

*(continued)*

281

# APPENDIX A    MALWARE

| Year | Designation | History | Behavior | Impact (USD) | Reference |
|---|---|---|---|---|---|
| 2011 | Duqu | Likely created by the same advanced actor(s) behind Stuxnet. Spread via crafted Microsoft Word documents. | Functioned as an espionage toolkit, gathering intelligence from industrial control systems and corporate environments. | Primarily intangible costs; economic impact in the millions (stolen trade secrets and R&D data). | https://www.cisa.gov/news-events/ics-alerts/ics-alert-11-291-01e |
| 2011 | Shylock (Caphaw) | Origin uncertain, though it targeted UK-based banking customers extensively. Distributed via compromised sites and phishing emails. | Focused on man-in-the-browser attacks to intercept and manipulate banking transactions in real time. | Over ~$10 million (direct financial theft from victims' accounts). | https://www.darkreading.com/cyberattacks-data-breaches/shylock-malware-resurges-targets-top-u-s-banks |

APPENDIX A  MALWARE

| | | | | |
|---|---|---|---|---|
| 2011 | GameOver ZeuS | An evolution of the Zeus banking Trojan, employing peer-to-peer communication to evade takedowns. | Targeted a wide range of financial institutions, harvesting login credentials and enabling unauthorized transfers. | Estimated in the hundreds of millions; the FBI and international partners eventually disrupted its infrastructure. | https://www.cisa.gov/news-events/alerts/2014/06/02/gameover-zeus-p2p-malware |
| 2012 | Flame | Attributed to nation-state actors, possibly the same collective behind Stuxnet and Duqu. Infected machines mainly in the Middle East. | Extraordinarily large and modular espionage platform, capable of recording audio, capturing screenshots, and logging keystrokes. | Difficult to tally, as its main aim was espionage rather than direct financial theft. Likely millions in investigation and remediation costs. | https://www.f-secure.com/v-descs/flame.shtml |

*(continued)*

APPENDIX A    MALWARE

| Year | Designation | History | Behavior | Impact (USD) | Reference |
|---|---|---|---|---|---|
| 2012 | Gauss | Another espionage-oriented malware tied to the same operators behind Stuxnet and Flame. Spread via USB sticks and spear phishing. | Targeted Lebanese banks, gathering financial credentials and account data. | Highly targeted; direct damages likely in the millions, with broader geopolitical implications. | https://notes.nap.edu/2012/08/24/gauss-malware-cyberattack-or-cyber-exploitation-nrc-reports-explain/ |
| 2013 | CryptoLocker | Thought to have Russian origins, primarily distributed via malicious email attachments and botnets like GameOver ZeuS. | Among the first high-profile ransomware to encrypt a victim's files and demand Bitcoin payment. | Over ~$3 million in ransom payments within the first few months, plus far higher costs in system recovery. | https://www.cisa.gov/news-events/alerts/2013/11/05/cryptolocker-ransomware-infections |

| | | | | |
|---|---|---|---|---|
| 2015 | Dridex | A direct descendant of Cridex, distributed via macro-enabled Word documents. Believed to be developed by Eastern European cybercriminal gangs. | Targeted banking credentials, forming botnets used to deploy further malware. | Hundreds of millions in bank fraud (especially against UK and US financial institutions). | https://www.cisa.gov/news-events/cybersecurity-advisories/aa19-339a |
| 2016 | Locky | Spread through malicious email campaigns, often disguised as invoices or shipping notifications. | One of the most disruptive ransomware families, encrypting files with a ".locky" extension. | Tens of millions in ransom payments and additional recovery costs for large and small organizations alike. | https://www.knowbe4.com/locky-ransomware |

*(continued)*

APPENDIX A   MALWARE

| Year | Designation | History | Behavior | Impact (USD) | Reference |
|---|---|---|---|---|---|
| 2016 | Cerber | Believed to be orchestrated by a professional ransomware-as-a-service group. Propagated primarily via email attachments. | Constantly evolved encryption tactics, sometimes including text-to-speech ransom notes. | Over ~$200 million in total ransom payments and damages. | https://www.sentinelone.com/blog/c3rb3r-ransomware-ongoing-exploitation-of-cve-2023-22518-targets-unpatched-confluence-servers/ |
| 2016 | TrickBot | Emerged from the Dyre banking Trojan codebase; run by organized cybercrime outfits in Eastern Europe. | Advanced modular Trojan capable of stealing credentials, spreading laterally in networks, and delivering other malware (e.g., ransomware). | Hundreds of millions in compromised data, fraud, and subsequent network remediation. | https://www.cisa.gov/news-events/cybersecurity-advisories/aa21-076a |

APPENDIX A  MALWARE

| | | | | |
|---|---|---|---|---|
| 2017 | WannaCry | Suspected North Korean involvement; exploited the EternalBlue vulnerability in Windows Server Message Block (SMB). | Propagated at lightning speed worldwide, locking down hospitals (NHS UK), telecoms, and factories. | Over ~$4 billion (including halted production lines and emergency IT overhauls). | https://www.csoonline.com/article/563017/wannacry-explained-a-perfect-ransomware-storm.html |
| 2017 | NotPetya | Linked to state-sponsored Russian actors, first unleashed via a Ukrainian tax software update. | Masqueraded as ransomware, but was actually a "wiper," permanently destroying data. | Exceeded ~$10 billion, hitting global shipping giant Maersk, pharmaceutical firms, and more. | https://www.cisa.gov/news-events/alerts/2017/07/01/petya-ransomware |

*(continued)*

287

APPENDIX A    MALWARE

| Year | Designation | History | Behavior | Impact (USD) | Reference |
|---|---|---|---|---|---|
| 2017 | Bad Rabbit | Hit primarily in Russia and Eastern Europe. Spread via drive-by downloads from compromised news/media websites. | Another ransomware variant related to NotPetya's code, shutting down systems and demanding Bitcoin ransom. | Low hundreds of millions, overshadowed by WannaCry and NotPetya, but still very disruptive. | https://blog.qualys.com/vulnerabilities-threat-research/2017/10/24/bad-rabbit-ransomware |
| 2018 | Emotet | Began as a banking Trojan from Eastern European groups but evolved into a botnet distributing other malware. | Excelled at harvesting email conversations, enabling highly effective phishing attacks. | Over ~$2.5 billion, factoring in widespread infections and secondary payloads. | https://www.cisa.gov/news-events/cybersecurity-advisories/aa20-280a |

| 2018 | SamSam | Believed to be operated by Iranian hackers, used brute force attacks on weak RDP credentials to penetrate networks. | Specialized in targeting city governments, hospitals, and universities, encrypting servers for high ransom demands. | Over ~$30 million in ransom fees, plus operational downtime losses. | https://www.cisa.gov/news-events/cybersecurity-advisories/aa18-337a |
| --- | --- | --- | --- | --- | --- |
| 2018 | Ryuk | Attributed to Russian cybercriminals, commonly distributed via TrickBot infections. | Focused on "big game hunting," targeting large enterprises and demanding multimillion-dollar ransoms. | Single attacks sometimes cost victims over ~$1 million in ransom; total damage is in the hundreds of millions. | https://www.sentinelone.com/cybersecurity-101/threat-intelligence/ryuk-ransomware/ |

(*continued*)

## APPENDIX A  MALWARE

| Year | Designation | History | Behavior | Impact (USD) | Reference |
|---|---|---|---|---|---|
| 2018 | GandCrab | Advertised on underground forums as a ransomware-as-a-service offering, presumably run by Eastern European threat actors. | Frequently updated, with affiliates distributing it via email spam and exploit kits. | Over ~$2 billion extorted before its operators announced "retirement" in 2019. | https://www.knowbe4.com/gandcrab-ransomware |
| 2019 | Maze | Possibly developed by a Franco-Russian group, delivered through phishing attacks and exploit kits. | Infamous for pioneering the "double extortion" tactic, publishing stolen data online if victims didn't pay. | Potentially hundreds of millions, with ransoms regularly topping six or seven figures. | https://www.cloudflare.com/learning/security/ransomware/maze-ransomware/ |
| 2019 | Sodinokibi (REvil) | Attributed to the same group behind GandCrab; leverages exploit kits, phishing, and supply chain attacks. | Popularized advanced double extortion methods, encrypting data, while threatening to leak sensitive info. | Many organizations paid million-dollar ransoms; cumulative damages are in the billions. | https://www.cybereason.com/blog/research/the-sodinokibi-ransomware-attack |

## APPENDIX A  MALWARE

| | | | | | |
|---|---|---|---|---|---|
| 2019 | LockBit | Linked to an organized Eastern European gang, distributed via email attachments or compromised websites. | Known for strong encryption and a quick, automated approach to scanning and encrypting networks. | Tens of millions in direct ransom payouts, with intangible losses running higher. | https://www.cisa.gov/news-events/cybersecurity-advisories/aa23-165a |
| 2020 | Conti | Operated by Wizard Spider (a well-known Russian cybercrime syndicate), often introduced via TrickBot or phishing. | Maintained a special "Conti News" site to publish leaked victim data, if ransom demands weren't met. | Caused over $100 million in global losses before the group's partial dissolution in 2022. | https://www.cisa.gov/news-events/alerts/2021/09/22/conti-ransomware |
| 2020 | Avaddon | Ransomware-as-a-service that proliferated through phishing emails, malicious ads, and exploit kits. | Employed double extortion, threatened to DDoS victims, and demanded ransoms in Bitcoin. | At least ~$40 million extorted prior to its abrupt shutdown in mid-2021. | https://cloud.google.com/blog/topics/threat-intelligence/chasing-avaddon-ransomware |

(*continued*)

291

## APPENDIX A   MALWARE

| Year | Designation | History | Behavior | Impact (USD) | Reference |
|---|---|---|---|---|---|
| 2020 | Evil Corp/ WastedLocker | Associated with the infamous Evil Corp cybercrime group, typically introduced by the Dridex botnet. | Tailored ransom amounts for large enterprises (often ~$500,000 to ~$10 million). | Tens of millions from ransoms, with some victims paying large sums to restore operations. | https://www.infosecinstitute.com/resources/malware-analysis/wastedlocker-malware-what-it-is-how-it-works-and-how-to-prevent-it-malware-spotlight/ |
| 2021 | DarkSide | Likely surfaced from Eastern Europe, leveraged phishing and compromised remote desktops to breach networks. | Involved in the high-profile Colonial Pipeline attack that disrupted fuel supply on the US East Coast. | The Colonial Pipeline ransom alone was ~$4.4 million (some later recovered), with total damages in the hundreds of millions affecting multiple organizations. | https://www.cisa.gov/news-events/cybersecurity-advisories/aa21-131a |

| | | | | |
|---|---|---|---|---|
| 2021 | BlackMatter | Viewed as a rebrand or successor to DarkSide, using similar tactics and code. | Continued double extortion, focusing on large corporate and critical infrastructure targets. | Dozens of victims paying ransoms in the millions each, cumulatively ballooning total damages. | https://www.cisa.gov/news-events/cybersecurity-advisories/aa21-291a |
| 2021 | Hive | Ransomware collective believed to be operating out of Eastern Europe, employing phishing and RDP compromises targeting Microsoft Exchange Mail Servers. | Specialized in healthcare sector attacks, quickly encrypting hospital systems and threatening patient care. | The FBI reported Hive extorted over ~$100 million from hundreds of organizations worldwide. | https://www.cisa.gov/news-events/cybersecurity-advisories/aa22-321a |

*(continued)*

# APPENDIX A  MALWARE

| Year | Designation | History | Behavior | Impact (USD) | Reference |
|---|---|---|---|---|---|
| 2021 | Kaseya Ransomware Attack | Orchestrated by the REvil gang, leveraged a zero-day in Kaseya's VSA software used by Managed Service Providers to turn a legitimate software deployment into malware. | A supply chain attack that simultaneously encrypted thousands of endpoints through a single compromised vendor. | Ransom demands reached ~$70 million; global impact included hundreds of businesses, total impact likely in the hundreds of millions of dollars. | https://www.cisa.gov/news-events/news/kaseya-ransomware-attack-guidance-affected-msps-and-their-customers |
| 2021 | Noberus (ALPHV/BlackCat) | A next-generation ransomware, possibly coded in Rust, associated with the BlackMatter/DarkSide lineage. | Highly customizable and modular, aiming at enterprise targets, with infiltration often via phishing or unpatched VPN software. | Known to extort large ransoms in the millions per incident, potentially adding up to tens of millions in short order. | https://www.cisa.gov/news-events/cybersecurity-advisories/aa23-353a |

APPENDIX A  MALWARE

| | | | | |
|---|---|---|---|---|
| 2022 | BumbleBee | A loader used by various criminal groups, introduced primarily through phishing campaigns with malicious ISO or VHD files. | Acts as an initial foothold for subsequent ransomware or data theft malware, facilitating large-scale intrusions. | Harder to isolate due to being a loader; however, associated attacks have demanded ransoms in the millions and inflicted wide-reaching damage. | https://securityaffairs.com/170112/malware/bumblebee-malware-attacks.html |
| 2023 | RedLine | A malware-as-a-service component designed to be embedded in other malware as an infostealer. | Although initially developed in 2020, its rise is notable in 2023 when embedded in seemingly legitimate software downloads. | Each copy of RedLine costs a malware developer between $100 and $200 per month to operate and then drives revenue based on the information stolen from users and sold on the dark web. | https://www.f-secure.com/us-en/articles/discover-top-types-of-malware-for-2023 |

*(continued)*

295

APPENDIX A   MALWARE

| Year | Designation | History | Behavior | Impact (USD) | Reference |
|---|---|---|---|---|---|
| 2024 | SocGolish | SocGolish is a downloader written in Java Script that socially engineers end users into downloading a faux web browser update. | The payload can be an infostealer, ransomware, or even remote surveillance tools depending on the implementation. | The costs associated with this malware have not been established. | https://www.cisecurity.org/insights/blog/top-10-malware-q4-2024#CoinMiner |

## APPENDIX A  MALWARE

From email worms of the late 1990s to sophisticated ransomware cartels of today, these digital plagues underscore how quickly malware evolves. What began with playful pranks and script-kiddie experiments has become a multibillion-dollar shadow industry. Only vigilance—through timely patching, implementation of the principle of least privilege and other robust cybersecurity practices, and international collaboration—can shield against the next unstoppable malware storm. The history of the most prominent malware helps us understand techniques and motives for potentially future attacks.

# APPENDIX B

# Exploits

While we've explored the definition of exploits, we have yet to review samples in detail and their specific implications. Below is a chronological rundown of 25 influential computer exploits that have shaped (and sometimes shaken) the Internet over the last quarter century. While some entries are vulnerabilities leveraged by multiple malware families, each stands out for its profound impact on security, global commerce, and everyday computing. Where possible, approximate financial impacts (in USD) and attributions are provided, though exact figures can vary and are estimates for perspective only.

> **Note** CVE stands for common vulnerabilities and exposures, a list of known cybersecurity vulnerabilities. The CVE list is maintained by the MITRE Corporation and reflected in NIST publications.
>
> MS refers to the public disclosure from Microsoft directly related to a security issue with one or more of their solutions.

## APPENDIX B   EXPLOITS

| Name | CVE/MS | Year | History | Notable behavior | Impact (USD) | Reference |
|---|---|---|---|---|---|---|
| Microsoft IIS Vulnerability | CVE-2001-0500 | 2001 | Exploited by Code Red and Nimda worms; allowed remote code execution on Windows 2000/NT servers. | Defacements ("Hacked by Chinese") and DoS attacks, including one targeting the White House. | $2–3 billion (due to lost productivity, downtime, and cleanup). | https://nvd.nist.gov/vuln/detail/cve-2001-0500 |
| SQL Server Resolution Service (Slammer) | CVE-2002-0649 | 2003 | Buffer overflow in Microsoft SQL Server's Resolution Service; possibly devised by underground hacking circles. | Spread at lightning speed, doubling infection rate every few seconds, knocking out ATMs, airline ticketing, and major Internet links. | Over $1 billion in emergency network reconfigurations and downtime. | https://nvd.nist.gov/vuln/detail/CVE-2002-0649 |

| | | | | |
|---|---|---|---|---|
| **Windows DCOM RPC (MS03-026)** | MS03-026 | 2003 | Leveraged by Blaster (Lovsan) worm to exploit a critical RPC flaw on Windows XP/2000/NT. | Caused infected systems to crash/reboot endlessly; worm threatened attack on Microsoft's Update site. | $500–600 million in direct damage and frantic patch deployments. | `https://learn.microsoft.com/en-us/security-updates/securitybulletins/2003/ms03-026` |
| **Windows LSASS (MS04-011)** | MS04-011 | 2004 | Sasser worm exploited a flaw in Local Security Authority Subsystem Service (LSASS) on Windows 2000/XP/Server 2003. | Infected PCs forced into endless reboot loops; spread automatically without user action, impacting banks, hospitals, home users. | ~$18 billion worldwide (shutdowns, lost productivity). | `https://learn.microsoft.com/en-us/security-updates/securitybulletins/2004/ms04-011` |

*(continued)*

## APPENDIX B  EXPLOITS

| Name | CVE/MS | Year | History | Notable behavior | Impact (USD) | Reference |
|---|---|---|---|---|---|---|
| Windows Server Service | CVE 2008-4250 | 2008 | Remote code execution via the Server Service on Windows XP/Vista/Server; became infamous as the Conficker worm's gateway. | Conficker formed massive botnets, disabled security tools, blocked antivirus sites, hit corporate/government networks worldwide. | Up to $9 billion in extended infections and disinfection efforts. | https://nvd.nist.gov/vuln/detail/cve-2008-4250 |
| Windows LNK Shortcut Exploit | CVE-2010-2568 | 2010 | Zero-day highlighted by the Stuxnet malware (allegedly a US–Israel cyber operation). | Merely viewing a malicious USB shortcut icon could execute code; Stuxnet targeted Siemens industrial control systems. | "Hundreds of millions" in damages; significant geopolitical consequences (Iran nuclear program sabotage). | https://nvd.nist.gov/vuln/detail/CVE-2010-2568 |

## APPENDIX B  EXPLOITS

| | | | | | |
|---|---|---|---|---|---|
| **RDP Vulnerability** | MS12-020 | 2012 | Flaw in Microsoft's Remote Desktop Protocol enabling remote code execution via specially crafted RDP packets. | Highly prized by cybercriminals for ransomware delivery or footholds in corporate networks. | Hundreds of millions in ransom/breach costs over time; many systems remained vulnerable for years. | https://learn.microsoft.com/en-us/security-updates/securitybulletins/2012/ms12-020 |
| **Heartbleed** | CVE-2014-0160 | 2014 | Bug in OpenSSL's "heartbeat" feature, discovered by Google Security and Codenomicon. Not tied to any one group but rapidly exploited in the wild. | Allowed theft of private keys, passwords, and other data from server memory with no authentication. | Potentially billions in patching, certificate reissues, and brand damage across major sites. | https://nvd.nist.gov/vuln/detail/cve-2014-0160 |

*(continued)*

## APPENDIX B  EXPLOITS

| Name | CVE/MS | Year | History | Notable behavior | Impact (USD) | Reference |
|---|---|---|---|---|---|---|
| Shellshock | CVE-2014-6271 | 2014 | A Bash shell vulnerability allowing extra commands to be appended via environment variables on Linux/Unix systems. | Remote code execution on web servers, IoT devices, etc. Worms emerged to auto-scan and exploit unpatched hosts. | Hundreds of millions in patching/cleanup; overshadowed by Heartbleed that same year. | https://nvd.nist.gov/vuln/detail/cve-2014-6271 |
| Android Stagefright | CVE-2015-3824 | 2015 | Multiple bugs in Android's media library (found by researcher Joshua Drake). | Simply receiving a malicious MMS could trigger remote code execution, affecting ~1 billion Android devices. | Major patching efforts by Google/OEMs; exact monetized damage unclear, but exposure was huge. | https://nvd.nist.gov/vuln/detail/CVE-2015-3824 |

APPENDIX B   EXPLOITS

| | | | | |
|---|---|---|---|---|
| **Dirty COW** | CVE-2016-5195 | 2016 | Privilege escalation bug in Linux copy-on-write mechanism, affecting multiple distributions and some Android devices. | Threat actors could gain root privileges, aiding lateral movement on servers or phones. | Millions in emergency patching across large Linux server farms. | `https://nvd.nist.gov/vuln/detail/cve-2016-5195` |
| **EternalBlue** | CVE-2017-0144 | 2017 | NSA SMB exploit leaked by Shadow Brokers. | Used by WannaCry ransomware (crippled NHS, Spanish telecoms) and NotPetya wiper. | WannaCry: more than $4 billion in damages; NotPetya: more than $10 billion globally. | `https://nvd.nist.gov/vuln/detail/cve-2017-0144` |

(*continued*)

## APPENDIX B   EXPLOITS

| Name | CVE/MS | Year | History | Notable behavior | Impact (USD) | Reference |
|---|---|---|---|---|---|---|
| **DoublePulsar** | No CVE; NSA backdoor | 2017 | NSA leak from the Shadow Brokers, functioned as a stealthy postexploitation backdoor. | Kernel-level code injection for ransomware or espionage tools, often used alongside EternalBlue. | Part of the same wave of exploits that caused billions in global disruptions (WannaCry/NotPetya). | `https://thehackernews.com/2017/04/windows-hacking-tools.html` |
| **Spectre** | CVE-2017-5753 and CVE-2017-5715 | 2018* | Hardware-level flaws in speculative execution affecting Intel, AMD, and ARM. Discovered by multiple researchers. | Allowed reading of other processes' memory (stealing encryption keys, etc.). | Billions in patching/performance overhead; brand damage for CPU vendors, but real-world exploits were rare. | `https://nvd.nist.gov/vuln/detail/cve-2017-5753` `https://nvd.nist.gov/vuln/detail/cve-2017-5715` |

| | | | | |
|---|---|---|---|---|
| **Meltdown** | CVE-2017-5754 | 2018* | Sibling of Spectre, specifically impacting Intel CPUs by breaking kernel/user space isolation. | Let malicious code access privileged kernel memory for passwords and secrets. | Substantial patching and redesign of OS kernels; performance penalties, limited in-the-wild exploitation. | https://nvd.nist.gov/vuln/detail/cve-2017-5754 |
| **BlueKeep** | CVE-2019-0708 | 2019 | A "wormable" vulnerability in older Windows RDP (XP, 7, Server 2008) enabling remote code execution without user interaction. | Hailed as "the next WannaCry," many tools (e.g., Metasploit) integrated exploits. | Hundreds of millions in remediation costs as organizations rushed to patch legacy systems. | https://nvd.nist.gov/vuln/detail/cve-2019-0708 |

*(continued)*

## APPENDIX B  EXPLOITS

| Name | CVE/MS | Year | History | Notable behavior | Impact (USD) | Reference |
|---|---|---|---|---|---|---|
| **SMBGhost** | CVE-2020-0796 | 2020 | Another wormable bug in SMBv3 on Windows 10 and Server 2019; Microsoft released emergency patches for EOL OSs to compensate for the flaw. | Allowed remote code execution with minimal user interaction; proof-of-concept exploits emerged quickly. | Tens of millions in urgent patching; not exploited at WannaCry scale, but underscored SMB's recurring issues. | https://nvd.nist.gov/vuln/detail/cve-2020-0796 |
| **Zerologon** | CVE-2020-1472 | 2020 | Cryptographic flaw in Netlogon authentication, discovered by Secura. | Threat actors could become Domain Admin by manipulating Netlogon messages; forced immediate domain controller patches. | Hundreds of millions in emergency security overhauls; massive breach risk for unpatched networks. | https://nvd.nist.gov/vuln/detail/cve-2020-1472 |

APPENDIX B  EXPLOITS

| | | | | | |
|---|---|---|---|---|---|
| **ProxyLogon** | CVE-2021-26855 | 2021 | Critical Microsoft Exchange Server chain discovered by Orange Tsai, initially exploited by state-sponsored actors. | Full email inbox and server privilege compromise; web shells installed for persistent espionage. | Billions in corporate email breaches, forensics, patching of on-premises exchange. | https://nvd.nist.gov/vuln/detail/cve-2021-26855 |
| **Print Nightmare** | CVE-2021-34527 | 2021 | Proof-of-concept for a Windows Print Spooler vulnerability was accidentally leaked. | Allowed local/remote privilege escalation by tricking Windows into installing malicious print drivers. | Millions spent on disabling spooler services or rapid patching in print-dependent enterprises. | https://nvd.nist.gov/vuln/detail/cve-2021-34527 |

*(continued)*

## APPENDIX B  EXPLOITS

| Name | CVE/MS | Year | History | Notable behavior | Impact (USD) | Reference |
|---|---|---|---|---|---|---|
| ProxyShell | CVE-2021-34473, CVE-2021-34523, CVE-2021-31207 | 2021 | Trio of Exchange Server RCE vulnerabilities found by Orange Tsai at Pwn2Own. | Chained exploits to deploy web shells on unpatched servers, leading to ransomware/data theft. | Tens to hundreds of millions in global cleanup; widely adopted by cybercriminals. | https://nvd.nist.gov/vuln/detail/cve-2021-34473  https://nvd.nist.gov/vuln/detail/cve-2021-34523  https://nvd.nist.gov/vuln/detail/cve-2021-31207 |
| Log4Shell | CVE-2021-44228 | 2021 | Remote code execution hole in Apache Log4j, widely used across countless Java applications. | Threat actors only needed to get the server to log a specific malicious string; exploited by nation-states and criminals. | Billions in frantic patching, code reviews, and forensics efforts worldwide. | https://nvd.nist.gov/vuln/detail/cve-2021-44228 |

APPENDIX B  EXPLOITS

| | | | | | |
|---|---|---|---|---|---|
| **Follina** | CVE-2022-30190 | 2022 | MSDT exploit triggered by opening or previewing a malicious Office document. | Allowed arbitrary code under the guise of Office "diagnostics"; used in spear phishing campaigns by cyber criminals/APTs. | Millions in urgent mitigation and patching, though smaller scale than Log4Shell. | https://nvd.nist.gov/vuln/detail/cve-2022-30190 |
| **Spring4Shell** | CVE-2022-22965 | 2022 | RCE flaw in the popular Spring Framework for Java. The disclosure quickly followed Log4Shell, prompting widespread concern. | Threatened many enterprise Java apps, enabling malicious commands on vulnerable servers. | Hundreds of millions in patch management costs; large-scale exploitation was relatively limited. | https://nvd.nist.gov/vuln/detail/cve-2022-22965 |

*(continued)*

311

## APPENDIX B   EXPLOITS

| Name | CVE/MS | Year | History | Notable behavior | Impact (USD) | Reference |
|---|---|---|---|---|---|---|
| MOVEit Transfer vulnerabilities | CVE-2023-34362 | 2023 | Zero-day in Progress Software's MOVEit file transfer solution, quickly abused by the Cl0p ransomware gang. | Massive data theft from banks, governments, and large enterprises reliant on MOVEit for secure file transfers. | Likely hundreds of millions in extortion demands, regulatory fallout, and remediation costs. | https://nvd.nist.gov/vuln/detail/cve-2023-34362 |
| Ivanti VPN | CVE-2024-21887 and CVE-2023-46805 | 2024 | This exploit allowed attackers to execute arbitrary code and compromise thousands of devices. | The impact was felt across a wide variety of industries that leveraged this solution. | It is estimated that thousands of devices worldwide where impacted and needed manual remediation. | https://socradar.io/top-10-exploited-vulnerabilities-of-2024/ |

*Spectre and Meltdown were discovered in 2017, but not publicly disclosed until 2018.

APPENDIX B   EXPLOITS

**Note**   Some entries reference Microsoft bulletins (e.g., MS03-026, MS04-011, MS12-020) instead of individual common vulnerabilities and exposures (CVEs). Where exact CVEs weren't explicitly provided in the text, the most commonly associated identifiers or the Microsoft bulletin reference are included.

# APPENDIX C

# Breaches

Over the past two decades, every vertical, government, and business has been shaken by cybersecurity breaches that have compromised sensitive information and disrupted services. Below is a chronological list of a few noteworthy cybersecurity breaches from 2005 to 2025, each accompanied by a summary for the event. Given the volume of publicly available data on thousands of breaches, I've selected these to best support our history lesson and provide the most value to readers, based on their background and impact.

# APPENDIX C  BREACHES

| Name | Month | Year | Background | Impact | Reference |
|---|---|---|---|---|---|
| **ChoicePoint data breach** | February | 2005 | Criminals posed as legitimate customers to access personal data (145,000+ individuals). ChoicePoint was a major data broker for credit/background checks. | Heightened awareness that unknown data brokers hold extensive personal information; prompted stricter identity theft regulations and highlighted the fragile nature of data brokerage. | https://www.ftc.gov/news-events/press-releases/2006/01/choicepoint-settles-data-security-breach-charges-pay-10-million-civil-penalties-5-million-consumer |
| **The TJX Companies breach** | January | 2007 | Retail parent company (T.J. Maxx, Marshalls) revealed at least 45 million credit/debit card records were stolen. Starting as early as 2005, hackers exploited weak wireless encryption to infiltrate corporate networks. | Shocked the retail industry; led to stronger wireless encryption standards and regulatory compliance requirements. The breach underscored how threat actors can remain undetected for extended periods. | https://www.computerworld.com/article/1650590/tjx-data-breach-at-45-6m-card-numbers-its-the-biggest-ever.html |

APPENDIX C  BREACHES

| | | | | |
|---|---|---|---|---|
| **Heartland Payment Systems breach** | January | 2009 | Malware on Heartland's payment processing system exposed over 100 million credit/debit card accounts. | At the time, the largest known breach of financial data; demonstrated that even security-focused companies can be vulnerable if they fail to keep pace with evolving threats. | https://www.darkreading.com/cyberattacks-data-breaches/heartland-payment-systems-hit-by-data-security-breach |
| **Epsilon breach** | March | 2011 | Email marketing provider used by many Fortune 500 firms suffered a phishing-related breach, exposing millions of customer names and email addresses. | Even basic personal data (names, emails) can enable large-scale targeted phishing; underscored the value threat actors place on any level of user information for future attacks. | https://www.darkreading.com/cyberattacks-data-breaches/epsilon-email-hack-exposes-bank-business-customers |

*(continued)*

317

## APPENDIX C  BREACHES

| Name | Month | Year | Background | Impact | Reference |
|---|---|---|---|---|---|
| **Sony PlayStation Network breach** | April | 2011 | Hack exposed personal info (including possible credit card details) of ~77 million PlayStation Network users; Sony shut down the network for weeks to remediate the environment, leaving gaming users without access to their systems. | Became a landmark breach for the gaming industry, revealing how entertainment platforms could be severely disrupted if security is undermined; raised consumer awareness of identity theft risks. | https://www.theguardian.com/technology/2011/apr/26/playstation-network-hackers-data |
| **LinkedIn breach** | June | 2012 | Initially 6.5 million hashed (but unsalted) passwords surfaced; later found to affect over 100 million user credentials that a threat actor could use to log in to the platform. | Reinforced the need for unique passwords and robust encryption; revealed professional networks can be prime targets. Note: this occurred before the wide adoption of MFA. | https://freshsec.com/blog/account-takeovers-follow-linkedin-data-breach-2012-and-2016/ |

APPENDIX C BREACHES

| | | | | |
|---|---|---|---|---|
| Adobe breach | October 2013 | Initially, three million encrypted credit card records and login data were reported stolen; later, total leaked records surpassed 150 million. | Diminished trust in large brands' security; prompted scrutiny of password encryption methods, given the risk of easily decrypted "encrypted" data if standards are weak. | https://krebsonsecurity.com/2013/10/adobe-breach-impacted-at-least-38-million-users/ |
| Target breach | December 2013 | Threat actors used stolen third-party HVAC vendor credentials to compromise point-of-sale (POS) systems. Exposed ~40 million credit/debit card numbers and personal data of ~70 million customers. | Exemplified the weakest link principle and triggered a US retail push toward EMV (chip-based) payments that had already been adopted in other geolocations. | https://www.idstrong.com/sentinel/that-one-time-target-lost-everything/ |

(*continued*)

## APPENDIX C  BREACHES

| Name | Month | Year | Background | Impact | Reference |
|---|---|---|---|---|---|
| Home Depot breach | September | 2014 | Similar approach to Target (third-party vendor credentials + POS malware). About 56 million payment card accounts exposed. | Showed big-box retailers remain attractive, high-value targets; emphasized that third-party remote access is a significant security risk. | https://ir.homedepot.com/news-releases/2014/11-06-2014-014517315 |
| JPMorgan Chase breach | August | 2014 | Names, addresses, emails, and phone numbers of 76 million households and 7 million small businesses stolen. | Demonstrated that even financial giants are vulnerable to large-scale exposure of contact information and caused major media concern despite no direct financial loss. | https://archive.nytimes.com/dealbook.nytimes.com/2014/10/02/jpmorgan-discovers-further-cyber-security-issues/ |

320

# APPENDIX C  BREACHES

| | | | | |
|---|---|---|---|---|
| **Anthem breach** | February | 2015 | Hackers stole personal data (~80 million customers and employees), including social security numbers and birthdates, from one of the largest US health insurers. | Marked health data as a prime target; compelled healthcare industry to intensify cybersecurity measures, given the sensitivity of medical and personal data. | https://www.insurance.ca.gov/0400-news/0100-press-releases/anthemcyberattack.cfm |
| **Office of Personnel Management (OPM)** | June | 2015 | More than 21 million federal employees' information was stolen (security clearance data, and electronic storage of biometric fingerprints). | Cited as one of the most damaging breaches in US government history, showcasing the espionage value of such data and its national security ramifications. | https://iapp.org/news/a/21-5-million-breached-in-second-opm-hack |

*(continued)*

# APPENDIX C  BREACHES

| Name | Month | Year | Background | Impact | Reference |
|---|---|---|---|---|---|
| **Yahoo breaches** | Unknown | 2016 | Two major breaches between 2013 and 2014 compromised three billion user accounts in total. Data included names, emails, MD5-hashed passwords, and security questions. | Unprecedented in scale; overshadowed other breaches of the era. Hurt Yahoo's acquisition deal with Verizon, lowering the sale price of Yahoo's core business by hundreds of millions. | https://www.darkreading.com/cyberattacks-data-breaches/deconstructing-the-2016-yahoo-security-breach |
| **Dropbox breach** | August | 2016 | 68 million user credentials (hashed and salted) from a 2012 intrusion surfaced online and the potential for password reuse heightened risk. | Illustrated the "slow burn" nature of breaches (data can remain dormant for years); underscored the importance of unique and non-reused passwords and password managers. | https://www.washingtonpost.com/news/the-switch/wp/2016/09/07/hacked-dropbox-data-of-68-million-users-is-now-or-sale-on-the-dark-web/ |

| | | | | | |
|---|---|---|---|---|---|
| **Equifax breach** | July | 2017 | Nearly 148 million Americans' data stolen (SSNs, birthdates, addresses) after Equifax failed to patch a known Apache Struts vulnerability. | Became emblematic of the stakes when any organization with sensitive information fails to patch critical vulnerabilities. The breach provoked public outrage and regulatory scrutiny, highlighting the fragility of consumer data at major financial data brokers. | https://archive.epic.org/privacy/data-breach/equifax/ |

*(continued)*

## APPENDIX C   BREACHES

| Name | Month | Year | Background | Impact | Reference |
|---|---|---|---|---|---|
| **Marriott/ Starwood breach** | November | 2018 | Hackers accessed Starwood guest reservation data since 2014, affecting up to 500 million records (passport numbers, personal details, etc.) over a four-year period. | Underscored the threat of long-term unauthorized access; highlighted merger/acquisition risks when inherited systems harbor latent vulnerabilities. | https://www.csoonline.com/article/567795/marriott-data-breach-faq-how-did-it-happen-and-what-was-the-impact.html |
| **Twitter hack** | July | 2020 | High-profile accounts (Barack Obama, Elon Musk, Bill Gates, etc.) hijacked via social engineering of Twitter employees. Tweets promoted a Bitcoin scam and resulted in a wide variety of malicious posts. | Very public demonstration of how insider tools and employee credentials are prime attack vectors. This breach shattered assumptions about social media giants' infallibility and strength of internal security controls. | https://thehackernews.com/2023/05/mastermind-behind-twitter-2020-hack.html |

APPENDIX C  BREACHES

| | | | | |
|---|---|---|---|---|
| SolarWinds supply chain attack | December 2020 | State-sponsored hackers compromised the SolarWinds Orion update process, distributing malicious code to thousands of organizations, including US federal agencies and Fortune 500 companies. | Showcased the monumental risk of supply chain attacks. The postmortem called for zero trust security models and rigorous integrity checks within the software development lifecycle. | https://www.techtarget.com/whatis/feature/SolarWinds-hack-explained-Everything-you-need-to-know |
| T-Mobile breach | August 2021 | Over 50 million current, former, and prospective customers had personal data stolen (names, SSNs, driver's licenses, phone numbers). | Reaffirmed telecoms as prime targets due to high-value personally identifiable information and underscored the need for advanced security protocols to protect large, centralized customer datasets. | https://www.cshub.com/attacks/news/iotw-hackers-steal-the-data-of-37-million-t-mobile-customers |

(*continued*)

APPENDIX C   BREACHES

| | | | | |
|---|---|---|---|---|
| **Okta technical support breach** | October | 2023 | Approximately 134 clients compromised through a supply chain breach when an end user inappropriately stored an integration secret in their personal account. The results were a threat actor gaining full visibility into their technical support system for the duration on the attack. | The breach was possible due to a stolen API key stored in a user's personal online profile. Threat actors then made a connection to Okta's support portal and where able to exfiltrate support tickets for a few weeks. These tickets contained sensitive information which allowed the threat actors to connect to individual clients IdP services. | https://www.beyondtrust.com/blog/entry/okta-support-unit-breach |
| **National public data** | August | 2024 | A total of 2.9 billion records for people in Canada and the United States including SSN, name, email, address, and phone numbers. | The breach was caused by a misconfigured database. | https://nordlayer.com/blog/data-breaches-in-2024/ |

Each of these breaches serves as a stark reminder that data security must never be an afterthought. From early cautionary tales (ChoicePoint, TJX) to the monstrous revelations of the 2010s (Yahoo, Equifax) and sophisticated supply chain strikes (SolarWinds), the journey of cybersecurity is littered with harsh history lessons. The cost of ignoring these lessons is dire: personal loss, large-scale catastrophes that can even imperil human lives, and the erosion of public trust and corporate valuations.

# APPENDIX D

# People

None of the history of cybersecurity is possible without people. Some have contributed groundbreaking innovations to improve cyber resilience, while others, with various motives, have worked tirelessly to threaten this reliance and exploit any weak links. To that end, below is a curated list of the most influential cybersecurity professionals (IMHO) who've significantly shaped the field over the past four decades. Each entry features a biography highlighting their key contributions, career milestones, and their impact on cybersecurity. While this is not a compendium of every single significant contributor, those recognized in this chapter influenced the community in ways that have long-standing repercussions for both offensive and defensive cybersecurity.

Note: The information for this section was compiled using Wiki Services, Google Searches, Open AI solutions, and other printed material. Attribution and references included may only be portions of the information based on all the sources available. As an author, I've done my very best to ensure the accuracy of all the biographies contained in this section.

APPENDIX D   PEOPLE

| Name | Biography |
| --- | --- |
| Matt Blaze | Matt Blaze is a renowned computer scientist and cryptographer best known for his pioneering work in secure systems, cryptography, and the intersection of technology with public policy. He obtained his Ph.D. in Computer Science from Princeton University, where he was mentored by leading figures in the field. Early in his career, Blaze garnered attention by discovering significant weaknesses in the Clipper Chip, a controversial encryption device proposed by the US government in the 1990s. His research and subsequent publications helped illuminate the perils of backdoor encryption and the potential for government overreach, influencing policy debates around lawful access to communications.<br><br>Throughout his academic career, Blaze has held faculty positions at major universities, including the University of Pennsylvania and Georgetown University, where he continues to lead groundbreaking research in cryptography and systems security. One of his most cited contributions is his work on trust management and distributed systems. In particular, his paper on "Policy Maker," coauthored with Joan Feigenbaum and Jack Lacy, significantly advanced how security policies are defined and enforced in decentralized networks. Beyond purely academic endeavors, Blaze is vocal about cybersecurity legislation and has frequently testified before the US Congress, offering expert insights into encryption, voting security, and surveillance laws.<br><br>In addition to his academic achievements, Blaze is actively involved in educating the broader public about cybersecurity risks. He maintains a widely read blog and social media presence, demystifying complex topics like cryptographic algorithms, digital forensics, and privacy legislation. His influence extends internationally; he regularly speaks at conferences such as Black Hat, DEF CON, and the RSA Conference, where his engaging talks inspire researchers, students, and policymakers alike. As a respected thought leader, Matt Blaze continues to shape the discourse on encryption, digital security, and privacy rights, solidifying his status as a towering figure in modern cybersecurity. |

(*continued*)

# APPENDIX D  PEOPLE

| Name | Biography |
|------|-----------|
| Whitfield Diffie | Whitfield Diffie, often regarded as one of the founding fathers of modern cryptography, revolutionized secure communications through his coinvention of public-key cryptography alongside Martin Hellman in the mid-1970s. Born in 1944, Diffie displayed an early aptitude for mathematics and logic, which later laid the groundwork for his groundbreaking research. The 1976 paper "New Directions in Cryptography," coauthored by Diffie and Hellman, introduced the world to the concept of key exchange and digital signatures, solving a major hurdle in cryptography: the secure distribution of encryption keys over insecure channels.<br><br>Before his landmark contributions, cryptography was largely the realm of government agencies, kept under tight secrecy. Diffie, however, believed in transparency and the democratization of secure communication tools. His pioneering ideas paved the way for protocols like the Diffie-Hellman key exchange, still widely used in secure web browsing, virtual private networks (VPNs), and countless other encryption-based applications. The direct result of his work is felt every time someone securely logs into an online bank account or sends an encrypted email.<br><br>Diffie's career has spanned academia, industry, and advocacy. He has held research positions at institutions like Stanford University and corporations like Sun Microsystems, where he continued to refine digital security protocols. His public stance against restrictions on encryption technology and his advocacy for privacy have led to significant shifts in technology policy in the United States and beyond. Diffie's arguments in the "crypto wars" of the 1990s were instrumental in expanding the legal use of strong encryption.<br><br>In recognition of his contributions, Diffie has received numerous awards, including the Turing Award in 2015, which is often described as the "Nobel Prize of Computing." Even as cryptographic methods evolve with quantum computing on the horizon, Whitfield Diffie's legacy remains a cornerstone in the fundamentals of secure communication, shaping the cybersecurity landscape for decades to come. |

*(continued)*

APPENDIX D    PEOPLE

| Name | Biography |
| --- | --- |
| Halvar Flake (Thomas Dullien) | Thomas Dullien, better known in the cybersecurity world by his moniker "Halvar Flake," is a highly respected researcher and entrepreneur. Born in Germany, Dullien initially gained fame for his exceptional skills in reverse engineering, vulnerability discovery, and software security analysis. Early in his career, he cofounded Saber Security, a company that developed seminal reverse engineering tools designed to analyze binary code for vulnerabilities. Under the brand Zynamics, these tools became industry standards, beloved by security professionals for their capabilities in dissecting malware and uncovering zero-day exploits.<br><br>Dullien's work has been extensively cited and referenced for its practical applications in incident response, malware forensics, and advanced vulnerability research. One of his most significant contributions is the development of BinDiff and BinNavi, tools that assist security experts in comparing different versions of binary code to pinpoint changes or potential security gaps. These innovations have helped simplify the complex process of dissecting and understanding malicious software, as well as patch analysis.<br><br>Beyond his technical achievements, Dullien is also known for his insightful talks at leading security conferences such as Black Hat, CanSecWest, and REcon. His presentations often delve into advanced concepts of exploitation and the economics of software security, challenging the status quo and nudging the industry toward more robust security measures. In 2011, Google acquired Zynamics, bringing Dullien's expertise in-house. He spent several years at Google Project Zero, the company's elite vulnerability research team, helping identify critical flaws in widely used software products.<br><br>An advocate for responsible disclosure, Dullien has been instrumental in setting ethical standards in the security research community. He frequently speaks about balancing transparency with corporate responsibility, emphasizing how coordinated vulnerability disclosure can help vendors fix issues before malicious actors exploit them. Halvar Flake's commitment to rigorous technical research and ethical responsibility continues to influence generations of cybersecurity professionals. |

*(continued)*

## APPENDIX D  PEOPLE

| Name | Biography |
|---|---|
| Dan Kaminsky | Dan Kaminsky (1979–2021) was a visionary security researcher and one of the most influential figures in the cybersecurity community. Best known for discovering a critical flaw in the domain name system (DNS) in 2008, Kaminsky's work prompted a global race to patch the Internet's foundational infrastructure. His discovery proved that threat actors could manipulate DNS responses, redirecting unsuspecting users to malicious websites, even if they typed in correct URLs. To mitigate the threat, Kaminsky coordinated a secret, rapid-response effort among major technology companies, DNS operators, and government agencies, a move that underscored his collaborative spirit and the industry's respect for him. |
| | Kaminsky's background combined curiosity, technical acumen, and a knack for explaining complex ideas in relatable ways. Before his seminal DNS research, he held roles at prominent security firms and contributed to open source projects, focusing on areas such as network security and cryptography. Post-DNS revelation, he became an advocate for better security practices and broader adoption of DNSSEC, a set of protocols designed to add cryptographic authenticity to DNS data. |
| | Beyond DNS, Kaminsky explored a myriad of other security frontiers, from cryptographic vulnerabilities in popular software to the challenges of trustworthy hardware. In addition to his research, he cofounded White Ops (now known as HUMAN), a cybersecurity company dedicated to preventing bot-based fraud and abuse on the Internet. Kaminsky also served on the boards of nonprofits, often advising on public policy issues related to Internet security. |
| | Equally known for his engaging and empathetic personality, Kaminsky frequently delivered keynote presentations at conferences like Black Hat and DEF CON, using humor and storytelling to underline the importance of cybersecurity. His talks demystified the intricacies of exploits and vulnerabilities for audiences both technical and nontechnical. While his untimely passing was a great loss, Dan Kaminsky's legacy endures in the safer and more aware digital ecosystem he helped create inspiring countless security researchers to follow in his footsteps. |

*(continued)*

APPENDIX D  PEOPLE

| Name | Biography |
|---|---|
| Eugene Kaspersky | Eugene Kaspersky is a Russian cybersecurity expert, entrepreneur, and the cofounder of Kaspersky Lab, one of the world's most recognized cybersecurity companies. Born in 1965, Kaspersky's aptitude for mathematics was apparent from an early age; he studied at a KGB-sponsored technical school focusing on cryptography and later worked for the Soviet defense ministry. This strong foundation in cryptographic theory and mathematical problem-solving set the stage for his future endeavors in the nascent antivirus industry. |
| | Kaspersky's interest in computer viruses began when his workstation was infected by the "Cascade" virus in 1989. Intrigued by the virus's workings, he analyzed its code and developed a program to remove it. This led him to create a suite of antivirus tools that eventually formed the basis of Kaspersky Lab. Officially founded in 1997, Kaspersky Lab grew rapidly into a global operation, garnering acclaim for its research-driven approach to malware detection. The company's antivirus solutions became staples for both enterprise and consumer markets, consistently ranking high in independent testing. |
| | Under Eugene's leadership, Kaspersky Lab has discovered and investigated some of the most notorious cyberespionage campaigns, including Stuxnet, Flame, and Gauss, which targeted critical infrastructure and government networks worldwide. Their detailed analyses of these complex threats not only highlighted the rise of state-sponsored cyberattacks but also helped define best practices in advanced threat detection and incident response. |
| | Eugene Kaspersky is also a vocal figure in the broader cybersecurity discourse. He has advocated for international cooperation against cybercrime, urging governments and private entities to work together on frameworks that transcend national boundaries. However, his company has sometimes been the subject of geopolitical controversies, particularly concerning alleged ties with Russian intelligence, a charge he has consistently denied. |

(*continued*)

APPENDIX D　PEOPLE

| Name | Biography |
|---|---|
|  | Despite the controversies, Eugene Kaspersky's impact on cybersecurity is undeniable. From pioneering antivirus research to public advocacy, he has played a pivotal role in shaping the threat intelligence landscape, ensuring that countless organizations worldwide can better protect themselves against ever-evolving digital threats. |
| Marc Maiffret | Marc Maiffret is widely recognized as a trailblazer in the field of cybersecurity. From a young age, his fascination with computers propelled him toward an unrelenting pursuit of digital innovation. Early in his career, he cofounded eEye Digital Security, a research firm that rapidly gained prominence by unveiling critical software vulnerabilities. Under Maiffret's guidance, eEye's researchers uncovered and disclosed high-impact flaws in Microsoft Windows and other widely used platforms, influencing industry protocols for vulnerability reporting. These findings not only showcased his technical prowess but also established his reputation as one of the foremost experts in identifying and mitigating cyber threats. |
|  | Maiffret's crowning achievement came in 2001 with his discovery of the notorious Code Red worm. This self-replicating piece of malware targeted Microsoft's Internet Information Services, exploiting a vulnerability that allowed it to compromise thousands of servers worldwide. Maiffret and his team quickly developed a patch and alerted organizations to the threat, effectively preventing further damage. This accomplishment solidified Maiffret's standing as a visionary thinker capable of outmaneuvering cybercriminals, while fostering safer online environments. His work on Code Red also underscored the importance of collaboration among software developers, security experts, and government agencies in the ongoing fight against global malicious attacks. |

(*continued*)

APPENDIX D   PEOPLE

| Name | Biography |
|---|---|
| | In addition to his groundbreaking discoveries, Maiffret testified before the US Congress, highlighting the urgent need for robust cybersecurity in public and private sectors. His real-world research and threat analysis informed lawmakers about emerging dangers and catalyzed conversations on stronger legislation. Over the years, he has championed public awareness through media appearances and high-profile speaking engagements. Renowned for his passion and ingenuity, Maiffret remains at the forefront of cybersecurity, advising top enterprises and contributing innovative solutions. His legacy endures as a testament to his unparalleled expertise and unwavering commitment to safeguarding the digital world. He continues shaping future standards as a leader in identity security. |
| Moxie Marlinspike | Moxie Marlinspike, born Matthew Rosenfeld, is a renowned cryptographer and privacy advocate best known for creating the Signal Protocol, the encryption backbone behind the Signal messaging app and other secure messaging platforms like WhatsApp and Facebook Messenger's "Secret Conversations." Originally a computer hacker with a deep fascination for cryptography, Marlinspike leveraged his technical prowess to develop user-friendly communication tools that prioritize privacy and security. |
| | Marlinspike's work gained prominence in the late 2000s and early 2010s, when he introduced a series of security tools and techniques aimed at protecting user data from unauthorized access. One of his most influential early projects was the SSLstrip tool, which exposed weaknesses in the way encrypted connections were handled, spurring the industry to address these flaws. Around the same time, he cofounded Whisper Systems, a company focused on end-to-end encryption products for mobile devices. |

*(continued)*

APPENDIX D  PEOPLE

| Name | Biography |
|---|---|
| | After Twitter acquired Whisper Systems in 2011, Marlinspike cofounded Open Whisper Systems (now known as the Signal Foundation) in partnership with Brian Acton. Under this organization, he continued to refine the Signal Protocol, making it not only secure, but also highly efficient and easy to use. This protocol quickly became a gold standard for end-to-end encrypted messaging, lauded by cybersecurity experts and human rights activists alike. |
| | Marlinspike's advocacy extends beyond building secure tools. He frequently discusses the ethics and implications of mass surveillance, believing that privacy is a fundamental human right. His public speaking engagements, blog posts, and cryptographic proofs highlight the necessity of robust encryption in an era of increasingly sophisticated cyber threats. In 2022, Marlinspike stepped down as CEO of Signal, emphasizing the need for diverse leadership and sustainable growth within privacy-focused organizations. Nonetheless, his influence on secure messaging and his commitment to individual privacy remain hallmarks of modern cybersecurity, inspiring developers and users worldwide. |
| Kevin Mitnick | Kevin Mitnick (1963–2023) was perhaps the most famous hacker in the world, transforming from a teenage phone phreaker and federal fugitive to a respected cybersecurity consultant and author. Born in Los Angeles, Mitnick's curiosity about telephone and computer systems led him down a path that blurred the lines between ethical hacking and criminal intrusion. He was known for his adeptness at social engineering, manipulating people into divulging confidential information, and for bypassing elaborate security systems of major tech and telecom companies. |

(*continued*)

APPENDIX D   PEOPLE

| Name | Biography |
|------|-----------|
|  | Mitnick's hacking exploits garnered widespread media attention in the 1980s and early 1990s, culminating in a high-profile FBI chase that ended with his arrest in 1995. Imprisoned for nearly five years, Mitnick's case sparked debates about the appropriate legal treatment for computer hacking and the ethics of "white hat" research. After serving his sentence, he reemerged in the cybersecurity field, but this time as a legitimate consultant guiding corporations on how to defend against the very tactics he once employed.<br><br>He founded Mitnick Security Consulting, advising Fortune 500 companies, government agencies, and individuals on how to shore up defenses against social engineering, network vulnerabilities, and other threats. Mitnick's expertise in social engineering techniques was particularly notable. He taught organizations to be wary of the human element, which is often the weakest link in any security chain.<br><br>Mitnick's transformation from outlaw hacker to revered security expert is also documented in his books, such as "The Art of Deception" and "Ghost in the Wires," which became bestsellers. In them, he candidly discussed his past exploits and offered guidance on preventing similar breaches.<br><br>Mitnick also served on the board of KnowBe4, a security awareness training platform, further extending his influence on cybersecurity education. Until his passing in 2023, Kevin Mitnick remained a vivid example of how hands-on expertise and an understanding of human psychology can be harnessed to build more robust cybersecurity practices worldwide. |

*(continued)*

APPENDIX D   PEOPLE

| Name | Biography |
|---|---|
| Katie Moussouris | Katie Moussouris is a trailblazing cybersecurity researcher and entrepreneur, widely recognized for her pioneering work in vulnerability disclosure policies and bug bounty programs. Moussouris' career spans influential roles at major tech organizations, including Microsoft, where she led the introduction of one of the industry's first formal bug bounty programs. This revolutionary initiative rewarded ethical hackers for identifying and disclosing security flaws in Microsoft products, setting a precedent that many other companies soon followed. |
| | After Microsoft, Moussouris founded Luta Security, where she continues to advise corporations and governments on handling vulnerability disclosures. Her expertise in creating secure channels for reporting vulnerabilities helps ensure that security researchers can collaborate ethically with organizations, reducing the risk of undisclosed exploits falling into the wrong hands. Among her major collaborations is her work with the US Department of Defense, where she was instrumental in launching "Hack the Pentagon," the first public bug bounty program for a US government agency. |
| | Moussouris has been an outspoken advocate for diversity and inclusion in the cybersecurity industry, frequently highlighting systemic barriers that prevent underrepresented groups from entering and thriving in the field. She also works tirelessly to promote coordinated vulnerability disclosure (CVD) as a global standard, emphasizing the need for legal safe harbors and responsible processes that protect security researchers from legal reprisals. |

(*continued*)

APPENDIX D    PEOPLE

| Name | Biography |
|---|---|
|  | In addition to her industry work, Moussouris regularly speaks at international conferences, such as Black Hat and RSA, contributing to the broader conversation on ethical hacking, bug bounties, and cybersecurity policy. Her influence can be seen in the widespread acceptance of bug bounty programs as a vital part of modern security strategies across sectors, ranging from finance and healthcare to government. By bridging the gap between hackers and institutions, Katie Moussouris has transformed vulnerability disclosure practices, making the digital world safer for everyone. |
| Gene Spafford | Eugene H. Spafford, often referred to as "Spaf," is a pioneering figure in the fields of cybersecurity and computer science education. Born in 1956, he earned his Ph.D. from the Georgia Institute of Technology and subsequently joined Purdue University, where he established the COAST Laboratory (later renamed CERIAS, Center for Education and Research in Information Assurance and Security). Under Spafford's leadership, CERIAS became a world-renowned hub for interdisciplinary research on information security, privacy, and cybercrime. |
|  | Spafford's contributions to cybersecurity extend far beyond academia. Early in his career, he coauthored the classic reference text "Practical UNIX Security," one of the first comprehensive guides to protecting UNIX systems. He also participated in the analysis of the Morris Worm incident in 1988, one of the first major cyberattacks to capture national attention. Through rigorous technical investigation, Spafford and other researchers laid the groundwork for modern intrusion detection and cybersecurity best practices. |

(*continued*)

## APPENDIX D  PEOPLE

| Name | Biography |
|---|---|
| | As an educator, Spafford has mentored countless students who have gone on to become leaders in academia, industry, and government. His teaching style, known for its clarity and emphasis on ethical and responsible security practices, has inspired generations of cybersecurity professionals. He also serves as a consultant and advisor to major organizations, including government agencies, such as the National Science Foundation (NSF) and the Department of Defense. Over the years, he has testified before US Congress on multiple occasions, providing expert guidance on pressing cybersecurity challenges, from critical infrastructure protection to intellectual property theft.<br><br>Spafford's numerous accolades, including awards from the National Cyber Security Hall of Fame, underscore his lasting impact. Through CERIAS, his publications, and his advisory roles, Gene Spafford has profoundly shaped cybersecurity's evolution. His balanced approach to research, education, and policy has led to a more robust understanding of both the technical and social dimensions of digital security, making him a cornerstone of the field for over three decades. |
| Bruce Schneier | Bruce Schneier is among the most widely recognized cybersecurity experts in the world, famed for his prolific writing, deep technical expertise, and incisive commentary on national security issues. Born in 1963, Schneier has authored numerous books, including *Applied Cryptography*, which became a seminal text for anyone seeking to understand the nuts and bolts of cryptographic algorithms and protocols. His subsequent works, like *Secrets and Lies* and *Data and Goliath*, examine the broader social and political implications of emerging technologies. |

(*continued*)

APPENDIX D    PEOPLE

| Name | Biography |
|---|---|
| | Schneier's interest in security extends far beyond cryptographic primitives. He has worked as a security consultant for various corporations, founded the influential firm Counterpane Internet Security (later acquired by BT), and has published hundreds of articles and essays dissecting the latest security threats, policy debates, and privacy concerns. Known for coining the term "security theater," Schneier often critiques measures that provide the appearance of security without genuine substance, especially in the context of airport screenings and national security policies.<br><br>Beyond industry, Schneier maintains active roles in academia and policy advisory. He has been a fellow at Harvard University's Berkman Klein Center for Internet & Society, where he researches and speaks on topics including election security, encryption policy, and the role of big tech in surveillance. He frequently testifies before government bodies worldwide to advocate for stronger data protection laws and balanced approaches to cryptographic regulation.<br><br>Schneier's public influence is bolstered by his widely read newsletter "Crypto-Gram" and his blog "Schneier on Security," platforms he uses to engage both specialists and laypeople. His approachable writing style demystifies complex security issues, encouraging readers to think critically about personal and organizational risks. Often described as a "security guru," Bruce Schneier's unique blend of technical depth, policy insight, and effective communication has made him a cornerstone of the global cybersecurity community for more than three decades. |

*(continued)*

# APPENDIX D  PEOPLE

| Name | Biography |
|---|---|
| Adi Shamir | Adi Shamir, born in 1952, is an Israeli cryptographer whose pioneering work has profoundly shaped modern cryptography and secure computing. Alongside Ron Rivest and Leonard Adleman, he coinvented the RSA cryptosystem in 1977, which became one of the first practical public-key cryptosystems for secure data transmission. The RSA algorithm's impact cannot be overstated: it remains a fundamental building block in everything from secure web browsing (HTTPS) to encrypted email and digital signatures. |
| | Shamir is also the "S" in the "SHA" (Secure Hash Algorithms) family, having contributed key insights to hash function design. Over the years, he has published seminal works on cryptanalysis, exploring ways to break or strengthen existing algorithms. Notably, his research into side-channel attacks has drawn attention to the fact that cryptographic implementations often leak information through physical channels like electromagnetic emissions or power consumption—a discovery that transformed the design and evaluation of secure hardware. |
| | Beyond RSA, Shamir has been instrumental in developing other cryptographic techniques. He coinvented Shamir's Secret Sharing, a protocol that divides a secret (like an encryption key) into multiple parts, which then must be recombined to access the original secret. This method has broad applications in secure backups, crypto asset custody, and corporate governance. |
| | Throughout his illustrious career, Shamir has served at top institutions, such as the Weizmann Institute of Science, where he mentored numerous students who went on to become leaders in the field. His contributions have earned him multiple accolades, including the Turing Award in 2002, which he shared with Rivest and Adleman. |
| | At a time when quantum computing threatens to disrupt current cryptographic algorithms, Shamir's ongoing research continues to guide the evolution of secure encryption. From fundamental innovations like RSA to advanced side-channel analysis, Adi Shamir's work remains at the forefront of cryptographic research, ensuring that global digital communications remain as secure as possible. |

*(continued)*

APPENDIX D  PEOPLE

| Name | Biography |
|---|---|
| Joanna Rutkowska | Joanna Rutkowska is a Polish computer security researcher whose groundbreaking work on stealth malware and virtualization-based security has positioned her as one of the most influential voices in the cybersecurity world. She first rose to prominence in 2006 after demonstrating "Blue Pill," a conceptual hypervisor-based rootkit that could render an operating system completely unaware it was being virtualized. This proof-of-concept shook the industry by revealing just how deeply malware could embed itself, challenging the reliability of existing detection methods. |
| | Rutkowska's fascination with low-level security mechanisms led her to explore trusted computing platforms and hardware-based security measures. She has consistently advocated for architectural changes to operating systems that prioritize minimal trust and reduced attack surfaces. This vision materialized in Qubes OS, a security-focused, open source operating system she cofounded. Qubes employs a compartmentalized design, isolating different activities (like web browsing, email, and sensitive tasks) into separate virtual machines or "domains," limiting the damage a successful attack can do. |
| | Beyond her technical achievements, Rutkowska has been recognized for her clear, no-nonsense approach to discussing security challenges. She frequently presents at conferences such as Black Hat, DEF CON, and the Chaos Communication Congress, diving into highly technical subjects while emphasizing responsible disclosure and practical defenses. Her work has influenced how both researchers and vendors approach vulnerability research, particularly around firmware and hardware-level exploits. |

*(continued)*

# APPENDIX D  PEOPLE

| Name | Biography |
|---|---|
| | Today, Qubes OS stands as a prime example of security by compartmentalization, adopted by privacy-conscious users, activists, and even international organizations. Rutkowska's contributions emphasize the importance of designing security from the ground up rather than relying solely on antivirus software or patchwork solutions. By challenging long-standing assumptions and demonstrating creative proofs-of-concept like Blue Pill, Joanna Rutkowska continues to push the boundaries of what's possible in secure computing, influencing product designs and inspiring a new generation of cybersecurity professionals. |
| Charlie Miller | Charlie Miller is a distinguished security researcher best known for his expertise in identifying critical vulnerabilities in consumer software, hardware, and automotive systems. Holding a Ph.D. in mathematics, Miller initially worked for the National Security Agency (NSA), where he developed a deep understanding of cryptographic methods and exploit development. He then shifted into the public sphere, where he gained fame for high-profile security disclosures that caught the attention of tech giants and global media alike. |
| | One of Miller's earliest claims to fame was his discovery of exploitable bugs in Apple's iPhone, MacBook batteries, and even the Safari web browser. Through meticulous research, he demonstrated that these vulnerabilities could compromise user data or potentially lead to remote code execution. His iPhone exploits were particularly notable for highlighting that even Apple's tightly controlled ecosystem was not immune to advanced hacking techniques. As a result, Miller's findings often compelled companies to release urgent patches, significantly improving the security of their products. |
| | In a collaboration with fellow researcher Chris Valasek, Miller made headlines by remotely hacking a Jeep Cherokee in 2015, demonstrating a critical vulnerability in the vehicle's Uconnect system. The duo could control the car's steering, brakes, and transmission—an alarming demonstration of how connected cars could be weaponized if left unprotected. Their research drove the automotive industry to adopt stricter cybersecurity practices, influencing regulatory discussions about the safety of autonomous and Internet-connected vehicles. |

*(continued)*

APPENDIX D  PEOPLE

| Name | Biography |
|---|---|
|  | Outside of hacking demos, Miller has worked as a security consultant for companies like Uber and Twitter, guiding them on how to strengthen their security protocols. His knack for discovering zero-day vulnerabilities and responsibly disclosing them to vendors has earned him numerous accolades, including multiple Pwn2Own awards. With each discovery, Charlie Miller reinforces the importance of consistent, robust security testing across every layer of modern technology. |
| Mikko Hypponen | Mikko Hypponen is a Finnish computer security expert and the Chief Research Officer at WithSecure (formerly F-Secure), a global cybersecurity firm based in Helsinki. With a career spanning over 30 years, Hypponen has dedicated his life to identifying and understanding emerging cyber threats, informing both industry and the general public about the evolving digital landscape. Early in his tenure at F-Secure, Hypponen rose to prominence by analyzing and containing computer viruses during a time when widespread malware outbreaks like "ILOVEYOU" and "Melissa" were making global headlines. |
|  | Hypponen's research interests are wide-ranging, extending from traditional computer viruses to sophisticated cyberespionage campaigns linked to state-sponsored actors. He has contributed significantly to global efforts that dismantled major botnets, including those behind some of the world's largest spam operations. His success in botnet takedowns has made him a sought-after voice for media interviews and documentary appearances, where he provides clear, relatable explanations of complex threats. |

*(continued)*

APPENDIX D  PEOPLE

| Name | Biography |
|---|---|
|  | In addition to his hands-on technical work, Hypponen is known for his dynamic conference talks and keynote speeches at events such as Black Hat and TED. He emphasizes the importance of privacy, free speech, and open Internet access, urging companies and governments alike to adopt balanced cybersecurity policies. Recognizing that global collaboration is essential for tackling cross-border cybercrime, he has also collaborated with Europol and other international law enforcement agencies to share threat intelligence. |
|  | Hypponen's approachable demeanor and knack for storytelling make him a household name in the cybersecurity community. He has authored numerous articles and research papers that delve into everything from the dark web to the rise of ransomware, influencing how both professionals and novices perceive cyber threats. Whether he's analyzing advanced persistent threats or advocating for user privacy, Mikko Hypponen's commitment to a safer digital future remains unwavering, making him one of the most trusted figures in cybersecurity today. |
| Window Snyder | Window Snyder is a highly respected cybersecurity expert whose career has spanned key roles at some of the largest and most influential technology companies, including Microsoft, Mozilla, and Apple. Beginning her career in the late 1990s, Snyder worked alongside pioneers in software security, honing her skills in threat modeling, vulnerability management, and secure software development practices. |
|  | One of Snyder's earliest achievements came during her time at Microsoft, where she helped develop the company's Security Development Lifecycle (SDL). The SDL revolutionized how Microsoft approached product design and coding, injecting security considerations at every stage of software development. This process significantly reduced the number of critical vulnerabilities discovered in Windows operating systems over time and became a model that other tech firms would later adopt. |

(*continued*)

APPENDIX D  PEOPLE

| Name | Biography |
|---|---|
| | After Microsoft, Snyder joined Mozilla as Chief Security Officer, guiding the development teams for Firefox to implement rigorous security protocols and quickly respond to emerging threats. Her leadership contributed to Firefox's reputation for being a more security-conscious browser alternative during a period when browser exploits were rampant. |
| | In subsequent roles at Apple and Intel, Snyder continued to champion secure design principles, particularly focusing on hardware-level security and firmware integrity. She has consistently stressed the importance of cross-organizational cooperation, recognizing that today's complex cyber threats transcend any single platform or device. In recent years, she cofounded a startup, Thistle Technologies, focused on securing connected devices, reflecting her commitment to end-to-end security in the expanding IoT landscape. |
| | Snyder frequently speaks at industry conferences, advocating for a holistic approach to cybersecurity that integrates user awareness, robust coding practices, and transparent disclosure policies. She underscores the importance of inclusivity and diversity in the security sector, believing that varied perspectives lead to more resilient solutions. Through her influential roles and steadfast dedication, Window Snyder has played a vital part in elevating the global standard for secure software and hardware development. |

*(continued)*

APPENDIX D   PEOPLE

| Name | Biography |
| --- | --- |
| Parisa Tabriz | Parisa Tabriz is a cybersecurity leader famed for her role as Google's "Security Princess," a title she humorously coined while leading the Google Chrome security team. With a background in computer engineering from the University of Illinois at Urbana-Champaign, Tabriz joined Google in 2007 and quickly gained recognition for her expertise in software security and vulnerability management. |
|  | Tabriz's most prominent work has been on the Chrome browser, where she spearheaded numerous security initiatives to protect billions of users around the world. Under her leadership, Chrome implemented features like site isolation, sandboxing, and advanced phishing detection, significantly reducing the browser's attack surface. She also led efforts to encourage widespread adoption of HTTPS, contributing to the "HTTPS Everywhere" movement that has radically increased the percentage of encrypted web traffic. |
|  | An advocate for ethical hacking and responsible disclosure, Tabriz manages Google's team of elite security researchers who hunt for vulnerabilities, not just in Chrome, but also in other products and third-party software. Her group's work has led to the discovery and responsible reporting of critical flaws, many of which could have otherwise been exploited by malicious actors. Beyond purely technical accomplishments, Tabriz champions diversity in the cybersecurity industry, frequently speaking about the importance of creating inclusive environments that can tap into a broader talent pool. |
|  | In recent years, Tabriz's influence has extended to broader product leadership at Google. She has been involved in strategic decision-making that affects how security is integrated across multiple services. Her ability to bridge the gap between deep technical expertise and organizational leadership has solidified her status as one of the most significant cybersecurity professionals of her generation. Whether promoting bug bounties, guiding vulnerability disclosure policies, or mentoring the next generation of infosec experts, Parisa Tabriz continues to shape the course of Internet security. |

(*continued*)

APPENDIX D   PEOPLE

| Name | Biography |
|---|---|
| Ron Rivest | Ronald Linn Rivest is an American cryptographer whose work underpins much of modern secure communications. Along with Adi Shamir and Leonard Adleman, he coinvented the RSA cryptosystem, which introduced the world to a practical method for public-key cryptography. Born in 1947, Rivest earned degrees from Yale and Stanford before joining the faculty at the Massachusetts Institute of Technology (MIT), where he would spend much of his influential career. |
| | Aside from RSA, Rivest's contributions are extensive. He designed symmetric-key encryption algorithms like RC4, which, despite known vulnerabilities in its older age, was once one of the most widely used stream ciphers in the world. Rivest also created a series of cryptographic hash functions (MD2, MD4, MD5), which were widely deployed before the discovery of critical weaknesses drove the field toward more robust alternatives. |
| | As an MIT professor, Rivest supervised numerous doctoral candidates who've gone on to push the boundaries of cryptography and computer science. His ability to blend theoretical rigor with practical implementation is often cited was a key reason for RSA's success. Because the invention of RSA solved the "key distribution problem," it effectively opened the door for secure digital transactions, online banking, and the broader ecommerce ecosystem. |
| | In later years, Rivest has been heavily involved in election security, co-developing systems like "Scantegrity," a cryptographically verifiable election protocol that enhances transparency and reduces the potential for voter fraud. He's a vocal advocate for the responsible use of encryption and often weighs in on debates about backdoors and government surveillance, emphasizing the inherent risks that come with undermining cryptographic integrity. |
| | From his foundational work on RSA to his ongoing research on voting protocols, Ron Rivest embodies the spirit of innovation that continues to drive cybersecurity forward. His ongoing influence in both academia and industry ensures that cryptography remains at the forefront of secure digital communication. |

*(continued)*

APPENDIX D  PEOPLE

| Name | Biography |
| --- | --- |
| Dragos Ruiu | Dragos Ruiu is a Canadian cybersecurity researcher and conference organizer who has profoundly influenced the global security community. Best known as the founder of the CanSecWest conference and the Pwn2Own competition, Ruiu has created platforms that have uncovered critical zero-day vulnerabilities in popular software and hardware. These events encourage ethical hackers to demonstrate real-world exploits in a controlled environment, subsequently leading to quick vendor patching and heightened public awareness of security flaws.<br><br>Ruiu's expertise spans both offensive and defensive security. As an independent researcher, he has explored complex topics like BIOS-level malware, air-gap attacks, and advanced persistent threats. Perhaps one of his most headline-grabbing investigations was "BadBIOS," a mysterious malware strain he hypothesized could traverse air gaps via ultrasonic signals. Although the research remained controversial and unverified, it sparked wider discussions about hardware and firmware vulnerabilities, underscoring the importance of investigating unconventional threat vectors.<br><br>Beyond his research, Ruiu's conferences, such as PacSec in Japan and EUSecWest in Europe, have a global footprint, uniting some of the world's top security minds. These gatherings serve as fertile ground for disclosure of groundbreaking vulnerabilities, from browser exploits to mobile device hacks. Pwn2Own, in particular, has become a hallmark event that challenges security researchers to find zero-day vulnerabilities in popular software, with prizes often reaching into the hundreds of thousands of dollars.<br><br>Ruiu's commitment to responsible disclosure and vendor collaboration has led to faster security updates and improved products, benefiting end users worldwide. His focus on community building has also fostered a culture in which ethical hackers can showcase their skills and be rewarded rather than persecuted. Through his research, conference organization, and spirited advocacy for responsible hacking, Dragos Ruiu has carved out an indispensable role in the cybersecurity landscape. |

(*continued*)

APPENDIX D   PEOPLE

| Name | Biography |
| --- | --- |
| Marcus Ranum | Marcus J. Ranum is a cybersecurity visionary credited with pioneering innovations in firewall technology and intrusion detection systems. Early in his career, Ranum worked at Digital Equipment Corporation (DEC), where he led the development of the DEC SEAL firewall, one of the first commercially available firewalls to emphasize application-level gateway controls. His work during this period helped define the foundational principles for modern network security, showing that filtering traffic at the application layer could provide more robust protection than simple packet filtering. |
| | Ranum later founded Network Flight Recorder (NFR), which specialized in network intrusion detection. His approach to intrusion detection integrated signature-based analysis with real-time monitoring, pushing the boundaries of what was possible in proactive threat detection. Over time, these technologies influenced how security professionals approached the defense of enterprise networks, leading to more sophisticated tools that monitor behavior as well as content. |
| | A passionate advocate for simplifying security, Ranum often critiques the industry's tendency toward complex, layered solutions that are challenging to maintain. He instead urges a back-to-basics approach that emphasizes strong architectural design, minimal exposure, and robust logging. His talks and writings are both technically insightful and provocatively critical, pushing peers to challenge assumptions and aim for clarity over complexity. |
| | Ranum's influence extends beyond product development. He has served on advisory boards and contributed to standards that guide cybersecurity best practices. A frequent keynote speaker, he has also authored articles in leading security journals, insisting that risk management must balance real-world user needs with rigorous threat modeling. Whether creating some of the earliest firewalls or championing a more reasoned approach to modern security challenges, Marcus Ranum's contributions have left a lasting imprint on network defense and the way professionals approach security. |

*(continued)*

## APPENDIX D   PEOPLE

| Name | Biography |
|---|---|
| Gary McGraw | Gary McGraw is a recognized authority on software security, having authored seminal books and articles that have shaped the way developers and security teams approach building secure software. Holding a dual Ph.D. in Cognitive Science and Computer Science, McGraw focused his early research on the psychology of software development and security flaws. This interdisciplinary perspective helped him articulate why security should be baked into the development lifecycle from the very start, rather than treated as an afterthought. |
| | McGraw cofounded Cigital (later acquired by Synopsys), where he served as Chief Technology Officer. Under his leadership, Cigital pioneered software security consulting, guiding Fortune 500 companies on best practices in code review, threat modeling, and architectural risk analysis. The influence of McGraw's company and his published works, particularly *Software Security: Building Security In* and *Exploiting Software*, brought software security from the fringes of IT into mainstream corporate governance. |
| | One of McGraw's major contributions is the development of the BSIMM (Building Security in Maturity Model), an empirical framework based on the observed security practices of dozens of organizations. The BSIMM helps companies assess and benchmark their software security initiatives against industry peers, offering a roadmap for continual improvement. This data-driven approach underscores McGraw's core philosophy: effective security practices can and should be measured, refined, and scaled across an organization. |
| | Over the years, McGraw has served as an advisor to various government agencies and academic institutions, emphasizing the need for better collaboration between industry, academia, and policymakers. A dynamic speaker and prolific writer, he has authored hundreds of articles, blog posts, and academic papers dissecting topics such as machine learning in security, cryptography, and software vulnerability trends. Through his pioneering research, consulting work, and educational outreach, Gary McGraw has left an indelible mark on the software security landscape, championing the idea that robust security begins at the code level. |

*(continued)*

APPENDIX D   PEOPLE

| Name | Biography |
|---|---|
| Tavis Ormandy | Tavis Ormandy is a high-profile security researcher and member of Google's Project Zero team, an elite group dedicated to discovering zero-day vulnerabilities in widely used software. From operating systems to antivirus products, Ormandy's work has been instrumental in identifying critical flaws that, if left unpatched, could pose severe risks to users worldwide. |
| | Ormandy's skill set combines low-level reverse engineering with a knack for spotting subtle design issues. Over the years, he has responsibly disclosed numerous vulnerabilities in products from major vendors like Microsoft, Adobe, and Symantec. His research often reveals systemic security lapses in software that many end users assume to be safe. For instance, Ormandy famously uncovered flaws in multiple antivirus engines that could be exploited remotely, flipping the script by demonstrating how security software itself can become a major attack vector, if not properly designed. |
| | What sets Ormandy apart is his commitment to timely and responsible disclosure. By adhering to Project Zero's rigorous 90-day disclosure policy, he pushes vendors to address flaws promptly, ensuring that end users receive patches before threat actors can exploit the vulnerabilities. While this approach has, at times, generated friction with software vendors, it has also forced faster action, leading to more secure products. |
| | Beyond discovering bugs, Ormandy actively contributes to the development of tools and methodologies that help other researchers in their hunt for software vulnerabilities. His published reports often include detailed analysis and proof-of-concept exploits, serving as invaluable educational resources for the wider security community. Whether he's dissecting obfuscated code or diving deep into cryptographic libraries, Tavis Ormandy's meticulous research helps raise the bar for software security across the board, ultimately making digital products safer for everyone. |

*(continued)*

APPENDIX D   PEOPLE

| Name | Biography |
|---|---|
| Dino Dai Zovi | Dino Dai Zovi is a cybersecurity expert and entrepreneur renowned for his deep technical skill and innovative approach to vulnerability discovery and exploitation techniques. He first gained mainstream attention when he, along with Shane Macaulay, won the Pwn2Own contest in 2007 by exploiting a zero-day vulnerability in Apple's MacBook. This high-profile feat demonstrated that Apple products, long considered by some users to be inherently secure, could indeed be compromised by determined threat actors.<br><br>Dai Zovi has worked in various roles across the security spectrum, from penetration tester and researcher to team lead at major tech companies. He is also a cofounder of Trail of Bits, a security consultancy that focuses on advanced research and building robust security tools. Under Dai Zovi's guidance, Trail of Bits has performed critical audits and security assessments for blockchain technologies, cryptographic libraries, and large-scale software platforms used by millions of users.<br><br>As an author, Dai Zovi co-wrote *The Mac Hacker's Handbook*, an influential text on Mac OS X exploitation. His candid and detailed breakdown of Apple's security model spurred more robust protections in subsequent macOS releases. He has also contributed extensively to the security community through talks at major conferences, sharing insights on topics like kernel exploitation, secure software development, and threat modeling.<br><br>A staunch advocate of educating the next generation of ethical hackers, Dai Zovi often emphasizes the value of public bug bounty programs and open platforms for vulnerability research. His hands-on expertise, combined with a willingness to share knowledge, has earned him a reputation as a go-to resource for both budding and seasoned security professionals. In a rapidly evolving threat landscape, Dino Dai Zovi's blend of technical acumen, entrepreneurial spirit, and community engagement continues to drive innovation in cybersecurity. |

*(continued)*

APPENDIX D   PEOPLE

| Name | Biography |
| --- | --- |
| Jon Callas | Jon Callas is a respected cryptographer, software engineer, and entrepreneur who has cofounded several companies dedicated to securing digital communications, most notably PGP Corporation and Silent Circle. Callas has been pivotal in advancing the usability and accessibility of encryption technology, making it feasible for the average user to protect their data in an era of pervasive surveillance. |
| | A graduate of the University of Maryland, Callas initially carved out a career in the tech sector with roles at Apple, where he contributed to security architecture. His passion for cryptography led him to co-develop PGP (Pretty Good Privacy) encryption, which quickly became an industry standard for secure email. Its blend of strong cryptographic methods with a relatively user-friendly interface brought end-to-end encryption to journalists, activists, and corporations worldwide, underscoring Callas' belief in the democratization of privacy tools. |
| | Later, Callas cofounded Silent Circle, a secure communication platform offering encrypted voice, video, and messaging services. The goal was to provide tools that weren't just theoretically secure, but also easy to incorporate into everyday workflows. As Chief Technology Officer, Callas oversaw the development of the company's products, ensuring they met rigorous standards for cryptographic robustness. |
| | Callas has also been an influential voice in the "Crypto Wars," advocating against government backdoors in encryption. He has testified before governmental bodies, defending the principle that secure encryption is an essential facet of modern life, not just for personal privacy, but also for economic and national security. |
| | Beyond his entrepreneurial ventures, Callas continues to serve as a mentor and advisor to emerging cybersecurity startups, helping them navigate the technical and ethical challenges of modern cryptography. |
| | By blending technical expertise with public advocacy, Jon Callas has played a crucial role in shaping the landscape of secure digital communication. |

*(continued)*

# APPENDIX D  PEOPLE

| Name | Biography |
|---|---|
| Brian Krebs | Bubbling with unrelenting curiosity, Brian Krebs has carved a niche as a leading figure in cybersecurity journalism. Born in 1972, Krebs was once just another inquisitive mind exploring the Internet's nascent frontiers. An unexpected infection by a computer worm in 2001 ignited his fascination with digital threats, nudging him onto a lifelong mission to demystify the dangers lurking online. |
| | Krebs began his career at *The Washington Post*, writing about computer security and building a reputation for his meticulous research. His columns soon transformed into the well-regarded "Security Fix" blog, which led him to uncover malicious networks, spam rings, and international hackers. Over the years, Krebs's stories placed him in the crosshairs of cybercriminals, inspiring the creation of his own independent platform, KrebsOnSecurity.com, in 2009. From data breaches to ransomware attacks, his investigations exposed vulnerabilities across the digital spectrum, spurring companies and governments to fortify their defenses. |
| | In 2014, Krebs published the New York Times bestseller *Spam Nation*, an exposé that dissected the rise of global cybercriminal enterprises. Recognized for his unyielding pursuit of the truth, Krebs has forged a reputation for fairness and authenticity, values paramount to his enduring influence in cybersecurity discourse. Though soft-spoken, he has weathered repeated retaliatory attacks, including a swatting incident meant to intimidate him into silence. |
| | Ultimately, Brian Krebs's work extends beyond headlines; it sparks a dialogue on the ethical intricacies of cyber defense, urging individuals and corporations alike to remain vigilant. With signature diligence, he continues to investigate, interpret, and illuminate the shifting contours of the digital realm. His passion for unveiling hidden threats, combined with a commitment to educating readers, has made him not merely a reporter, but an indispensable watchdog, revealing a high-stakes world at the edge of our screens. His legacy stands as a testament to unwavering integrity in journalism. |

*(continued)*

APPENDIX D   PEOPLE

| Name | Biography |
|---|---|
| HD Moore | HD Moore is the creator of Metasploit, one of the most influential penetration testing frameworks in cybersecurity history. Released initially as an open source project in 2003, Metasploit quickly gained traction among both legitimate security professionals and malicious hackers. Through Metasploit, users could leverage a modular architecture to develop and execute exploits against various systems, streamlining the process of vulnerability testing. Under Moore's guidance, Metasploit became a flagship tool for ethical hackers, helping organizations identify and remedy security flaws before cybercriminals could exploit them.<br><br>Moore's journey into cybersecurity began in his youth, driven by a deep fascination with the inner workings of computer systems. This curiosity evolved into a career spanning multiple roles, including penetration tester, security researcher, and Chief Research Officer at Rapid7, the company that acquired Metasploit in 2009. At Rapid7, Moore led efforts to expand the Metasploit framework and integrate it into comprehensive security solutions, cementing its status as an industry standard for vulnerability assessment and red teaming.<br><br>Beyond Metasploit, Moore has been involved in high-profile vulnerability research and responsible disclosures. He's uncovered major security flaws in widely used products, often prompting swift action from vendors. His approach to disclosure balances ethical responsibility and a drive for improving the overall security ecosystem.<br><br>A regular presence at conferences like DEF CON and Black Hat, Moore's talks often dive into the technical nuances of exploit development and the shifting strategies threat actors use. He has also championed knowledge sharing, encouraging up-and-coming security researchers to learn the ropes through Metasploit and other open source initiatives. Thanks to Moore's contributions, penetration testing and vulnerability management have become more approachable fields, enabling countless security professionals to better defend their networks. Today, Metasploit remains a cornerstone tool in the cybersecurity toolkit, a testament to Moore's enduring legacy. |

*(continued)*

## APPENDIX D   PEOPLE

| Name | Biography |
|---|---|
| Christopher Wysopal ("Weld Pond") | Christopher Wysopal, also known by his hacker handle "Weld Pond," is a pioneering cybersecurity researcher and entrepreneur who played an influential role in shaping modern vulnerability disclosure practices. A member of the legendary hacker collective L0pht, Wysopal coauthored groundbreaking advisories in the 1990s that exposed critical flaws in operating systems, routers, and other infrastructure. This work provided early warnings about the fragility of Internet-connected systems, eventually compelling companies to take vulnerability reporting more seriously. |
| | Wysopal was among the L0pht members who famously testified before the US Congress in 1998, warning that they could shut down the Internet within 30 minutes. Their testimony spurred public debate on cybersecurity, pushing legislative bodies and federal agencies to consider the significance of robust digital defense. This hearing has since become an iconic moment in cybersecurity history, highlighting the ethical hacker community's crucial role in revealing systemic weaknesses. |
| | Following his tenure at L0pht, Wysopal cofounded Veracode in 2006. As CTO and CISO, he led the development of the company's cloud-based platform for automated application security testing. Veracode's solutions focused on static and dynamic code analysis, helping companies discover and fix security flaws early in the software development lifecycle. The company's success was a major milestone for application security, illustrating the market's growing desire for scalable, automated solutions. |
| | Throughout his career, Wysopal has advocated for transparency in security research. He authored papers and delivered keynotes that encouraged ethical disclosure policies, bridging the gap between security researchers and software vendors. He has also served on various government advisory boards, influencing cybersecurity standards at the highest levels. Thanks in large part to Christopher Wysopal's pioneering efforts, from L0pht advisories to cutting-edge application security, modern organizations are more prepared to handle vulnerabilities in a responsible, collaborative fashion. |

## APPENDIX D  PEOPLE

These individuals represent a broad spectrum of cybersecurity expertise, from cryptographic pioneers and legendary hackers to modern-day bug bounty champions and secure software evangelists. Their work has collectively raised the bar for digital safety, proving that cybersecurity is as much about groundbreaking research and technical acumen as it is about ethical responsibility and community collaboration.

# APPENDIX E

# Crime Syndicates

Below are ten of the most noteworthy cybercriminal groups from across the last decade whose actions are enough to keep CISOs awake at night. This list is a short story of ill-gotten gains and the corporate victims left reeling in their wake.

> **Note** This list was compiled from public information from MITRE, CISA, and various vendors.

## APPENDIX E  CRIME SYNDICATES

| Name | A.K.A. | Background | History | Impact (USD) | Reference |
|---|---|---|---|---|---|
| Lazarus Group | Hidden Cobra | Alleged North Korean state-sponsored group known for high-profile heists (e.g., Sony Pictures breach) and sophisticated hacking campaigns. Particularly active in targeting financial institutions via the SWIFT system. | Sony Pictures (2014), Bangladesh Bank (2016), and various financial institutions in Southeast Asia. | Estimated over $100 million in theft and damages, potentially up to $200 million. Uses custom malware, destructive wipers, and spear phishing to strike at financial assets. | https://attack.mitre.org/groups/G0032/ |
| Carbanak | Anunak/ Cobalt | Specializes in large-scale financial sector heists, infiltrating banks and ATM networks. Manipulates core banking databases to siphon funds into hacker-controlled accounts. | Attacks on 100+ financial institutions across Europe, Asia, and America. Multiple ATM "jackpotting" incidents worldwide. | Over $1 billion stolen to date, with individual thefts netting $2.5 million–$10 million each. Primarily uses phishing with custom Carbanak malware and RATs to gain access to critical transaction systems. | https://attack.mitre.org/groups/G0008/ |

APPENDIX E  CRIME SYNDICATES

| | | | | |
|---|---|---|---|---|
| **Indrik Spider** | Dridex Gang | Infamous for the Dridex banking Trojan (harvesting user credentials), later pivoting to high-stakes ransomware. Runs multimillion-dollar extortion campaigns against organizations. | Dozens of US and UK financial institutions affected—Travelex allegedly ransomed for $6 million (2019–2020). | US authorities estimate over $100 million in cumulative damages. Phishing emails and Dridex Trojan used for credential theft, lateral movement, and eventual ransomware deployment. | https://attack.mitre.org/groups/G0119/ |
| **APT28** | Fancy Bear | Believed to be linked to Russian military intelligence. Conducts espionage (rather than ransom) campaigns, focusing on data exfiltration and politically charged leaks. | DNC breach (2016), multiple European government/defense agencies, international sporting organizations. | Financial impact is difficult to pin down; victims have spent millions hardening networks postattack. Notable for spear phishing, zero-day exploits, and leaking stolen data at strategically sensitive times. | https://attack.mitre.org/groups/G0007/ |

*(continued)*

## APPENDIX E   CRIME SYNDICATES

| Name | A.K.A. | Background | History | Impact (USD) | Reference |
|---|---|---|---|---|---|
| **Gold Southfield** | REvil, Sodinokibi | Ransomware group famed for multimillion-dollar demands and "double extortion" (data theft plus encryption). Gained notoriety through high-profile hits like the Kaseya supply chain attack in 2021. | JBS Foods ransom ($11 million in 2021), Kaseya supply chain attack affecting hundreds of downstream companies. | Likely over $200 million in total damages (ransom, downtime, and lost business). Operates a ransomware-as-a-service (RaaS) model and leverages aggressive negotiation tactics postinfection. | https://attack.mitre.org/groups/G0115/ |
| **FIN7** | Anunak, links to Carbanak | Often intersecting with Carbanak activities. Targets restaurant, hospitality, and retail industries for payment card data. Known to masquerade as legitimate cybersecurity firms to gain trusted access. | Breaches at Chili's, Arby's, Chipotle, and other major chains. Over 100 US companies were breached across the service industry. | Over $1 billion in stolen card data, according to law enforcement. POS infiltration and spear phishing as vendor communications are common; massive costs in remediation and credit monitoring for affected customers. | https://attack.mitre.org/groups/G0046/ |

## APPENDIX E  CRIME SYNDICATES

| | | | | |
|---|---|---|---|---|
| **DarkSide** | *(none given)* | Emerged in 2020, running ransomware operations like a polished "business." Gained huge notoriety by attacking Colonial Pipeline, causing major fuel disruptions in the United States. Claimed they donated part of ransoms to charity. | Colonial Pipeline (2021), various manufacturing and healthcare targets in the United States and Europe. | Colonial Pipeline ransom was $4.4 million (partially recovered); total disruption and damages soared into the tens of millions. Specializes in double extortion with carefully orchestrated ransom negotiations. | https://www.cisa.gov/news-events/cybersecurity-advisories/aa21-131a |
| **Wizard Spider** | TrickBot Syndicate | Behind the TrickBot Trojan, which evolved from a banking Trojan to a modular cybercrime tool. Associated with Ryuk and Conti ransomware operations, often striking hospitals and municipal targets. | Healthcare organizations in the United States and Europe. Local governments and school systems in the United States. | Over $100 million in combined ransoms plus severe disruption to public services. Attack vectors include botnet spam, TrickBot for privilege escalation, and subsequent ransomware deployment. | https://attack.mitre.org/groups/G0102/ |

*(continued)*

365

# APPENDIX E  CRIME SYNDICATES

| Name | A.K.A. | Background | History | Impact (USD) | Reference |
|---|---|---|---|---|---|
| APT29 | Cozy Bear | Another Russian state-linked advanced persistent threat (APT), more covert than APT28. Specializes in espionage against governmental, security, and research targets. Expert at maintaining stealthy, long-term footholds. | US State Department and White House (2014–2015), SolarWinds Orion supply chain compromise (2019–2020), COVID-19 vaccine research labs. | Difficult to quantify; likely hundreds of millions in damage when factoring in stolen data and large-scale security overhauls. Uses multilayered backdoors, patient recon, and stealthy infiltration. | https://attack.mitre.org/groups/G0016/ |
| Cl0p | CLOP | Financially motivated ransomware group, first emerging around early 2019 as a CryptoMix variant. Known for its "double extortion" model (data encryption and exfiltration) targeting large enterprises. | Accellion FTA (2021) and MOVEit Transfer (2023) campaigns, affecting hundreds of organizations. | Initial access via extensive phishing campaigns, exploitation of known software vulnerabilities, and remote desktop protocol (RDP) compromises. | https://www.cisa.gov/news-events/cybersecurity-advisories/aa23-158a |

**Note** Financial impact figures and specific targets reflect reported or estimated values (USD); actual totals may vary as investigations and attributions evolve.

In the last decade, these ten groups have left a trail of digital chaos costing billions in direct financial loss, not to mention tarnished reputations, compromised trade secrets, and sleepless nights in IT war rooms around the globe. From ransomware rings masquerading as legitimate businesses to espionage outfits that cloak themselves in sovereign immunity, the diversity of threat actors operates at a level of sophistication that challenges even the most hardened cybersecurity defenses.

# APPENDIX F

# Social Engineering

As we have been discussing attack vectors, crime syndicates, and the malware used to compromise organizations, we've repeatedly laid bare that, often, the biggest weakness is us, human beings. In this appendix, we've curated a list of 15 significant social engineering–driven cyberattacks from roughly the past decade (2015–2025). Each entry pairs a high-level narrative with essential facts: the nature of the social engineering technique, a snapshot of how the breach unfolded, and the estimated financial or business impact.

APPENDIX F   SOCIAL ENGINEERING

| No. | Attack name | Year | Technique used | How it played out | Estimated financial/ business impact (USD) | Reference |
|---|---|---|---|---|---|---|
| 1 | Anthem data breach | 2015 | **Phishing/ spear phishing** | Crafted emails prompted employees to click malicious links, harvesting credentials and allowing hackers to access vast personal health data. | ~$115 million settlement; significant reputational damage in healthcare sector. | https://www.cs.bu.edu/~goldbe/teaching/HW55815/presos/anthem.pdf |
| 2 | FACC CFO scam | 2016 | **Business email compromise (BEC)/CEO fraud** | Threat actors spoofed the CEO's email, persuading the CFO to transfer funds into a fraudulent account. | ~$54M loss; severe shareholder impact and legal fallout. | https://www.trendmicro.com/vinfo/us/security/news/cybercrime-and-digital-threats/austrian-aeronautics-company-loses-42m-to-bec-scam |

370

| | | | | | |
|---|---|---|---|---|---|
| 3 | DNC email leak | 2016 | **Spear phishing** | Customized emails fooled staffers into resetting credentials on fake sites, leading to widespread email and document leaks. | Hard-to-quantify monetary losses; legal fees and national reputational harm. | https://www.cnn.com/2016/07/24/politics/dnc-email-leak-wikileaks/index.html |
| 4 | Multiple organizations (WannaCry) | 2017 | **Phishing + exploit (EternalBlue)** | Ransomware rapidly spread through unpatched Windows systems; initial infection vectors included phishing emails carrying malicious attachments. | ~$4 billion global losses; UK NHS alone spent ~$100 million in remediation. | https://www.bbc.com/news/world-39919249 |

*(continued)*

APPENDIX F  SOCIAL ENGINEERING

| No. | Attack name | Year | Technique used | How it played out | Estimated financial/business impact (USD) | Reference |
|---|---|---|---|---|---|---|
| 5 | Pathé BEC scam | 2018 | **Business email compromise (BEC)** | Spoofed executives from Pathé's French HQ convinced the Dutch branch to transfer multiple large sums to fraudulent accounts. | ~€19 million (≈ $22 million) lost; executives were dismissed postincident. | https://www.helpnetsecurity.com/2018/11/14/pathe-bec-scam/ |
| 6 | Toyota Boshoku Corporation | 2019 | **BEC/ impersonation** | Carefully faked emails posing as a trusted partner led employees to approve substantial invoice payments to scammers' accounts. | ~$37 million unauthorized transfer; triggered intense internal audits. | https://www.cpomagazine.com/cyber-security/toyota-subsidiary-loses-37-million-due-to-bec-scam/ |

| | | | | | |
|---|---|---|---|---|---|
| 7 | Twitter hack | 2020 | **Phone-based spear phishing** | Hackers convinced Twitter employees with admin rights to reveal credentials, then took over high-profile accounts (Elon Musk, Bill Gates, etc.) to push a Bitcoin scam. | ~$200 thousand direct scam revenue; major reputational/regulatory repercussions. | https://digitalcommons.kennesaw.edu/cgi/viewcontent.cgi?article=1089&context=jcerp |
| 8 | Barbara Corcoran hack | 2020 | **BEC/impersonation** | Criminals spoofed the email of Corcoran's assistant (and the writing style), tricking her bookkeeper into wiring $400 thousand for a supposed real estate renovation. | ~$400 thousand initially lost; majority eventually recovered. | https://www.cnn.com/2020/02/27/business/barbara-corcoran-email-hack-trnd/index.html |

*(continued)*

APPENDIX F  SOCIAL ENGINEERING

| No. | Attack name | Year | Technique used | How it played out | Estimated financial/ business impact (USD) | Reference |
|---|---|---|---|---|---|---|
| 9 | Magellan Health phishing | 2020 | **Phishing (malicious link)** | Employees clicked on a link in a seemingly legitimate internal memo; threat actors installed malware, moved laterally, and exfiltrated sensitive data. | >$1.4 million in remediation, legal fees; thousands of individuals' data exposed. | https://www.scworld.com/analysis/magellan-health-settles-for-1-43m-after-data-breach-delayed-notification |
| 10 | Colonial Pipeline Attack | 2021 | **Credential stuffing and social engineering** | Threat actors tested leaked credentials until gaining VPN access, then deployed ransomware on critical systems controlling a US fuel pipeline, forcing an operational shutdown. | $4.4 million ransom paid; broader economic impacts due to fuel supply disruption. | https://www.techtarget.com/whatis/feature/Colonial-Pipeline-hack-explained-Everything-you-need-to-know |

374

| | | | | | |
|---|---|---|---|---|---|
| 11 | Ubiquiti breach | 2021 | **Insider threat and social engineering** | An internal developer manipulated credentials and data access, then attempted to extort ransom by staging the attack as an external hack. | Impact in tens of millions; major stock fluctuation and investigation. | https://www.theverge.com/2021/3/31/22360409/ubiquiti-networking-data-breach-response-whistleblower-cybersecurity-incident |
| 12 | Twilio hack | 2022 | **SMS phishing ("smishing")** | Threat actors sent bogus "reset" texts to Twilio staff, capturing Okta credentials and compromising some internal systems and customer data. | Unknown direct losses: costs included incident response and possible fines. | https://www.twilio.com/en-us/blog/august-2022-social-engineering-attack |

*(continued)*

# APPENDIX F  SOCIAL ENGINEERING

| No. | Attack name | Year | Technique used | How it played out | Estimated financial/ business impact (USD) | Reference |
|---|---|---|---|---|---|---|
| 13 | Uber hack | 2022 | **MFA fatigue and social engineering** | Threat actors flooded a contractor's phone with repeated MFA requests until the victim approved one by mistake, gaining internal network access and leaking screenshots. | Undisclosed direct losses; significant brand damage and investigation. | https://www.bu.edu/ articles/2022/what- you-need-to-know- about-uber-data- breach/ |
| 14 | Microsoft/ Lapsus$ breach | 2022 | **Employee phishing and credential theft** | Lapsus$ group tricked or coerced employees into revealing sign-in codes; exfiltrating source code and bragging on social media. | Financial impact undisclosed; costly code leaks and security overhauls. | https://www.cisa. gov/sites/default/ files/2023-08/CSRB_ Lapsus%24_508c.pdf |

APPENDIX F  SOCIAL ENGINEERING

| 15 | Mailchimp hack | 2022 | **Social engineering of support staff** | Impersonating legitimate users and employees, threat actors convinced Mailchimp staff to grant access to accounts, then utilized compromised mailing lists to launch widespread phishing campaigns. | Exact losses unknown; brand damage and multiple client restitution steps. | https://mailchimp.com/newsroom/march-2022-security-incident/ |

377

## APPENDIX F  SOCIAL ENGINEERING

While social engineering has been around almost as long as the word "gullible," many readers may be surprised at how easily it can be performed. If you have any doubts, search the Internet for a "Tree Octopus" or who is really behind the "John Titor" story. The results may surprise you.

# Index

## A

Adobe, 29, 97, 319, 353
Advanced persistent threats (APT), 28, 29, 44, 87, 97, 127, 149, 160, 177, 346, 350, 363, 366
Agentic AI, 13, 93, 94
Altair, 11
Anti-spyware, 144, 146–148, 150, 187
Antivirus, 16, 26, 64, 66, 67, 74, 86, 90, 127, 139, 144–151, 165, 187, 274, 302, 334, 335, 344, 353
Apple, 11, 12, 16, 32, 63, 99, 120, 139, 169, 344, 346, 347, 354, 355
ARPANET, 7–9, 18, 67, 144
Arup, 111
Ashley M., 33, 108
Attack vectors, 1–41, 44, 46, 71, 77–82, 87–89, 99, 110, 111, 113, 125, 126, 130, 131, 135, 143–145, 150, 152, 153, 155, 158, 159, 171, 173, 174, 176, 184, 185, 187, 188, 191, 195, 196, 199, 204, 209, 217, 232, 257, 263, 324, 353, 365

Aurora, 29, 97
Authentication, 5, 7, 9, 10, 55, 71, 73, 135, 157, 166, 168, 184, 185, 189–196, 205, 218, 220–222, 224, 226, 252–254, 257, 261, 263, 266, 268, 303, 308

## B

Backup, 34, 66, 88, 89, 259, 261, 262, 342
Berners-Lee, T., 17
BeyondTrust, 27
Biometrics, 166, 181, 193–195, 261, 321
Thomas, B., 67
Brute force, 78, 200, 218, 220, 289
Bug bounty, 35, 51, 52, 98, 101, 121, 338, 339, 348, 354, 359
Bulletin board systems, 12

## C

California consumer privacy act (CCPA), 38, 45, 113, 237, 241, 249, 267
Cat and mouse, 26, 35, 39, 83, 90, 101, 130, 139, 257

# INDEX

CERN, 17
Certified information systems security professional60 (CISSP), 27
ChatGPT, 46, 138
Checkpoint, 211
Cheswick, W., 19
ChoicePoint, 105, 316, 327
Cisco, 19
Cloud attack vectors
Code rem, 96, 220
Common vulnerabilities and exposure2 (CVE), 55, 57, 77
Common vulnerability scoring system (CVSS), 56, 57, 77
Computer fraud and abuse Act (CFAA), 14, 20
Conficker
Confused deputy, 93, 94
COVID, 89, 109, 366
Creeper, 67, 69, 144
Cryptography, 4, 20, 119, 200, 330, 331, 333, 334, 336, 342, 349, 352, 355
CryptoLocker, 65, 88, 108, 284
Cybersecurity information sharing Act (CISA), 35, 114

# D

Data loss prevention, 30, 111, 144, 147, 150, 176–181
Data loss prevention (DLP), 30, 144, 150, 176–181

Denial-of-service, 25, 37, 44, 76, 84, 86, 232
Disclosure, 45, 53, 55, 98, 101, 120, 121, 136, 177, 239, 240, 242, 243, 249, 332, 338, 339, 343, 344, 347, 348, 350, 353, 357, 358
Distributed denial-of-service (DDoS), 25, 37, 44, 68, 70, 71, 104, 105, 232, 236, 238
Dot-com, 21, 23–28
Double extortion, 34, 111, 129, 290, 291, 293, 364–366
Draper, J., 10
Dwell time, 45, 127, 175, 229, 231–238

# E

ECCN, 20
eEye digital security, 27, 84, 273, 335
Elk cloner, 16, 63
Encryption, 3, 4, 9, 20, 37, 38, 62, 75, 81, 90, 91, 111, 112, 119, 130, 140, 144, 154, 155, 157, 161, 163, 168, 199–201, 205, 233, 259, 260, 263, 286, 291, 306, 316, 318, 319, 330, 331, 336, 337, 341, 342, 349, 355, 364, 366
Endpoint detection and response (EDR), 66, 100, 144, 151–153, 160, 223, 232

Endpoint protection platforms
	(EPPs), 144, 149–151
Engima
Eniac, 3
Equifax, 33, 108, 323, 327
Estonia, 105
EternalBlue, 99, 287, 305, 306, 371
Exfiltration, 77, 81, 152, 155, 246,
	252, 363, 366
Exploitation techniques,
	97, 354

# F

Facebook, 32, 35, 37, 98, 135, 181,
	281, 336
Federal bureau of investigation
	(FBI), 10, 283, 293, 337
Firewalls, 19, 20, 25, 29, 75, 81, 86,
	100, 108, 119, 140, 144, 150,
	154–160, 164, 165, 169, 170,
	173, 179, 209, 279, 351

# G

General data protection regulation
	(GDPR), 34, 45, 115–117,
	157, 167, 170, 178, 183, 186,
	193, 195, 198, 237, 241,
	249, 267
Google, 29, 32, 35, 97, 98, 139, 229,
	332, 348, 353
Gramm-Leach-Bliley Act
	(GLBA), 25

# H

Hacktivism, 107
Health insurance portability and
	accountability act (HIPAA),
	25, 167, 170, 183, 186, 193,
	195, 198, 205, 241, 249
Heartbleed, 35, 303, 304
Honeypots, 223
Hopper, G., 6, 50

# I

Identity and access management
	(IAM), 94, 166, 167, 179,
	181–187, 191
Identity attack vectors, 184, 191,
	196, 217
Identity defined security alliance, 35
Identity governance, 31, 187–189, 228
Identity theft, 2, 19, 103, 123, 158,
	281, 316, 318
I LOVE YOU, 84, 273
Industrial control systems (ICS),
	30, 69, 97, 281, 282, 302
Insider threats, 11, 31, 39, 93, 152,
	186, 197, 210, 375
International business machines
	(IBM), 7, 8, 11, 12, 27, 95,
	131, 236
International monetary fund
	(IMF), 113
Internet of things, 36, 101
Internet of things (IoT), 36, 37, 40,
	101, 347

Intrusion detection systems (IDS), 20, 25, 100, 156, 159, 160, 165, 179, 209, 260, 351

## J
Juniper, 19

## K
Keyloggers

## L
Lateral movement, 81, 143, 157, 158, 163, 212, 217-229, 233, 248, 253, 305, 363
Least privilege, 30, 39, 53, 63, 69, 74, 93, 94, 96, 144, 181, 183, 186, 191, 197, 198, 210, 212, 223-225, 248, 254, 258, 259, 297
LinkedIn, 32, 106, 107, 135, 318
Log4j, 100, 310
Log4Shell, 100, 310, 311

## M
Machine learning, 35, 38, 90, 149, 151, 158, 160, 170, 181, 189, 253, 352
Macro, 19, 64, 66, 285
McAfee, 16, 145
Melissa, 19, 64, 272, 274, 345

Meltdown, 99, 307
Metasploit, 27, 307, 357
Microsoft, 18, 19, 23, 24, 35, 64, 68, 84-86, 88, 95, 96, 98, 120, 121, 139, 259, 272, 273, 275, 282, 293, 299-301, 303, 308, 309, 313, 335, 338, 346, 347, 376
Mirai, 37
MITRE, 35, 78, 82, 299, 361
Morris, R.T., 18
Morris worm, 18, 68, 70-72, 76, 258, 339
MOVEit, 90, 312, 366
Multifactor Authentication (MFA), 135, 157, 166, 184, 185, 190, 191, 193-196, 221, 222, 226, 252, 261, 266, 268, 376
Mydoom, 86, 276

## N
National institute of standards and Technology (NIST), 24, 200, 206, 299
Network segmentation, 99, 157, 158, 223, 224, 260, 261
Nigerian prince, 134, 135
Nimda, 23, 84, 85, 95, 274, 300
NotPetya, 33, 89, 257, 288, 305, 306

## O
1%, 257

## P

Passkeys, 181
Patch management, 59, 86, 101, 173, 207, 214, 227, 259, 311
Payment card Industry data security standard (PCI DSS), 34, 157, 167, 170, 195, 198, 205
Payment card industry (PCI), 34, 113
Penetration testing, 27, 51, 59, 174–176, 203, 255, 263, 357
Pentesting, 174, 175
Phreaking, 10, 13, 14
Privacy laws, 178
Privileged access management (PAM), 31, 100, 176–199, 210, 212, 215, 225, 228, 254, 255
Privilege escalation, 73, 80, 213, 222, 309, 365

## Q

Quantum computing, 36, 38, 40, 130, 199–201, 331, 342
Quantum computing and cybersecurity, 36

## R

Ransomware-as-a-service (RaaS), 34, 130, 286, 364
Ranum, Marcus J., 19, 351
Reaper, 67, 144
Remote access, 5, 81, 163, 166–168, 218, 220, 221, 224, 226, 235, 236, 320
Reputation, 21, 24, 33, 43–46, 59, 123, 129, 150, 158, 165, 178, 181, 186, 205, 231, 232, 237, 239, 244, 252, 265, 266, 268, 335, 347, 354, 356, 367, 370, 371, 373
Resource access control facility (RACF), 7
Return on investment (ROI), 45, 231–238
Risk management, 25, 28–36, 43, 87, 172, 249–250, 351
Rootkits, 64, 72–76, 107, 343

## S

Sarbanes-Oxley act (SOX), 25, 183, 198, 205, 206
Sasser, 85, 86, 277
Script kiddies, 12, 14, 43, 125, 297
Secrets, 15, 20, 29, 31, 87, 89, 103, 128, 133, 135, 165, 177, 194, 225, 251–256, 282, 307, 326, 333, 336, 340, 342, 367
Secure remote access, 163, 166–168, 224, 235, 236
Security information event management (SIEM), 168–171
Shellshock, 35, 304

INDEX

Single sign-on (SSO), 184, 185, 190–193
Sniffed, 20, 161
Snyder, W., 120, 346, 347
SolarWinds, 37, 46, 90, 100, 110, 325, 327, 366
Sony, 64, 74, 75, 106, 107, 318, 362
Spectre, 99, 306, 307, 312
SQL injections, 21, 54, 99
Stuxnet, 30, 65, 69, 87, 88, 97, 106, 281–284, 302, 334
Supply chain, 2, 35, 37, 44, 77, 90, 91, 100, 110, 112, 245–250, 252, 290, 294, 325–327, 364, 366

## T

Target, 19, 23, 32, 33, 43, 58, 69, 81, 86, 89, 96, 104, 107, 111, 124, 128, 136, 137, 140, 174, 234, 251, 293, 294, 318–321, 325, 364–367
Titor, J., 103, 378
Tomlinson, Ray, 9
Trojan horses, 18, 86, 87, 124, 223
Twitter, 32, 120, 135, 258, 324, 336, 345, 373

## U

UNIVersal automatic computer (UNIVAC), 3
UNIX, 68, 71, 73, 76

## V

Virtual private networks (VPN), 110, 154, 157, 160, 162, 163, 331
Vulnerability assessment, 59, 172, 173, 227, 228, 255, 273, 357
Vulnerability management, 22, 27, 171–176, 229, 346, 348, 357

## W, X

WannaCry, 10, 33, 65, 88, 89, 99, 257, 259, 288, 305–308, 371
Wiener, Norbert, 6

## Y

Yahoo, 33, 322, 327
Y2k, 83, 103, 125

## Z

Zatko, Peiter, 120
Zero day, 2, 29, 31, 34, 51–53, 65, 77, 88, 91, 96–98, 100, 101, 126, 128, 149, 204, 220, 265, 294, 302, 312, 332, 345, 350, 353, 354, 363
Zero trust (ZT), 35, 39, 53, 77, 111, 139, 144, 166, 214, 224, 249, 325
Zeus, 87, 280, 283, 284

GPSR Compliance
The European Union's (EU) General Product Safety Regulation (GPSR) is a set of rules that requires consumer products to be safe and our obligations to ensure this.

If you have any concerns about our products, you can contact us on

ProductSafety@springernature.com

In case Publisher is established outside the EU, the EU authorized representative is:

Springer Nature Customer Service Center GmbH
Europaplatz 3
69115 Heidelberg, Germany